Wartime Shanghai

Wartime Shanghai

Edited by
Wen-hsin Yeh

London and New York

First published 1998 by Routledge
11 New Fetter Lane, London EC4P 4EE

Simultaneously published in the USA and Canada
by Routledge
29 West 35th Street, New York, NY 10001

Typeset in Times by Solidus (Bristol) Limited
Printed and bound in Great Britain by
Biddles Ltd, Guildford and King's Lynn

British Library Cataloguing in Publication Data
A catalogue record for this book is available from the British Library

Library of Congress Cataloging in Publication Data
A catalogue record for this book has been requested

ISBN 0-415-17441-4

Contents

	List of illustrations	vi
	List of contributors	viii
	Acknowledgments	ix
1	**Prologue: Shanghai besieged, 1937–45**	
	Wen-hsin Yeh	1
2	**Introduction: the struggle to survive**	
	Wen-hsin Yeh	18
3	**Ambiguities of occupation: foreign resisters and collaborators in wartime Shanghai**	
	Bernard Wasserstein	24
4	**The other Japanese community: leftwing Japanese activities in wartime Shanghai**	
	Joshua A. Fogel	42
5	**Chinese capitalists and the Japanese: collaboration and resistance in the Shanghai area, 1937–45**	
	Parks M. Coble	62
6	**Projecting ambivalence: Chinese cinema in semi-occupied Shanghai, 1937–41**	
	Poshek Fu	86
7	**Urban warfare and underground resistance: heroism in the Chinese secret service during the War of Resistance**	
	Wen-hsin Yeh	111
8	**Urban controls in wartime Shanghai**	
	Frederic Wakeman, Jr.	133
9	**The purge in Shanghai, 1945–46: the Sarly affair and the end of the French Concession**	
	Marie-Claire Bergère	157
	Bibliography	179
	Index	192

Illustrations

Maps

1   Political capitals in wartime China, 1940   xi
2   Shanghai and its vicinity   xii
3   *Gudao* Shanghai: the International Settlement, 1937–41   xiii
4   Unoccupied Shanghai: the French Concession, 1937–45   xiv
5   Hongkou: the Japanese district in Shanghai   xv

Plates

The plates can be found between pp. 110 and 111.

1   Chinese refugees swarm into the foreign areas, August 1937
2   Suzhou Creek, flowing into the Huangpu River, separated the Japanese-occupied area from the Anglo-American International Settlement
3   Police quell a rice riot in the International Settlement, 1940
4   Chinese exchange shops in the International Settlement
5   Shanghai, 1940
6   Wang Jingwei on the third anniversary of the puppet regime in Nanjing, 1942
7   Wang Jingwei and German envoys to the Nanjing puppet government
8   Wang Jingwei and his entourage on a pilgrimage to a Meiji shrine in Japan, 1941
9   Zhu Minyi, Minister of Foreign Affairs in Wang Jingwei's puppet government, signing the agreement with the French consul by which the French Concession reverted to the Chinese, July 22, 1943
10 The commander-in-chief of the Japanese Army surrenders to the commander-in-chief of the Guomindang army, He Yingqin
11 Wang Jingwei, 1940
12 Wang Jingwei reviewing puppet army troops
13 Nanjing massacre, December 1937
14 The Fifth Plenum of the Third Central Committee of Wang's puppet Guomindang, in front of Sun Yat-sen's tomb

15 The British Club in Shanghai, rebuilt in 1909, reputedly with the longest bar in the world
16 The major buildings along the Shanghai Bund: the Hong Kong and Shanghai Banking Corporation building, the Maritime Customs House, the Broadway Mansion, the Bank of China, and Sassoon Building
17 A Japanese soldier and a Chinese woman in the occupied zone
18 Japanese soldiers marching into the International Settlement, December 9, 1941

Contributors

Marie-Claire Bergère is a Professor at the Centre d'Etudes Chinoises, Institut National des Langues et Civilisations Orientales, Université de la Sorbonne Nouvelle, Paris. She is author of *Sun Yat-sen* (Fayard, 1994) and *The Golden Age of the Chinese Bourgeoisie* (Cambridge University Press, 1989).

Parks M. Coble is a Professor of History at the University of Nebraska-Lincoln who specializes in the history of Republican China and Sino-Japanese relations. He is the author of *Facing Japan: Chinese Politics and Japanese Imperialism, 1931–1937*, published in the Harvard East Asian Monograph Series, 1991.

Joshua A. Fogel is Professor of East Asian History at the University of California, Santa Barbara. His most recent book is *The Literature of Travel in the Japanese Rediscovery of China, 1862–1945* (Stanford University Press, 1996).

Poshek Fu teaches modern Chinese history at the University of Illinois, Urbana-Champaign. Author of *Passivity, Resistance, and Collaboration: Intellectual Choices in Occupied Shanghai, 1937–1945*, he is currently working on issues of Chinese cinema and Hong Kong identity.

Frederic Wakeman, Jr. is Haas Professor of Asian Studies and Director of the Institute of East Asian Studies at the University of California, Berkeley. His most recent book is *Policing Shanghai 1927–1937* (University of California Press, 1995).

Bernard Wasserstein is Professor of History at Oxford University. His most recent work is *Vanishing Diaspora: The Jews in Europe Since 1945* (Harvard University Press, 1996).

Wen-hsin Yeh is Professor of History and Chair of the Center for Chinese Studies at the University of California, Berkeley. Her most recent book is *Provincial Passages: Culture, Space, and the Origins of Chinese Communism* (University of California Press, 1996).

Acknowledgments

The seven contributed chapters of this book represent the fruit of years of scholarly interaction and collaborative effort. So many individuals and institutions have contributed to this process that it may not be possible for us to acknowledge all our debts. The chapters have their origins in larger projects pursued respectively by each individual contributor that are designed to answer different questions. All are responses, however, to perceived new developments in the field. Foremost among these are the opening up of major archival collections in China in the 1990s, and the systematic publication of documentary materials that accompanied this accessibility. We find ourselves gaining access consequently for the first time since 1945 to primary sources on Shanghai during the War of Resistance (1937–45).

The end of the Cold War and the tragic conclusion of China's democratic spring in June 1989, which spurred new thoughts on the meaning of modern history, formed the backdrop of a second set of factors that led to new reflections. The reconceptualizing contributed to the undermining of the once-dominant revolutionary teleology—an established historiography intent upon explaining the victory of the Chinese Communist Party and its socialist revolution in 1949. Old ideas about heroes and villains came under scrutiny, along with a reevaluation of emotionally charged issues such as Chinese nationalism. It became possible thereafter for a reconsideration to take place on issues such as collaboration and resistance during China's War of Resistance against the Japanese.

As the contributors pursued respective research over the course of these several years, our paths invariably crossed. Ideas were exchanged as conversations took place in the reading rooms of the Shanghai Municipal Archives, of the Shanghai Municipal Library, of the East Asian Collection of the Hoover Institution, of the microfilm section of the National Archives, as well as in the conference rooms of the Shanghai Academy of Social Sciences and of Fudan University. Several of us recall the camaraderie of doing research in the heat under Shanghai's August sun, and taking refuge in the air-conditioned facilities of the former French Club or the high-vaulted atrium of the Hong Kong-based Shanghai Hilton. The organization of panels for scholarly meetings followed naturally enough. The idea for a volume was born after a particularly well received presentation at the 1994 annual meeting of the American Historical Association in San Francisco that was organized by Poshek Fu and chaired and commented on by Wen-hsin Yeh. With the funding support of the Luce Foundation, a workshop was subsequently convened in Berkeley in December 1994 to sharpen the focus of the collaborative endeavor.

To all our friends and critics of the above-named institutions, especially to former and present directors Han Weizhi and Shi Meiding of the Shanghai Municipal Archives and to President Zhang Zhongli of the Shanghai Academy of Social Sciences, we wish to express our warmest thanks for making it possible for us to carry out our research in this heady decade of reform in China.

The following individuals deserve special thanks for reading and commenting on early drafts of chapters in this volume: Sherman Cochran, William Kirby, and participants of the Cornell Seminar on Shanghai; Andrew Barshay, Lydia Liu, Elizabeth Perry, Shu-mei Shih, Zhang Jishun, and participants of the Berkeley Seminar on Shanghai. Both seminars were made possible by a grant from the Luce Foundation, which also afforded generous support for two multiple-year collaborative research projects centered respectively at Berkeley and Cornell. Shana Brown offered invaluable research assistance on the maps and the illustrations. Elinor Levine coordinated single-handedly both the Luce-sponsored workshop in Berkeley and the final publication of this volume. Their contributions are gratefully acknowledged.

All attempts have been made to locate copyright holders of material used in this book. If any attribution or acknowledgment is missing it would be appreciated if contact could be made care of the publishers so that this can be rectified in any future edition.

W.Y.

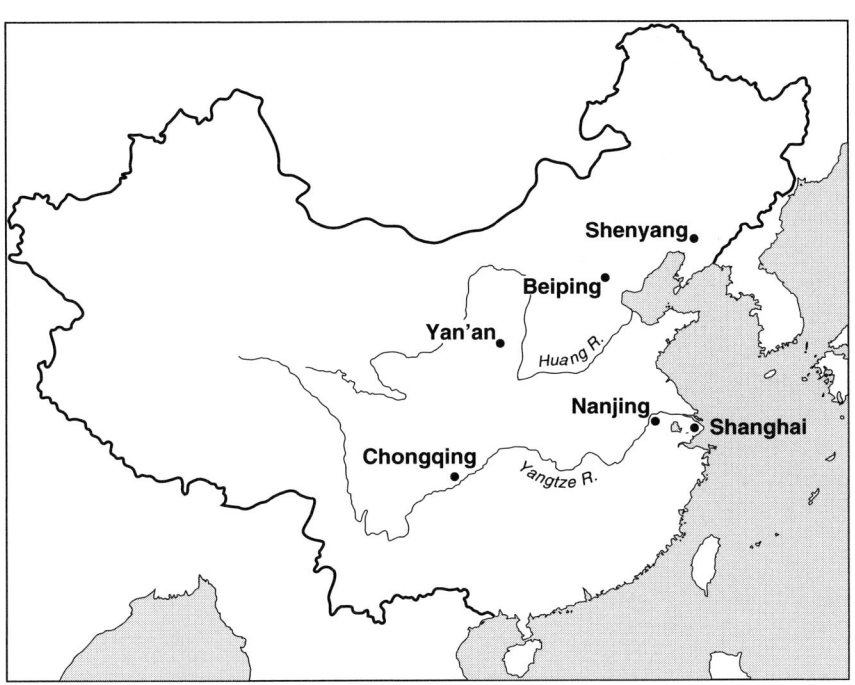

Map 1 Political capitals in wartime China, 1940

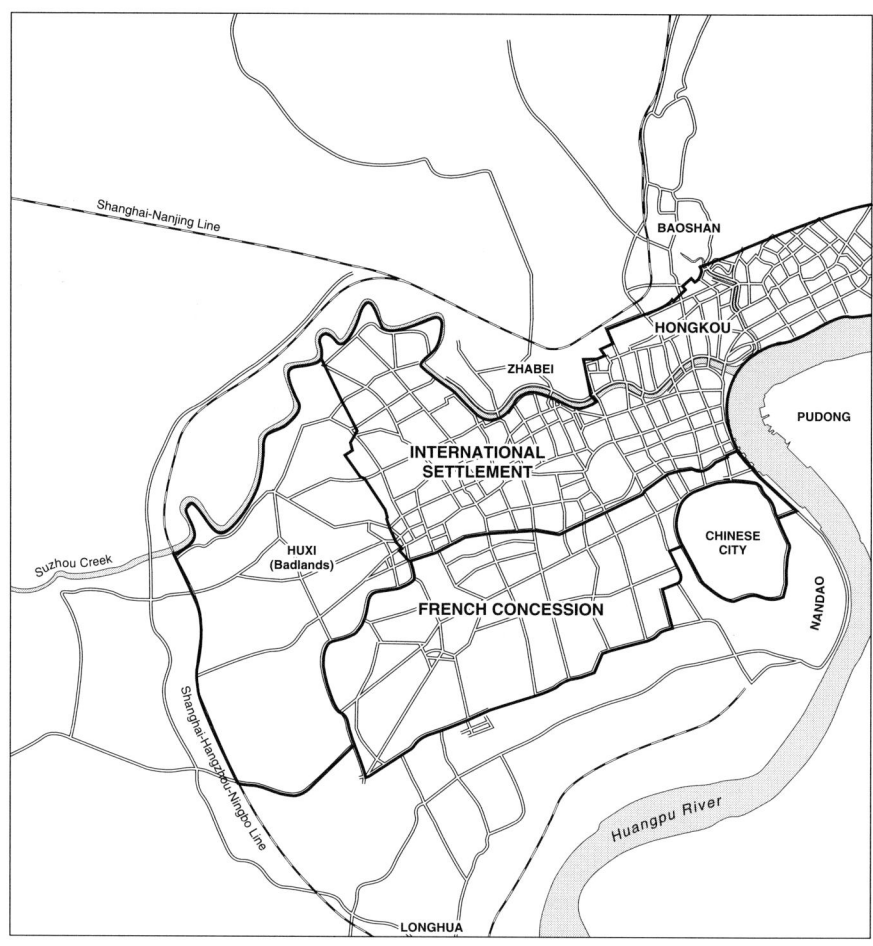

Map 2 Shanghai and its vicinity

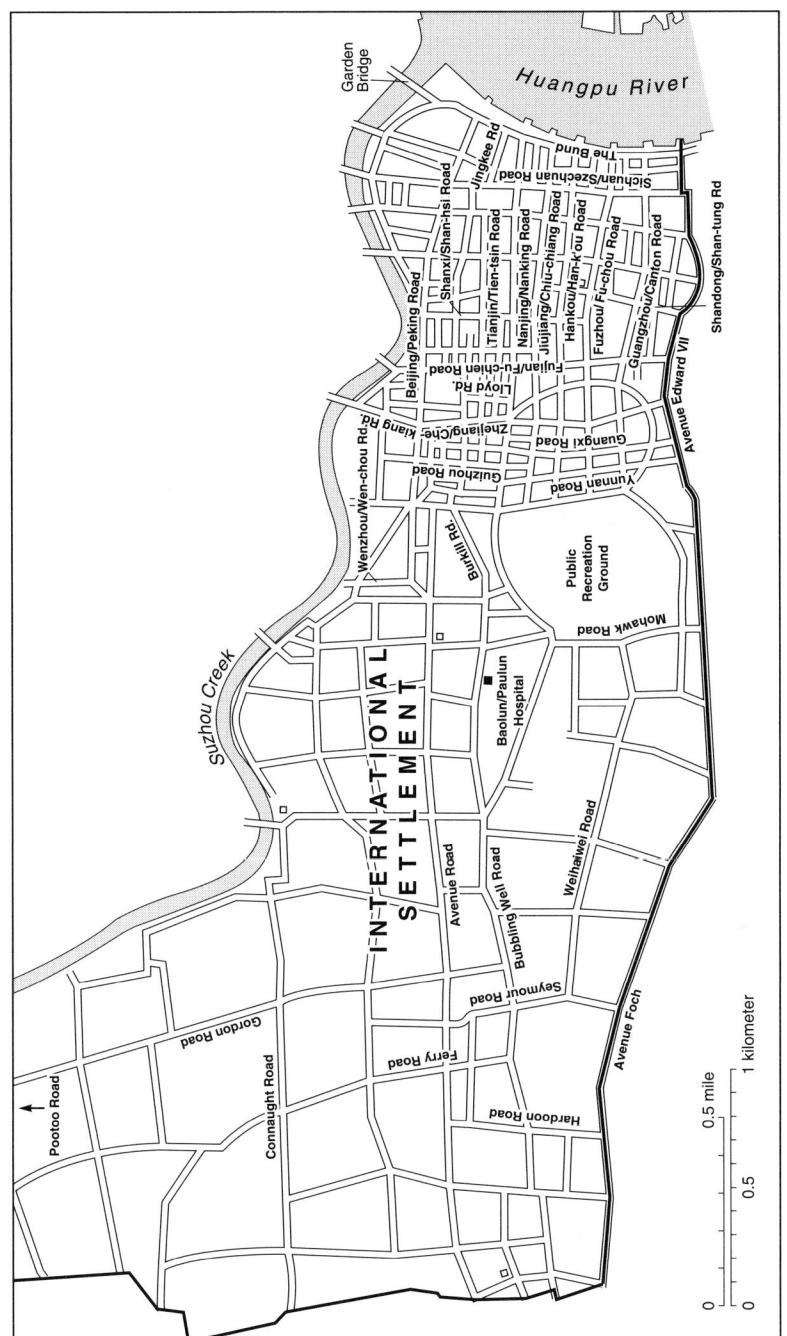

Garden
Bridge

Huangpu River

Jingkee Rd
Sichuan/Szechuan Road
The Bund
Shanxi/Shan-hsi Road
Tianjin/Tien-tsin Road
Nanjing/Nanking Road
Hankou/Han-k'ou Road
Jiujiang/Chiu-chiang Road
Fuzhou/Fu-chou Road
Guangzhou/Canton Road
Shandong/Shan-tung Rd
Avenue Edward VII
Beijing/Peking Road
Fujian/Fu-chien Road
Lloyd Rd.
Zhejiang/Che-kiang Rd.
Guangxi Road
Guizhou Road
Yunnan Road
Wenzhou/Wen-chou Rd.
Butkill Rd.

Suzhou Creek

I N T E R N A T I O N A L
S E T T L E M E N T

Public
Recreation
Ground

Mohawk Road

Baolun/Paulun
Hospital

Avenue Road

Bubbling Well Road

Weihaiwei Road

Seymour Road

Ferry Road

Avenue Foch

Hardoon Road

Connaught Road

Gordon Road

Pootoo Road

0   0.5 mile
0   0.5   1 kilometer

Map 3 Gudao Shanghai: the International Settlement, 1937–41

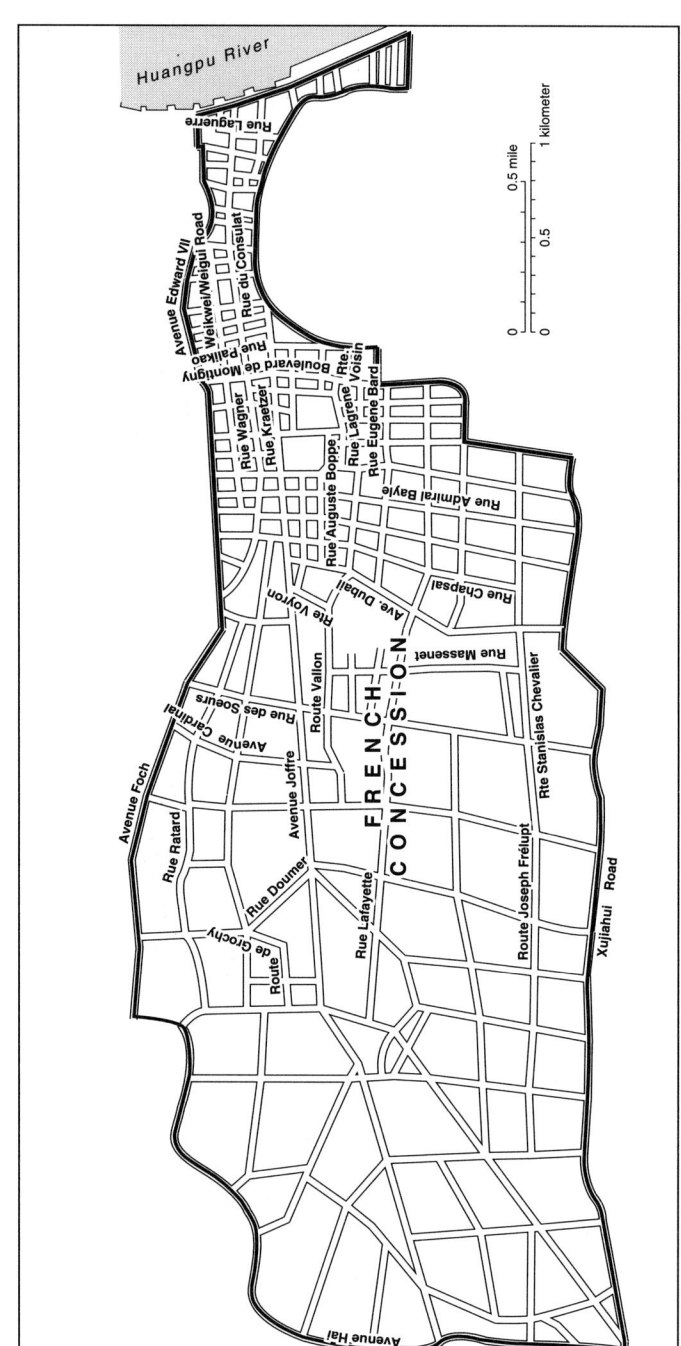

Map 4 Unoccupied Shanghai: the French Concession, 1937–45

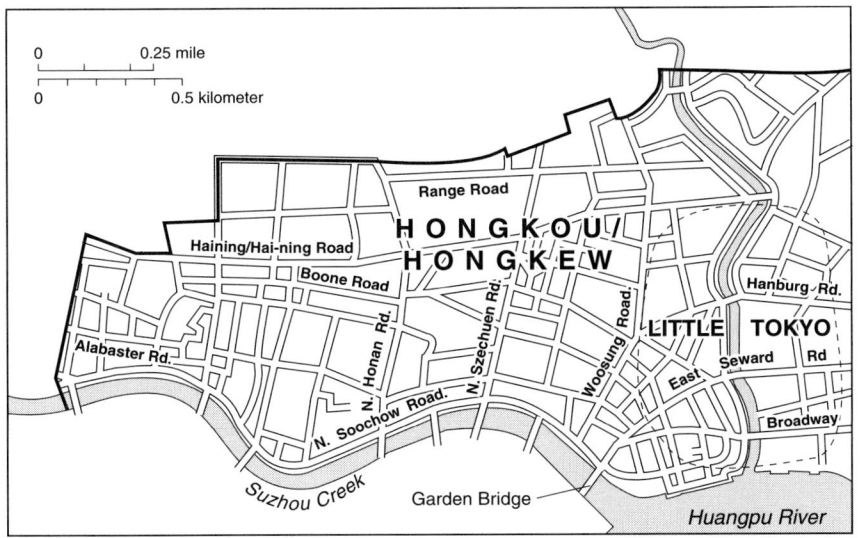

Map 5 Hongkou: the Japanese district in Shanghai

1 Prologue

Shanghai besieged, 1937–45

Wen-hsin Yeh

Shanghai in the 1930s was one of the most sophisticated and complex metropolises in the world.[1] When the Japanese launched their assault on the Chinese parts of the city in August 1937, Shanghai also became the first major city to come under the impact of concerted attack by armored columns and bomber armadas in the mechanized warfare of World War II. The fighting disrupted the well established patterns of relationships among the city's various constituent components.[2] With the fall of the Chinese city to the Japanese, it also thrust upon the unoccupied sectors—the International Settlement and the French Concession—the new tasks of survival in a hostile environment. The financial, manufacturing, publishing, and entertainment industries continued to thrive. The political autonomy that the largely British and American concession authorities sought to maintain *vis-à-vis* the Japanese, however, was precarious at best. On the morning Japan bombed Pearl Harbor (December 8, 1941), Japanese troops in Shanghai simultaneously moved into the International Settlement and occupied the entire city.

Different parts of Shanghai thus fared differently during the War of Resistance (1937–45). Besides the conflicts between the Chinese and the Japanese, there were divisions that traced their origin to the wars and treaties between China and European powers in the nineteenth century. Chinese resistance against Japanese aggression took place in the context of a broader nationalism that had been developing for decades against colonial influence and imperialist expansion, formal as well as informal. This contextual complexity meant that those occupying different positions in the city experienced the war differently, from perspectives unique to themselves. What, for example, did it mean to be a European instead of a Chinese in the International Settlement during the war? How significant was it to be a nationalist instead of a socialist in the city? Did the war forge among Shanghai's diverse population a new sense of community, or did it simply serve to underscore the differences that had fragmented Shanghai society? What sorts of new consciousness did the war foster? And what were the legacies of these eight years, when Shanghai, the center of Chinese modernity, was exposed to the most violent forms of war and occupation?

In the years since 1945, in a climate dominated by the civil conflicts between the Nationalists and the Communists, few attempts have been made to come to terms with the history of wartime Shanghai in its full complexity. General histories published in China and Taiwan offer cursory treatment, if at all, of the subject, painting quite often a picture of sharp contrasts between resistance and collaboration, heroes and traitors, patriotism and treason. Not only has the interpretive framework been constraining; much has been left utterly unexplored about the happenings as such.

The war, with the ceaseless reconfigurations of national strategies and local tactics, the demands on the front line as well as in the home base in Tokyo or Chongqing, and the ever shifting balance of power among the contestants, was a critical juncture in Shanghai's modern transformation. It also meant different things to different people at different points in time. This is not the place to offer a detailed account of the political events that took place during the war. Several general trends none the less deserve to be noted to provide a backdrop to the specificities of war in Shanghai.

WARFARE IN SHANGHAI

The war broke out in Shanghai on August 13, 1937, and ended in August 1945. The eight years in between can be divided into two phases: a *gudao* (lone islet) period when all parts of the city except the International Settlement and the French Concession were taken by the Japanese, and a full occupation period ushered in by the Japanese seizure of the International Settlement in December 1941. The French Concession, by then under a council appointed by the Vichy government, was spared the occupation. It was, instead, handed over to a Japanese-backed Chinese puppet regime—the Wang Jingwei regime in Nanjing—subsequent to the conclusion of a treaty in 1943 in which the French relinquished their extraterritoriality.[3]

The *gudao*, as it happened, was formed in a period of heavy fighting in 1937, and was made possible by European treaty privileges in China. The heavy fighting had much to do with Chiang Kai-shek's resolve, in the aftermath of the Japanese attack in August on Shanghai, to reverse his long-held policies followed up to that point, and to opt for armed resistance instead of negotiated peace. Chiang launched a full-scale campaign of resistance, and ordered, over the course of the following weeks, over seventy battalions of Chinese troops into the Shanghai area.[4]

The ensuing battle of Shanghai, which ended in late October with the retreat of Chinese troops, was one of the most fiercely contested struggles in China's War of Resistance (1937–45) against Japan. It pitched a patchwork of Chinese troops, hastily assembled, against a smaller yet much better equipped Japanese force. The Japanese, intent upon delivering a knockout blow, eventually beefed up their military strength to 200,000 men. The Chinese, with an aroused civilian public that was mobilized to stand behind the military, put up a determined resistance. By the time Chinese troops abandoned their attempt to defend Shanghai, they had exacted a toll of 50,000 Japanese casualties. They had also left behind nearly 300,000 dead and wounded of their own.

The troops that pulled out of Shanghai withdrew westward along the highways and railroads in the direction of Nanjing. Five weeks later, Nanjing, the Nationalist capital, also fell. The fall of that city set the stage for the infamous Japanese rape and massacre of the city's civilians. The number of dead was said to be as high as 200,000. By mid-December 1937, nearly 10,000 of the approximately 25,000 men who graduated between 1929 and 1937 from the Central Military Academy, Chiang Kai-shek's prized officer training institution, had been killed in the fighting. Nearly one-third of the entire Chinese military force under Nationalist command had also fallen on the battlefield.[5]

Within a matter of but three months, then, large parts of the lower Yangzi delta region, the heartland of China's modern industry and commerce, were laid to waste, and numerous mills, shops, schools, and factories—in some cities up to 90 percent—were destroyed by incendiary bombs and artillery fire.[6] The affluent as well as the destitute gathered their family members and took to the road. Some followed the retreating troops up the Yangzi into China's vast interior. Others went into hiding either among the peasants in the countryside or up into the hills and provincial borderlands. Shanghai's International Settlement and the French Concession, which had promptly declared their neutrality as soon as armed conflict broke out, were seen by all as a haven in a land of conflagration.

The thin line drawn by Suzhou Creek, which bounded the northern limits of the International Settlement, became a zone of demarcation between two worlds. North of the creek the explosions of aircraft, machine guns, rifles, and hand grenades reverberated in the air in a sky darkened by the smoke arising from crumbling structures and smoldering buildings. South of the creek, from the roofs, balconies and windows of multiple-storeyed modern buildings—the International Hotel, the China Hotel, the Nine Heavens pub—crowds of men and women looked down into the war zone with the aid of binoculars. A contingent of 500 men, assigned by the Nationalist army to guard the general warehouse of the Bank of China, the Bank of Communications, the Central Bank, and the Farmers' Bank, thus carried out their mission on the north bank in full view of the concerned spectators in the concessions. These fighters, of course, also spared time to receive visitors who navigated across the creek to salute their determined resistance.[7]

Nationalist state-owned enterprises set the example by moving their operations and valuables into the concessions. The Bank of China directed its Nanjing personnel to report to Shanghai. The Central Bank moved its currency reserves into the vaults in the concessions. Many schools, newspapers, and even government departments moved their archives and equipment into the International Settlement both for safe keeping and for continuous operation under the protection of the British and the American flags.

Refugees, similarly, poured into the ten square miles of the conjoined foreign concessions from all parts of the lower Yangzi, swelling the population from 1.5 million to 3 million by mid-September and increasing the size of the average household to thirty-one people. Concession authorities and charitable organizations turned schools, temples, and public places into hundreds of refugee shelters. Tens of thousands of men and women none the less clogged the back alleys and laid down their bedding on the city's sidewalks. Rental charges skyrocketed while sub-rentals multiplied. By late fall, entire shanty towns, in defiance of municipal codes and ordinances, sprang up along the edges of the concessions—home to the new arrivals who now tried to make their living as day laborers and itinerant peddlers.[8]

As the Chinese part of the city lay in ruins, the foreign concessions not only maintained an appearance of business as usual, but further entered a period of war-stimulated boom, thanks to the increased demand generated by the sudden influx of wealth and people. One major source of increased demand for a foothold in the *gudao* was none other than the Nationalist government, which had, by late 1938, relocated its wartime capital to Chongqing. The Nationalist authorities had always relied upon Shanghai as a source of capital and tax revenue. They had also always accorded Shanghai its due recognition as the national capital of media, public opinion, political intelligence, and propaganda, and designed their own organs accordingly. With the outbreak of the war and with the relocation of the central government into the isolation of the interior, it became all the more important that the state hold on to this window to the outside world via the International Settlement.

The pre-war International Settlement, especially the quarter-square-mile area along the Bund, had long been an established center of multinational banking, where a large number of foreign and Chinese-owned enterprises, including the Bank of China and the Bank of Communications, had maintained their head offices. The sub-district on Wangping Street, which lay a few blocks inland behind the Bund, meanwhile, was where a large number of major Chinese newspapers and publishing houses had clustered—a sort of Fleet Street to the Bund's Wall Street. With these institutions in place, the *gudao* emerged, after the fall of Nanjing, as a strategically critical site for a Nationalist presence in the lower Yangzi region. The state transferred into the International Settlement a vast amount of resources and personnel under its control. With the quiet support of the British and the Americans in Shanghai, state-owned banks continued to fly the Chinese national flag atop their office buildings while successfully maintaining the circulation of the fabi, the Nationalist currency, as the legal tender in the lower Yangzi. Critical Nationalist government and party organs, including the official wire service, the Central News Agency, were allowed not only to open up liaison offices but also to build radio stations. A whole network of finance and information was set up that linked Shanghai with Chongqing.

The sudden increase of the wealthy among the city's population provided a second source of demand that stimulated the boom in the city. Theaters, hotels, restaurants, night clubs, amusement parks, and gambling casinos were in high demand. Fiction writers made a fortune serializing old-fashioned mandarin duck and butterfly romances that had little to say on current events.[9] With the production of historical melodramas, the film industry entered a period of growth that—as Poshek Fu suggests in Chapter 6—could almost be considered golden in its history.

After a brief interval, many textile mills, formerly situated elsewhere, relocated in the Settlement and resumed their operation under foreign registration. Chinese entrepreneurs rushed to move their plants from the interior to take advantage of the abundance of labor due to the refugee populations, the access to raw materials, the accumulation of liquid capital in the Shanghai banks, and, above all, the sense of relative safety from war. They regained their productive energy soon enough, and small enterprises pro-liferated in response to rising demand, creating the economic conditions for the "flourishing" of the *gudao*.[10] The stock market and the commodity exchange traded at a level of activity and total capitalization that well exceeded their pre-war record. Trade organizations and social clubs, such as the Bankers' Association, the Chamber of Commerce, and the YMCA, not only retained their pre-war level of activism but also went on to spawn ancillary organizations that mobilized the city's middle class for a variety of causes. The social pages of journals and newspapers were crowded with announcements of fund-raisers such as amateur theatrical performances and sewing campaigns for soldiers on the front line.[11] The *gudao*, so actively linked by an army of smugglers with the hinterland, bounced back to such a high level of prosperity, with such minimal structural disturbance of well established patterns of social and economic lives, that the war, far from leveling off inequalities between the rich and the poor, increased the disparity and intensified the stratification.

PUPPET REGIME

Early in 1938, as the Japanese gave up attempts to bring Chiang Kai-shek to the negotiation table for a speedy resolution of the state of war, they adjusted their policies from invasion to occupation, and sought to work out efficient ways that might permit them to hold Chinese territories securely with a minimal drain on their energy. Instead of creating one puppet regime for all occupied territories in China, however, political prudence combined with conflictual factional interests within the Japanese camp led to the creation of multiple collaborationist governments: in Manchuria, as was done in 1931, in north China, as was accomplished in late 1937, and in central China. The occupied sectors of Shanghai, to be sure, had been placed under a puppet municipal government headed by a local collaborator named Su Xiwen as soon as the city fell. For the right candidate to head a puppet regime in Nanjing with nominal responsibilities over all of central China, the Japanese none the less regarded it necessary to seek out political figures of national stature, and such prospective collaborators turned out to be concentrated in Shanghai's foreign concessions. Japanese recruiters, representing the military, the military intelligence, and the Foreign Ministry, thus busied themselves proffering deals in Shanghai—in rivalry as well as in cooperation among themselves.

Several notable Chinese—Zhou Fengqi, Tang Shaoyi—were approached by the Japanese in 1938 for this purpose. Before the discussions could yield practical results, however, these men were felled, one by one, at the hands of assassins dispatched by the Juntong, the military intelligence service under the command of General Dai Li in Chongqing. Only two men, Liang Hongzhi and Wang Jingwei, escaped attempts on their lives to head puppet regimes in Nanjing. Liang, a back-up choice, was a native of Fujian, a former student in Japan, an old-fashioned politician who had served in the Beijing government prior to the ascent of the Nationalists to power in 1927, and a willing collaborator who believed in peace with the enemy. A man of some status but with no viable political base, Liang was handled by his new friends without much ceremony. In anticipation of the launching of the new Reform government in Nanjing, for example, Liang and his entourage of Cabinet members were cooped up in a Shanghai hotel room for weeks prior to their projected date of inauguration. When they were taken finally by train to Nanjing, they saw a dismal place that had scarcely recovered from the devastation of the recent massacre. Liang and his companions took the trip only to be told, after having spent more days waiting in the dark, that the inauguration had been rescheduled, and the entire group was to be returned to Shanghai for more waiting.

Wang Jingwei's collaboration with the Japanese, by comparison, developed along a different path. Wang was a veteran follower of Sun Yat-sen and a senior member of the Nationalist Party, who held government positions second in public standing only to Chiang Kai-shek. His unannounced departure from Chongqing in December 1938 to meet with the Japanese shook the Nationalist establishment to its core. Shortly after Wang's arrival in Hanoi in January 1939, Chongqing sent assassins to take his life. The agents of Juntong misidentified their intended target, however, and instead gunned down Wang's long-time aide in his bed. Wang, shocked and infuriated, made his way to Shanghai in May. There he convened a "Sixth Congress of the Nationalist Party" and outlined the blueprint of a Nationalist government in Nanjing that was to seek peace and to fight socialism within an East Asian Sphere of Co-prosperity led by the Japanese.[12]

The creation of the Wang regime was arguably the single most important development during the conflict when it came to setting the tone of wartime politics. As Chiang Kai-shek's Chongqing government came to be identified with war and resistance, Wang Jingwei's Nanjing government was equated with peace and collaboration. In his public speeches and writings Wang Jingwei drew upon Buddhist imageries and compared himself to a tender-hearted pacifist assuming great personal sacrifice in an endeavor to succor the multitude. His regime probably deserves greater credit than it has received for procuring food for urban residents and sheltering the civilian population from harsher forms of Japanese brutality. It is perhaps precisely for this reason that the rise of a full-blown puppet regime flying the Nationalist Party flag in the lower Yangzi valley set off a period of intense rivalry between Chongqing and Nanjing for resources, allegiance, and legitimacy, which powerfully colored nearly all aspects of life in wartime Shanghai.

One of the most conspicuous areas of the presence of the Wang regime involved the creation of an armed secret service on the fringes of the International Settlement.[13] Built on funds and ammunitions received from the Japanese, the service was run by Nationalist and Communist intelligence turncoats who recruited their agents from Shanghai's notorious gangs. Known as No. 76 for its street address on Jessfield Road, the organization took the Juntong as its top enemy. In close collaboration with the Japanese, No. 76 by and large succeeded, by the end of 1939, in neutralizing the threat that Chongqing underground agents posed to Chiang Kai-shek's political enemies in Shanghai. The attacks and counterattacks between the two led to much bloodshed on both sides. It also delivered the city into the grip of urban terrorism.

To stifle pro-Chongqing expression in the International Settlement, for example, No. 76 agents targeted editors of newspapers that cheered resistance. They staged drive-by bombings that blew up editorial offices and killed the occupants. They also drew up a hit list containing the names of eighty-some journalists. After abducting and killing Cai Juntu, the publisher of a small weekly, the agents severed his head and placed it on display atop the light pole across the street from Cai's office. Terrorist acts of this sort, combined with the establishment of pro-Wang news organs and publishing enterprises in the International Settlement under the direction of Wang's propaganda chief Lin Bosheng, delivered a powerful message to the city's reading public on the hazards of political resistance.[14]

A second major target of terrorist attack were the financial institutions that pledged loyalty to Chongqing. In addition to office bombs and mail threats, No. 76 carried out large-scale operations in retaliation for Chongqing underground actions against the Wang faction. In one of these instances, the Wang agents simultaneously struck the dormitories of the Jiangsu Provincial Bank and the Bank of China, mainstays of Chongqing financial institutions in Shanghai, shortly after midnight on March 22, 1941. In the Jiangsu Bank dormitory, they roused twelve men out of their beds, lined them up against the wall, and sprayed bullets that led to the death of seven on the spot. In the case of the latter, they ransacked the Bank of China's living quarters, rounded up 128 employees and took them away at gunpoint. The men were eventually returned and released. The puppet police agents departed, however, only after they had randomly singled out three men and murdered them in the presence of their families.[15] Thanks to the activism of No. 76, the years from 1939 to 1941 recorded hundreds of cases of kidnapping, murder, and attempted assassination.

A second area in which the Wang regime made its presence felt concerned control over economic resources and the push for the circulation of the *Zhongchu juan*, paper notes issued by the regime's newly established central bank, the Zhongyang chubei yinhang (Central Reserve Bank). Much of the regime's revenue depended, as Frederic Wakeman has shown, upon its dealings with the gambling casinos in the Shanghai badlands—so much so that it amounted to a "Monte Carlo regime."[16] With the *Zhongchu* notes as an additional vehicle, the new "Nationalist government" of the Wang faction sought to seize control of Shanghai's banking world. It made the *Zhongchu* notes the legal tender of exchange in all occupied areas. It required all enterprises to pay salaries in these notes.[17] The overall effect of the regime's measures was such that Communist guerrilla fighters and Nationalist underground agents alike were compelled to stock up on *Zhongchu* notes in order to avoid detection as they slipped in and out of the variously occupied zones.

By dint of the military's ability to set up checkpoints and to control routes of transportation, meanwhile, those in Shanghai felt the pressure of Japanese interference in their economic lives. After the fall of the mid-Yangzi town of Anqing in the summer of 1938, for example, the Japanese military touched off an economic crisis in the city by closing off shipping between Shanghai and other Yangzi ports, thus severing the city's connections with its central China hinterland. Two years later, with the establishment of the Vichy regime in France, Saigon fell under the sway of the Japanese and Shanghai's well-being was further threatened with the disruption of maritime routes to Southeast Asia.

This ability to choke off critical routes of transportation leading to the "lone islet" gave the Japanese considerable leverage in control over the flow of raw materials and the distribution of finished products. The puppet regime, with a new central bank at its disposal, was poised, meanwhile, to create a trading environment with a currency barrier that promised to complicate the exchange of goods between the city and its surrounding countryside.

The lines that had been drawn around the *gudao* by extraterritoriality, to be sure, had always been permeable to political turmoil around it. The establishment of the Wang regime in Nanjing ushered in a phase both of heightened tension between the two rival factions of the Guomindang and of an increasingly energetic penetration of puppet influence into the city. It drove home to many in the *gudao* their personal stake in making certain political choices. In the shadow of urban terrorism, and under the threat of an economic blockade, the *gudao* seemed a far cry from a safe haven, and the pursuit of an ordinary life uninvolved with politics seemed suspect indeed. The gap between the rich and the poor, which had brought so much disparity to their respective war experiences, had shown few signs, meanwhile, of being narrowed. The rise of the Wang regime as an enemy and as an alternative to the Chiang government in the lower Yangzi introduced a new dimension of political division to an urban society that was already stratified by differences in wealth.

ALLEGIANCE AND DIVISION

This division between Chongqing and Nanjing, which essentially pitted one faction of Chinese against another, was certainly a prominent theme in wartime Shanghai politics, but not the only one. Although the Japanese were the makers and backers of the puppet regime, tension soon arose between the patron and the client as the Wang regime, insisting that its semblance of legitimacy and its usefulness to the peace movement depended on it, persisted in demanding greater autonomy. The points of friction covered not only issues of rights to tax revenue, the conduct of diplomacy, and control over the police force, but also the building of a military presence under the banner of the Wang regime. It has been argued, indeed, that almost as soon as the Wang regime was formally inaugurated in Nanjing, a subtle shift took place in the three-way contests involving Nanjing, Chongqing, and Tokyo. It was not long before the Japanese came to perceive in their allies in peace as much of a challenge to their domination of China as in their enemies in war.[18]

A second source of variation has to do with the Chinese Communists, a party to the second United Front with the Nationalists in the Chinese War of Resistance against the Japanese. The Communists and the Nationalists had been locked in deadly civil conflict with each other since 1927, which was suspended only in 1936 under tremendous domestic political pressure. In the early years of the Sino-Japanese war, as the Nationalists bore the brunt of Japanese military attack and withdrew from the cities in coastal China, the Communists, sometimes in collaboration with the Nationalists via the organs of the United Front and other times on their own, were able to develop new strength in the cities as well as in the countryside in Japanese-occupied areas.

In *gudao* Shanghai, Communist organizers found a receptive audience among the city's lower middle-class urbanites—the salaried employees, especially the younger clerks and newly recruited trainees of banks, the customs, the postal service, insurance companies, trading firms, bookstores, publishing houses, and department stores. These men and women, many new to the city and of precarious financial standing, were active participants in workplace-based associations that provided their members with a certain degree of collective security in an economy of monetary inflation and material scarcity. The members were also readily mobilized for amateur drama and other social activities that raised funds for the war effort and refugee relief—campaigns that at the same time attacked the city's pro-Nationalist top elites as collaborators who, for material rewards, had sold out to the enemy.[19]

Activists in the Shanghai Communist Party cells maintained close contacts with the New Fourth Army, which was conducted, until late 1940, out of the Jiangnan area. This underground Communist network linked the urban organizers with rural guerrilla fighters, and cut across the Japanese line that separated the *gudao* from the occupied zone. At the same time, rivalry between the Communists and the Nationalists brought much strain to the United Front. Mutual suspicion between the two, coupled with competition for territorial bases behind the enemy lines, culminated in the New Fourth Army Incident in Shanghai's hinterland in January 1941, when Nationalist troops attacked the Communists and captured one of its top commanders. The incident severely tested joint support for the United Front. The two partners in resistance thereafter went their separate ways.[20]

A third source of variation, finally, had to do with ideological divisions within the Japanese operation in China that divided the rightwing military officers in the field from the left-leaning staff researchers on China. The stories of the Sorge spy ring and the case involving the Research Division of the South Manchurian Railroad Company are well known and have been told elsewhere.[21] The intricacies of Japanese involvement with the Chinese in Shanghai, as Joshua Fogel's Chapter 4 in this volume makes amply clear, dated well back into the pre-war years. The multiple connections between Chinese and Japanese socialists in the city, whether under the organizational infrastructure of the Comintern or through intellectual influence, can be traced further back to the very founding of the Chinese Communist Party in 1921. This history, with all its density in personal ties and mutual influences between the Chinese and the Japanese, was heavily present in the foreign concessions in Shanghai, where the urban Chinese socialist movement was born.[22] Informal networks existed within the *gudao*, where lines formed on the basis of ideological affinity crisscrossing bonds that stemmed from national allegiance. This condition prevailed despite the official lines drawn up in Japan proper, which treated socialists as public enemies.

JAPANESE OCCUPATION

The *gudao* gave way to full occupation on December 8, 1941. That day, Japanese airplanes struck and sank British and American gunboats moored in the Huangpu river in a pre-dawn attack. Japanese troops marched across Suzhou Creek and posted sentries at all major intersections in the International Settlement. Chinese-language proclamations, issued jointly by the supreme commands of the Japanese navy and army in the Shanghai area, appeared on bulletin boards in the street, announcing the military's goodwill to "assure the security" of the civilians in the International Settlement. After a brief meeting with the Japanese consul in Shanghai, the Shanghai Municipal Council announced that its personnel, British as well as American, were to remain on duty as before, although a Japanese officer was immediately assigned to assume command of the Settlement police force.[23]

Almost immediately after the occupation, the Japanese took active measures to disperse the heavy concentration of population—over 3 million in total—that had built up in the concessions since 1937, in the hope of alleviating civilian pressure on urban resources. An elaborate system involving the issuance of travel permits, the creation of checkpoints, the channeling and monitoring of movements, the registration of household memberships, and the certification of travel bureaus developed. Over 600,000 people, consisting mainly of the poor and the unemployed, were eventually returned to the countryside, although many also managed to find their way back to the city.

Subsequent Japanese measures in Shanghai were most notable for attempts in two areas: control over the city's population and over the allocation of resources. There were several objectives to these measures: to enhance the security of the city for the occupiers, to reduce its drain on vital resources and personnel, and, if more could be hoped, to sustain Shanghai's economic productivity to contribute to Japan's war effort. The means that were employed drew heavily upon the presence of the military police, which was supplemented by the use of the existing Settlement, French Concession, and puppet police forces. In the most tangible demonstration of the power of this combined force, urban life ground to a halt as banks, bookstores, and department stores in the International Settlement were ordered to shut down. Nanjing Road, the busiest street for commerce and traffic, was cut up into small sections by the erection of sandbags, barricades, and barbed wire. The British-owned tramways, which had performed such a critical function in keeping the arteries of this congested city freely flowing, were ordered to curtail hours of operation and to reduce lines of service. Electrical consumption per unit, which had been indispensable in keeping the city's entertainment quarters ablaze at night, was capped at a drastically reduced level. This forced the city's bars and dance halls to truncate their hours and to turn off their neon signs. Instead of the glamour, the crowds, and the stream of traffic in the first years of the war, Shanghai was subdued into quiet inactivity enshrouded in darkness. Arbitrary application of barbed wire and checkpoints further compartmentalized the city into scores of neighborhoods, each vulnerable to a disciplinary blockade that subjected the residents to a total denial of basic necessities such as food and water.[24]

In February 1942, the Shanghai Municipal Council and the French Concession carried out Japanese orders to conduct household registration throughout the city. The data collected included information on the employment of the occupants. Armed with this input, occupation authorities singled out certain neighborhoods—in the Settlement as well as in Nanshi—where pro-Chongqing sentiment was believed to be running high, for "anti-terrorism drills." Residents were given training exercises so that they would have no excuse not to collaborate with the police in the event of incidents against the Japanese. These neighborhoods, furthermore, were organized into "citizens' associations," which, like the *baojia* in the countryside, were held collectively responsible for neighborhood security.[25] As an ultimate measure of sure control, heads of households were issued rice coupons only if their pacifist conduct was vouched for by the heads of these associations.[26]

The outbreak of the Pacific war placed heavy demands on the warring parties for fresh resources. It also cut off maritime trade and deprived Shanghai of critical access to overseas shipments. The occupation authorities thus moved to regulate the allocation of resources. Restrictions were placed on the total quantities of permissible private purchase and storage of vital staples such as rice, cooking oil, and coal. Free circulation of currency was also curtailed when holders of bank accounts were told that their withdrawals in cash must stay within a certain limit. Although rapid inflation in daily necessities was briefly averted, residents of Shanghai felt the pinch of material scarcity, and rice lines appeared throughout the city. Those of lower middle-class income—shop clerks, elementary school teachers, handicraftsmen, and workers—were the most seriously inconvenienced by the new measures. Among the truly destitute, the rising cost of rice drove some to robbery in attempts to lay their hands on food. Others perished in the unusually harsh winter of 1942.[27] Those with means and connections meanwhile resorted to hoarding for profit. Yuan Ludeng, Wen Lanting, and Lin Kanghou, chairs appointed by the Nanjing regime to head the control boards of rice, cooking oil, and grain, and leading figures in banking circles under the Wang regime, became known as "the three elders" and the wealthiest individuals in occupied Shanghai.[28]

As the war in the Pacific intensified, an ever-growing list of goods was placed under special control: gasoline, motor vehicles, metal, rubber, medicine, lumber, fuel, dye, and construction materials.[29] The assets of Chongqing government banks had been seized shortly after the Japanese took the city. Those in the foreign banks and trading houses likewise had been either frozen or confiscated. The *Zhongchu* notes of the Wang regime triumphed over the *fabi* and became the legal tender required in all payments of tariffs, taxes, and court fees. The Nanjing government and the occupation authorities tied the pricing of the restricted goods to the issuance of their notes. They also pressured Settlement banks and financial institutions to adopt the practice of crediting account values in *Zhongchu*. These measures of currency and economic control placed large quantities of goods under a unified system of buying and selling at regulated prices handled by licensed dealers. Transport of these goods required the presentation of special passes issued by the military police. The measures, furthermore, channeled the goods to supply the needs of the military before satisfying the demand of the civilians.

But, despite the presence of their military police, it is doubtful whether the Japanese were successful in mastering control of the city. The complexity of Shanghai's social scene permitted the city to elude even the determined grasp of the Nationalists' Shanghai Public Security Bureau in the pre-war years. The outbreak of the war further introduced new lines of division into the city's political life. Both the Communist Party and the Nationalist secret service exploited the intricate network of personal ties and social connections for their own purposes. Neither, of course, showed much enthusiasm for the framework set by the Wang regime and the Japanese for peace. The Wang regime, meanwhile, was itself deeply riven by bitter power struggles between the "peace faction" of Nationalist Party collaborators who ran the government in Nanjing and the secret service chiefs at 76 Jessfield Road in Shanghai who were the main perpetrators of urban terrorism.[30] Much of the feuding had to do with the control of economic resources and the police force. These conflictual lines of allegiance among the Nationalists, the Communists, and the Wang regime divided Shanghai society under Japanese occupation. The controlled economy, meanwhile, bred its own resistance and disorder. As the inflationary pressure on the *Zhongchu* notes climbed, an active black market developed outside the regulated trade.[31] Aided by the Nationalists and the Communists, each with their respective needs, a whole underground economy took shape that spilled across the patrolled borders drawn by the puppet and the Japanese military police.

With the disruption of maritime trade, inland trade with Chongqing-controlled areas became all the more attractive. Ancient routes across mountain paths and along river valleys regained vitality. Traffic through the Qiantang river valley in Zhejiang, which linked Shanghai via the waterways south of the Yangzi with Anhui, Jiangxi, and Guangdong, opened up viable channels of trade and travel destined eventually for Chongqing. These routes went through areas where Nationalist military commands had maintained a certain presence *vis-à-vis* the Japanese. Counterfeit notes gained wide circulation in these zones of contested political control. Corruption was rampant where smugglers readily bore the cost of such border transactions.

In the city itself, power struggles and corruption combined to undermine the efficacy of the measures of control. The inflation that had been spiraling since 1942 seriously eroded the standing of the city's middle class. With large sectors of the city's established businesses placed under price control and state regulation, those who owned capital, including the financial institutions, saw few outlets for their money except stocks and commodities. A speculative mood prevailed, and well-being was seen to hinge upon the intent of the occupation authorities as well as upon the political fortunes of the market patrons. Rumors about imminent controls on gold in late March 1942, for example, sent the price of the metal plummeting. But the controls did not materialize. Gold prices in the black market bounced back to a high level in July, as did the value of gold on the commodity exchange.

Once again, wartime conditions in Shanghai intensified the disparity between the rich and the poor. In the final years of the war, the spectacular wealth enjoyed by a diminishing number of winners in these struggles contrasted sharply with the deprivation of the multitude. More than any other time during the war, wealth was seen as closely connected with access to political power in a system widely perceived to be unprincipled and unjust. Those with political connections with the state machinery and inside information reaped huge profits playing the stock and commodity markets. So much of the speculators' fortune rode upon the durability of the Japanese military and the Wang regime that rumors and reports on the war front readily sparked fluctuations as the Pacific war went on.[32]

As the tide turned against the Japanese in the Pacific, things also began to unravel for the Wang regime in Nanjing. Wang Jingwei died in 1944 in a

Tokyo hospital. A fierce power struggle broke out in the last days of his regime. Chen Gongbo and Zhou Fohai, the surviving leaders of the peace movement, opened up secret communications with the Nationalists as well as the Communists when they saw that their days in Nanjing were numbered. These last-minute efforts came too late and were of too little use to change these men's political fate at the conclusion of the war. In the fall of 1945, Chen Gongbo was put on trial as a collaborator by the returning Nationalists and was subsequently sentenced to death. Zhou Fohai died in prison while awaiting trial. Many others who had prospered during the occupation period—Yuan, Wen, and Lin, the three elders of Shanghai's banking circle, for example—saw their property confiscated and were thrown into prison.

The end of the war and the defeat of the Japanese did not bring the restoration of the International Settlement and the French Concession. The Allies had renounced their nineteenth-century treaty rights in China during the war. The end of the foreign concessions brought to the point of closure a whole century of European imperialism in China, and gave the returning Nationalists a city that was, for the first time in nearly a century, administratively unified.

The Nationalist rule of the city after the war was to last, however, for less than four years. Shanghai's takeover by the Communists in the late 1940s was determined, in one sense, by forces distant from the city—by the numerous battles fought in Manchuria and north China that ended in Nationalist failure, and by the success of the Communists' much lauded strategy of "surrounding the city with the countryside." But the transition of Shanghai to Communism was the outcome not only of Nationalist military failure but also of Communist political victory. When the People's Liberation Army marched down Nanjing Road in May 1949 an entire underground network emerged from all walks of life to assure the continuous smooth functioning of the city. The seeds of this moment had been planted well before the outbreak of the civil war. In retrospect, it was the Communists who stood to gain most in Shanghai's eight-year struggle under the military power of the Japanese.

NOTES

1 A considerable body of scholarship has been developed in recent years on the urban history of Shanghai in the first half of the twentieth century. Marie-Claire Bergère's important book *The Golden Age of the Chinese Bourgeoisie, 1911–1937*, Cambridge, 1989, related Republican China's failed democratic institutions to the relationship between the city's financial elites and the political authorities. Parks Coble, in *The Shanghai Capitalists and the Nationalist Government, 1927–1937*, Cambridge, Mass.: Harvard University Press, 1980, refutes the Maoist thesis that the Nationalist regime was bourgeois in class composition. Sherman Cochran, *Big Business in China: Sino-Foreign Rivalry in the Cigarette Industry, 1890–1930*, Cambridge, Mass.: Harvard University Press, 1980, provides a pioneering perspective on the Shanghai-based international business operations. Joseph Fewsmith, *Party, State, and Local Elites in Republican China: Merchant Organizations and Politics in Shanghai,*

1890–1930, Honolulu: University of Hawaii Press, 1985, examines middle-class political power at the street level. Emily Honig, *Constructing Chinese Ethnicity: Subei People in Shanghai, 1850–1980*, New Haven: Yale University Press, 1992, sheds important light on places of origin and urban identity. Bryna Goodman's *Native Place, City, and Nation: Regional Networks and Identities in Shanghai, 1853–1937*, Berkeley: University of California Press, 1995, offers the most sophisticated treatment of the subject to date. Concerning the lower levels of Shanghai society, Emily Honig, in *Sisters and Strangers: Women in the Shanghai Cotton Mills, 1919–1949*, Stanford: Stanford University Press, 1986, shows that working-class consciousness in Shanghai was conspicuous only by its absence. Elizabeth Perry, in *Shanghai on Strike: The Politics of Chinese Labor*, Stanford: Stanford University Press, 1993, examines the division of the labor force into levels of skill and groups of common places of native origin while exploring the political significance of such divisions to affiliations with the Nationalists versus with the Communists. Other scholars devote their attention to the social tension and political unrest that troubled the city for most of the Republican period (1919–49). Jeffrey Wasserstrom, in *Student Protests in Twentieth Century China: the View from Shanghai*, Stanford: Stanford University Press, 1991, analyzes the symbolic mediation of collective political protests. How the city was administered and whether it was effectively patrolled was masterfully explored by Frederic Wakeman in *Policing Shanghai*, Berkeley: University of California Press, 1995, which also presents a sweeping view of the various aspects of urban life. How the newly ascendant Guomindang regime established control over this complicated city via the Shanghai municipal government from 1927 to 1937 is the subject of Christian Henriot's important study *Shanghai, 1927–1937: Municipal Power, Locality, and Modernization*, Berkeley: University of California Press, 1993, English translation by Noel Castelino. On the other side of law and order, there is Brian Martin's informative treatment of the career of Du Yusheng in *The Shanghai Green Gang: Politics and Organized Crime, 1919–1937*, Berkeley: University of California Press, 1996, Gail Hershatter, *Dangerous Pleasures: Prostitution and Modernity in Twentieth Century Shanghai*, Berkeley: University of California Press, 1996, and Christian Henriot, *Belles de Shanghai: prostitution et sexualité en Chine aux XIXe–XXe siècles* (English edition forthcoming, Cambridge University Press). Few of the above, however, treat Shanghai during the war. The only exceptions are Poshek Fu, *Passivity, Resistance, and Collaboration: Intellectual Choices in Occupied Shanghai, 1937–1945*, Stanford: Stanford University Press, 1993, which focuses on literary activities, and Frederic Wakeman, Jr, *The Shanghai Badlands: Wartime Terrorism and Urban Crime, 1937–1941*, New York: Cambridge University Press, 1996.

2   On administrative divisions of pre-war Shanghai and for a brief sketch of the city's social history, see Frederic Wakeman, Jr, and Wen-hsin Yeh, "Introduction," in *Shanghai Sojourners*, Berkeley: Institute of East Asian Studies, University of California at Berkeley, 1992, pp. 1–14.

3   On the French Concession during the war, see Chapter 9 in this volume. Both concessions were handed over to the Wang regime in July 1943. The Wang government marked the occasion by a prompt and thorough renaming of all streets bearing foreign names—King Edward Road in the International Settlement, for example, became Shanghai Road, while Foche Road, the main thoroughfare in the French Concession, became Taishan Road. Zheng Zu'an, "Jindai Shanghai chengshi fengmao de bianqian" [Changing faces of modern Shanghai], paper presented at conference on modern Shanghai, Shanghai Academy of Social Sciences, August 1994.

4   Tao Juyin, *Gudao jianwen: Kangzhan shiqi de Shanghai* [Things seen and heard on

the lone islet: Shanghai during the War of Resistance], Shanghai: Renmin chu-banshe, 1979, p. 12. On the political history of this period leading up to the Sino-Japanese War, see Parks Coble, *Facing Japan: Chinese Politics and Japanese Imperialism, 1931–1937*, Cambridge, Mass.: Harvard University Press, 1991.

5   Lloyd Eastman, *Seeds of Destruction*, Stanford: Stanford University Press, 1984, p. 144. See also Lloyd Eastman, "Nationalist China during the Sino-Japanese War, 1937–1945," in John K. Fairbank and Albert Feuerwerker, eds, *The Cambridge History of China* XIII, "Republican China, 1912–1949," Part 2, pp. 547–608, Cambridge: Cambridge University Press, 1986.

6   See Chapter 5 in this volume.

7   When the main Nationalist force withdrew, these men, cheered on by volunteers who brought them food and supplies from across the river, persisted in their resistance, which they did not give up until late in November. Tao Juyin, *Gudao jianwen*, p. 15.

8   Tao Juyin, *Gudao jianwen*, pp. 3–4.

9   Edward Gunn, *Unwelcome Muse: Chinese Literature in Shanghai and Peking, 1937–1945*, New York: Columbia University Press, 1980.

10   See Chapter 5 in this volume.

11   See, for example, the "Yule xinwen" [Entertainment news] section in the various issues of *Yinqianjie* [Financial circle], the publication of Shanghai's banking employees, in 1938 and 1939.

12   Tao Juyin, *Gudao jianwen*, pp. 53–9. Huang Youlan, *Kangri zhanzheng shiqi de heping yundong* [The so-called peace movement during the War of Resistance], Beijing: Jiefangjun chubanshe, 1988, pp. 136–41; Huang Meizhen and Zhang Yun, *Wang Jingwei jituan panguo toudi ji* [An account of how Wang Jingwei and his followers betrayed the nation and joined the enemy], Kaifeng: Henan renmin chubanshe, 1987, pp. 142–59.

13   See Chapter 7 in this volume. See also Wakeman, *Shanghai Badlands*, pp. 80–92.

14   For an eye-witness account of urban terrorism of this period, see Zhu Zijia (Jin Xiongbai), *Wang zhengquan de kaichang yu shouchang* [The beginning and end of the drama of the Wang regime], I–IV, Hong Kong: Chunqiu zazhi she, 1959–61; V–VI, Hong Kong: Wuxingji shubao she, 1964, 1971.

15   Tao Juyin, *Gudao jianwen*, p. 90. Wakeman, *Shanghai Badlands*, pp. 119–23. Cheng Naishan's novel *The Banker*, trans. Britten Dean, San Francisco: China Books and Periodicals, 1992, is a fictionalized account of the story of the Bank of China during the war. Cheng's grandfather was a senior manager with the bank in Shanghai during those years.

16   Wakeman, *Shanghai Badlands*, pp. 107–10.

17   For an overview of banking and finance in wartime Shanghai, see Wang Jishen, ed., *Zhanshi Shanghai jingji* [Wartime Shanghai economy], Shanghai: Shanghai jingji yanjiu suo, 1945, pp. 1–59. See also D. K. Lieu, "The Sino-Japanese Currency War," *Pacific Affairs* 12, 4 (1939), pp. 413–26.

18   Gerald E. Bunker, *The Peace Conspiracy: Wang Ching-wei and the China War, 1937–1941*, Cambridge, Mass.: Harvard University Press, 1972, and John Hunter Boyle, *China and Japan at War, 1937–1945: The Politics of Collaboration*, Stanford: Stanford University Press, 1972.

19   Wen-hsin Yeh, "On the Republican Origin of the Communist *Danwei*," in William Kirby and Marie-Claire Bergère, eds, *China's Mid-century Transition*, Cambridge, Mass.: Harvard University Press, forthcoming.

20   Lyman Van Slyke, "The Chinese Communist Movement during the Sino-Japanese War, 1937–1945," in Fairbank and Feuerwerker, *The Cambridge History of China* XIII, Part 2, pp. 609–83. On the New Fourth Army Incident of January 1941, see especially pp. 665–71.

21 Chalmers Johnson, *An Instance of Treason: Ozaki Hotsume and the Sorge Spy Ring*, expanded edition, Stanford: Stanford University Press, 1990.

22 Wen-hsin Yeh, *Provincial Passages: Culture, Space, and the Origins of Chinese Communism*, Berkeley and Los Angeles: University of California Press, 1996, pp. 219–225; Peter Zarrow, *Anarchism and Chinese Political Culture*, New York: Columbia University Press, 1990, pp. 31–58.

23 Tao Juyin, *Gudao jianwen*, pp. 99–101; Wasserstein, *Student Protests*, p. 9.

24 Tao Juyin, *Gudao jianwen*, pp. 114–26.

25 See Chapter 8 in this volume.

26 Shanghai Municipal Archives, ed., *Riwei Shanghai shi zhengfu* (Puppet Shanghai Municipal Government), Shanghai: Dang'an chubanshe, 1988, pp. 254–6.

27 Tao Juyin, *Gudao jianwen*, pp. 118–29.

28 Wang Jishen, *Zhanshi Shanghai jingji*, pp. 108–48.

29 Commodities that came under economic control were placed under special boards that approved all transactions involving these goods. Ownership became legal only after registration. Tao Juyin, *Gudao jianwen*, p. 227.

30 Huang Meizhen and Zhang Yun, *Wang Jingwei*, pp. 315–23.

31 Tao Juyin, *Gudao jianwen*, pp. 225–35.

32 Tao Juyin, *Gudao jianwen*, pp. 170–6.

2 Introduction

The struggle to survive

Wen-hsin Yeh

Those who lived through this war struggled for survival in an environment of complex politics with diffused meaning. Local politics intersected with national events and international divisions of much longer duration and far-reaching scope. Yet local politics was not purely derivative; the locale had its significant role to play in shaping the contests at a higher level. What was so striking about wartime Shanghai was that no single issue or ideological position had been able to lay a sweeping claim on the allegiance or loyalty of all individuals in the city, thanks to this ceaseless mixing and reconfiguring of politics on all levels. Shanghai consequently entered the war not as one civic entity, but as a mosaic of ethnic and sub-ethnic communities each with its own diverse origins and destinations. No black-and-white distinction could be drawn between resistance and collaboration, since few could agree upon what they were standing for, although all recognized in the Japanese a common enemy.

Bernard Wasserstein's chapter (Chapter 3), which examines the conduct of the city's Europeans, including the public administrators of the foreign concessions, shows how many people had readily opted for collaboration instead of resistance. The 50,000-some Europeans in wartime Shanghai had arrived there, first of all, from a variety of places under diverse circumstances. The French, the Russians, and the European Jews (who counted among the city's newest arrivals) were geographically isolated from home and politically at sea with lost bearings. "None could look to a clearly focused political home. None felt a sense of community either with the surrounding Chinese population or with the rest of the deeply fissured European groups in Shanghai. That most of them opted for a policy of accommodation rather than resistance may be regarded, in the circumstances, as a natural and unsurprising response to an impossible situation" (p. 27).

The city's 10,000 or so British and Commonwealth citizens and the smaller number of Americans, who called themselves " Shanghailanders" and traced their connections with the city to a much earlier time, behaved in many ways in just as compromising a manner. Wasserstein shows that despite the availability of opportunities to flee, they stayed on, went along with the

enemy, and "facilitated the smooth handover and functioning of the administration of Shanghai with its port, its major industries and other strategic
facilities under Japanese auspices" (p. 28). This service to the Japanese could
be viewed as collaboration, because it surely aided the Japanese war effort.
When confronted with the accusation of treason at a later time, some defended
themselves by arguing that their first duty was to the international community
in Shanghai. Others insisted that they had been instructed by the British
government to cooperate or that they had never been instructed to act
otherwise.

British-owned enterprises, like the British-controlled public services, went
on conducting business as usual. Some even went so far as to claim
unabashedly the priority of their business interests over the national interest,
and insisted upon the importance of preserving their established positions in
China.

The considerations of the " business collaborators" contrasted with a third
type, dubbed the "anti-imperialist collaborator" by Wasserstein, such as the
half-Chinese, half-British Lawrence Kentwell. The former saw the war as a
threat to their established interest. The latter saw wartime disruption as
presenting a new opportunity. Kentwell occupied himself during the war with
the production of violently anti-British and pro-Japanese propaganda. Race
was the main factor on his mind, and the war gave him hope that European
racial discrimination against the Chinese would be suitably redressed.
Kentwell thus did not simply go along with the Japanese but actively
contributed his service to their cause.

The war, however, was ineffectual as an instrument against racial
contempt, even when national alliances cut across racial divides. The
Japanese and the Germans did not work well together in Shanghai. Nor did
the Shanghailanders and the Shanghaiese succeed in gaining each other's full
confidence as allies in war. Japanese war propaganda, meanwhile, addressed
its Chinese targets as brothers of common cultural heritage and ethnic
descent, and urged joint efforts in the creation of an East Asian Sphere of
Co-prosperity that would assert itself against European colonialism. Wasserstein concludes that racial inequality, which was the central political idea that
animated European Shanghai, "helped distort loyalties, weaken the links tying
individuals to political communities, and open a pathway for the descent into
treason" (p. 39). What happened during the war went a long way in explaining
the end of European Shanghai in the post-war order of the city.

The Japanese in Shanghai, by contrast, faced communal fissures of a
different sort. Japanese civilians, as Joshua Fogel shows in Chapter 4, had
built a full-fledged community in Hongkow, complete with banks, schools,
churches, newspapers, shops, beauty salons, a health service, a police force,
and a wide array of investment interests. This was the result of a significant
rise of Japanese sojourning in China in the mid-1930s, and these civilians did
not hesitate to clamor for a tough Japanese stance to protect their concerns in
Shanghai.

Japanese intellectuals, especially those with socialist leanings who studied China, however, did not see themselves at ease in these communities. Firmly rooted in a pacifist creed, they found themselves deprived of a political homeland. These men frequented bookstores and coffee shops and mingled with their fellow left-leaning Chinese writers, playwrights, and translators in salons and reading societies. Together they built a network of left-wing intellectuals that cut across national boundaries and placed personal political convictions above the state's mandate to adhere to its chosen policies.

The central figure in this informal network, Uchiyama Kanzo, survived the years of war and the subsequent civil conflicts by steadfastly maintaining an impeccably apolitical stance. The same tendency to steer clear of partisan choices and strong commitment characterized the wartime politics of many private Chinese industrialists—producers of textiles, flour, matches, and other consumer goods who had been left behind in Shanghai by the Nationalist government to fend for themselves. These entrepreneurs, as Parks Coble shows in Chapter 5, did everything possible to keep themselves in control and their businesses alive. Not unlike their British counterparts, Chinese business-men in occupied areas were preoccupied with survival, and it was not uncommon for them to put their business considerations before national concerns. Neither patriots nor collaborators by choice, many families of capitalists dispatched their various constituent branches to invest with opposing political camps simultaneously, splitting political risks in the face of uncertainty. Coble argues that this strategy of political diversification within the same family network, observed repeatedly in a significant number of cases, allowed the capitalists as a social group to survive remarkably well during the war. Even though some ended up being charged as collaborators, enough members of the same family would have cultivated sufficiently strong political ties elsewhere to salvage the family's fortunes as a whole under changing circumstances.

Poshek Fu's Chapter 6, which examines the rise of the film industry on the *gudao*, affirms this theme of distance from national politics. Fu shows that Zhang Shankun (1905–56), the most visible and profitable entrepreneur of Chinese cinema during the war, prospered as a prolific producer of low-budget historical romances which enjoyed major commercial success. Zhang's films—and those of his rivals and imitators—contained few overt political messages. They transported the minds of the film industry's growing audience to the realms either of the distant past or of folkloric sentimentalism. The films were neither explicitly patriotic nor collaborationist. They were popular and commercially successful among the city's large number of recent sojourners, according to Fu, precisely because they seemed so utterly uninvolved with contemporary events.

The Press Bureau of Japan's Central Expeditionary Army in Shanghai, however, kept a close watch on the film industry. Film producers lived constantly in the shadow of urban terrorism. Marketing and distribution of film products beyond the confines of the *gudao*, especially to the occupied provinces in central China and to Southeast Asia, were vulnerable to Japanese blockade and intervention. Political pressure had certainly been applied, furthermore, on Chinese producers to make films that promoted Japanese ideas of East Asian co-prosperity.

By simply refusing to be anything other than a mere businessman mindful of the box office, Zhang and others defied the political pressure from the occupation authorities to produce propaganda. On the other hand, there was certainly a war raging, and the industry thrived by closing its eyes to that war. The conduct of the film industry during wartime in Shanghai was thus full of moral ambiguity. Zhang and his colleagues, unlike the peacemakers of the Wang regime, were not active contributors to the Japanese war effort. Neither did they, on the other hand, put up much of a resistance to hinder that campaign. Together with the British administrators, the Chinese capitalists, and even the Japanese socialists of the city, Shanghai film producers went about their business as usual, contributing to a sense of peace and even normalcy under the shadow of war and occupation. This peace, so studiously and singlemindedly maintained, coexisted in close proximity with widespread violence and misery. It was a normalcy built upon cowed acceptance of brute force and injustice, tenable only on the implicit recognition that the survival of one's self and immediate family should come before that of any larger community.

There were, to be sure, overt acts of resistance in the form of attacks on Japanese personnel and assassinations of their prospective Chinese allies. Yeh's Chapter 7 draws attention to the secret service agents of Chongqing who were armed to act and war with their rivals of No. 76. Recruited and trained by the Nationalist government to carry out paramilitary missions against the regime's declared foes and rivals, these men clearly did not think primarily of the survival of the self. Their resistance, on the other hand, was a matter less of moral choice than of duty and profession. The resistance stemmed, furthermore, less from individual determination to defend values and norms rooted in the everyday life of the locale than from a state's organized response when facing fundamental threats to its interest and authority. The brotherhood that these men formed had but tenuous connections with the urban milieu that was uniquely Shanghai.

What seems striking about wartime politics in Shanghai, on balance, was not quite so much the organized struggles between contenders for state authority—the Wang regime vs. the Chongqing authorities, the Japanese vs. the Chinese, the Nationalists vs. the Communists—as the institutionalization of the coercive power of the state over the population. Wakeman's Chapter 8, which describes the installation of mechanisms of urban control under the Japanese occupation authorities, documents the extension of the household registration system (*hukou*) into the foreign concessions and the creation of the urban militia (*baojia*) there after 1941. The control system put in place by the Japanese, Wakeman notes, "remained intact" when the Nationalists liberated the city in 1945. "Identity cards (*shenfenzheng*) were issued by the Guomindang authorities, and the household registration infrastructure survived, just as it would persist through 1949 and the period of Communist 'Liberation' as well" (p. 150). As the civilians of the city preoccupied themselves with issues of sheer survival, state authorities worked to enhance their grip on the amorphous urban society. One of the lasting legacies of the war years turned out to be the continuous development of mechanisms of state control, which appeared to have a life of their own that cut across national as well as ideological divisions.

One form of state authority unequivocally came to an end in Shanghai in 1945. As Marie-Claire Bergère's Chapter 9 shows, the war marked the conclusion of European Shanghai and the colonial form of rule in the city. The moment arrived with the arrest of Roland Sarly, assistant director of police in what had been the French Concession, during the night of December 14, 1945, by the Nationalist garrison force. Sarly, who had served as an inspector with responsibility for external affairs in the municipal police force of the Wang Jingwei government from August 1943 to March 1945, was accused of collaboration and treason. He had turned over to the Japanese for torture and execution Nationalist soldiers and Chongqing agents who had sought refuge in the French Concession. He was also corrupt in his handling of the controls over the prices and rationing of goods. Unlike his British counterparts in the Shanghai Municipal Police, however, Sarly, as he was appointed by the Vichy regime, was not interned by the Japanese. He was consequently arrested by the Nationalists after the Japanese defeat and brought before the High Court of Shanghai for trial.

The choice between collaboration and resistance in wartime Shanghai, to be sure, was a matter of much ambiguity. By Bergère's analysis, "Japanese militarism was not founded upon the same ideological basis or the same ambitions as Nazism. The presence of Western imperialism complicated the political choices of Chinese patriots. And the growing strength of the Communists encouraged the conclusion of secret alliances between Chongqing and Nanking or even with the Japanese" (p. 163). But the trial of Sarly's alleged treason, as it unfolded in the Shanghai courtroom in 1945–6, was not so much about collaboration and resistance during the war as about post-war contestation between the Chinese and the French authorities over the latter's extraterritoriality in the city. After much diplomatic maneuvering behind the scenes, Sarly was let go in the end. The French, meanwhile, gave up their claims in China proper in exchange for the withdrawal of Nationalist troops from northern Indochina.

Bergère's chapter draws attention to the courtroom politics in post-war trials of collaboration and resistance. Numerous individuals, Chinese as well as foreign, were put on trial for collaboration and treason. Those who were found guilty not only received jail sentences but also saw their properties confiscated and their reputation destroyed. Individuals stood trial, however, often to serve the purposes of the state. To try Sarly as a Japanese collaborator was to allow the Nationalists a chance to assert their legitimacy *vis-à-vis* the former colonialists. To try Chen Gongbo and his fellow collaborationists of the Nanjing regime, similarly, was to allow the returning Nationalists a chance to vindicate Chongqing's war policies *vis-à-vis* the peace faction. The state's action, to be sure, could not be completely divorced from popular sentiment. This use of the courtroom none the less gave the state yet another way to exercise its authority against Shanghai's civilian population as it saw fit. The end of the war saw in the city, in short, a further constriction of the civil society that seemed to have such a promising start in the mobilizational campaigns for patriotism before the Japanese assault began.[1]

NOTE

1 Upon the return of Chiang Kai-shek's Nationalist government to the lower Yangzi, many who had prospered under the Wang Jingwei regime, including a number of popular women writers, were accused of collaboration with the enemy and punished in various ways. There was no equivalent to the "Vichy syndrome" in subsequent Chinese political life, however, that drew upon constructions of wartime experience in Shanghai. Like the Chiang Kai-shek government in Chongqing, the Wang regime claimed legitimacy as an heir to the Nationalist Party of Sun Yat-sen. Although Wang was himself an early activist in the 1911 revolution and a major rival to Chiang Kai-shek within the Nationalist Party, he was no national hero of Pétain's stature. Nor did the division between Wang and Chiang fall along lines of tension either in terms of social background, social policies, regional histories, political ideologies, or religious beliefs. Collaboration with the Japanese, furthermore, did not implicate the Wang regime in atrocities against targeted sectors of the population on racial or ethnic grounds. The Wang regime, within limits, had functioned, in fact, as a sort of buffer between the Japanese military and the Chinese civilians in the lower Yangzi region. Wang died before the end of the war and thereby escaped standing trial as a traitor. The Nationalists and the Communists soon moved towards the civil war that concluded with a Communist victory. Both parties, despite their civil conflicts, subscribed to the same notion of a unified China of territorial integrity under the governance of one centralized state. The Wang regime, given its willingness to settle for partial autonomy under Japanese tutelage, was marginalized in subsequent Chinese historial narratives as a regional episode of transient significance. On recent French reconsiderations of resistance and collaboration during World War II, see especially Henry Rousso, *The Vichy Syndrome: History and Memory in France since 1944*, trans. Arthur Goldhammer, Cambridge, Mass.: Harvard University Press, 1991.

3   Ambiguities of occupation

Foreign resisters and collaborators in wartime
Shanghai

Bernard Wasserstein

Collaboration was a widespread, indeed pervasive, phenomenon throughout
the European, North African and Asian territories occupied by the Axis
powers in World War II. In the immediate aftermath of the war it was
generally defined and interpreted as the reverse of the coin of resistance. More
recently, as the passions of indictment and apologetics have diminished, both
collaboration and resistance have come to be seen as ambiguous and complex
phenomena, including more grey than black and white. This is the case both
for the European theater, in the works, for example, of H. R. Kedward
and Paul Jankowski on occupied France and Isaiah Trunk on the Jewish
Councils in Eastern Europe, and for the Chinese theater in, for example, Poshek
Fu's recent book on intellectuals in wartime Shanghai.[1] In the case of occupied
China it has long been recognized that a simple typology of "resistance" and
"collaboration" is almost useless in understanding the shifting loyalties of
many local warlords and political figures associated with the Guomindang.
Indeed, in the Chinese instance neither a black–white collaborator–resister
dichotomy nor a continuum between the two poles seems to accord with
historical reality. The triangular Chongqing–Communist–puppet taxonomy
which lay at the back of much early post-war writing on the subject is also
now generally regarded as superficial and inadequate.

It may be helpful to consider the phenomena of resistance and collaboration using the metaphor of a palimpsest: political loyalties and alignments
were repeatedly formulated, partly erased, then reformulated to meet
changing circumstances and needs. The little sub-case of the foreign
communities in Shanghai may seem, at first glance, exotic and too isolated
from both the Chinese and the European experiences of occupation to tell us
much about either of these larger theaters. But a spotlight thrown on this tiny
sideshow may illuminate some of the larger patterns of collaboration and
resistance in the war. In particular, this chapter examines the reasons that led
so many foreigners in Shanghai to opt for collaboration rather than
resistance—in a few cases to opt for both.

Collaboration, even if defined in the rather narrow version from the *Oxford
English Dictionary* as "traitorous cooperation with the enemy", was certainly
a more common phenomenon among Europeans in Shanghai than resistance

even if we accept, for the moment, the broad *OED* definition of resistance as "organized covert opposition to an occupying or ruling power"—which, be it noted, does not seem to require any armed action. A report prepared for the US Office of Strategic Services a few weeks after the end of the war estimated that "some 200 white persons, men and women" collaborated with the enemy. They were said to have

> informed on the underground, led the way to the hiding places of secret wealth, furthered Japanese and other Axis propaganda by working for controlled newspapers and broadcasting from controlled radio stations. Some helped the Japanese [the report continued] in their dirtiest work—torture, kidnapping, murder, extortion.[2]

Out of a European population of more than 50,000, the figure of 200 collaborators seems relatively small. Yet even a brief examination of the behavior of Europeans and other foreign citizens in Shanghai between the Japanese occupation of the International Settlement on December 8, 1941, and September 7, 1945, the date on which General Toii Minfu of the Japanese Thirteenth Army formally surrendered Shanghai to General Chen Shu-sun of the Third Chongqing Army, suggests that the figure is underestimated and that collaboration cannot be dismissed as a marginal phenomenon.

This is demonstrable even if we pass over with the most cursory of reviews three of the largest European groups in Shanghai at the time: the 25,000 Russians, the European Jewish refugees, who numbered at least 18,000, and the French, of whom there were about 2,700 civilians plus about 1,000 troops. While varying numbers of individuals engaged in active collaboration (in the narrow sense of working for Japanese security organs and so forth), all three of these communities as a whole may be said to have arrived, in different ways, at some form of accommodation and *modus vivendi* with the new order.

The Shanghai Russians, most of them "White" anti-Communists who had arrived as refugees towards the end of the Russian civil war, tended almost instinctively to see the Nazis as liberators rather than invaders of their homeland. The leading Russian newspaper, *Shanghai Zaria*, expressed the general feeling on December 26, 1942, when it supported pro-Japanese statements by Ataman Semenov, the White Russian leader in Dairen (whose son served as a Japanese nominee in the Foreign Affairs section of the Shanghai Municipal Police until 1944). The paper declared: "Russian immigrants [in Shanghai] are for the New Order and demonstrate full loyalty to the Nipponese Empire." Some younger elements in the community, assiduously courted by Soviet propagandists, whom the Japanese permitted to operate in Shanghai until 1945, argued that the Stalin regime should be regarded as temporary and that all Russians should rally to the defense of the national hearth; few, however, heeded this call.[3] At least fifty-six Russians in Shanghai worked directly for Japanese security organs during the war—for the gendarmerie, for the Japanese Naval Bureau, for the Special Political

Police of the puppet regime at 76 Jessfield Road, or for other bodies.[4] In addition, a large number worked for the Shanghai Municipal Police. Towards the end of the war many of the Russians changed their tune opportunistically and some applied for Soviet citizenship, leading to their repatriation after the war—often direct to prison camps.

The refugee Jews, while naturally anti-Nazi, were not particularly hostile to the Japanese—to whom many of them felt gratitude for affording them an escape hatch from Nazi Europe. When the Japanese took hostile measures against them, most notably their virtual internment in the Hongkew district between 1943 and 1945, the Jews tended to attribute the actions to German pressure on the Japanese—although the evidence suggests that, in so far as the Japanese in Shanghai took advice from anyone on the Jewish issue, they looked not to local Nazi representatives but to fanatically antisemitic "White" Russian advisers to the Naval Bureau and the police. In general, the Jews preserved an attitude of studied neutrality towards the Far Eastern war. Apart from some underworld figures, few engaged in active collaboration, though a small number served in the municipal police at least until 1943. Jewish newspapers in German, Russian and Yiddish continued to appear in Shanghai under Japanese censorship through most of the occupation. The Japanese even permitted some quasi-political activity by Zionist groups—particularly the rightwing Betar movement, which had a long record of sympathy for Japanese militarist expansion in East Asia. The few Jews who had contacts with British intelligence or resistance elements for the most part belonged not to the European refugee community but to the older-established Baghdadi Jewish merchant colony, many of whose members held British citizenship.

As for the French business community and the pro-Vichy administration of the French Concession, evidence now available shows that anti-Allied feeling was widespread, mainly in the sense of pro-Vichy loyalty but, in some cases, of pro-Axis and pro-Japanese activity. The French consul-general from 1940 to 1943, Roland de Margerie, had been *chef de cabinet* to Prime Minister Reynaud and was regarded as opposed to the armistice. (He was sent to Shanghai after the fall of France for that very reason.) Yet he served the Vichy regime loyally in the Far East throughout the war—his local German counterpart, Consul-general Martin Fischer, with some insight, categorized him as an *attentiste*.[5] It would hardly be going too far to say that after June 1940 the primary target of French hostility in Shanghai appears to have been not the Germans but the British. In 1942 the French club, the Cercle Sportif Français, barred membership to any British or Americans.[6] Perhaps this was in response to Japanese pressure—but the move undoubtedly reflected the anti-Anglo-Saxon feelings of many Frenchmen in Shanghai at the time.

From mid-1940 to early 1941 a Free French group in Shanghai headed by R. Egal, a local wine merchant, carried on Gaullist propaganda and sent sixty-five men to fight in De Gaulle's forces. Initially Egal's activities were welcomed by the British embassy. But just as De Gaulle proved to be a thorn in the side of Churchill and Roosevelt, so Egal's own "headstrong behavior" came to be considered an embarrassment by some British diplomats and officials in the Far East. There was a palpable sense of relief in British official circles when pro-Vichy elements engineered his arrest and removal from Shanghai to Hanoi in April 1941.[7] The British secured his release on condition that he furnish an undertaking not to engage in further political activities.[8] Although he was able to return to Shanghai briefly the following autumn, Free French activity there effectively ended then. Under the Japanese occupation a French judge, Georges Rivelain-Kauffman, led a small group that maintained connections with French resistance in Indochina and with the Chongqing regime; but the local French police, apparently in collusion with the Japanese, kept him under close surveillance.

A contingent of about 1,000 French infantry, composed partly of Annamite troops, was the only military unit of a European power (apart from a small force of Italian marines) to remain in the city after the departure of the last British troops in 1940 and of the American marines in November 1941. Apart from occasional parades in the French Concession, the French soldiers remained in their barracks until they were humiliatingly disarmed on the orders of Japanese military authorities on March 10, 1945.[9] No resistance was offered on that occasion.

The equivocal behavior of many of the French in Shanghai led to a settling of accounts at the end of the war. The commander of the French garrison, Colonel A. J. F. Artigue, expressed shame at his conduct the previous March and shot himself in the head: "Ils m'ont trompé! Nous aurions dû nous battre," he said.[10] (De Gaulle sent him a message of sympathy, exonerating him of any dishonor; he died of his wound two years later.) The director of the French Concession police force, Captain L. Fabre, committed suicide. Fabre's deputy, Roland Sarly, was arrested by the Chinese and charged with collaboration with the Japanese. Perhaps to forestall further arrests by the Chinese, the French themselves arrested a local French Nazi, Paul-François Tosoli, in January 1946, and spirited him away aboard a cruiser to Saigon— occasioning a diplomatic storm over the alleged infringement of Chinese sovereignty.

Each of these three groups found itself in a peculiar position, not only geographically isolated but also politically at sea with lost bearings. None could look to a clearly focused political home. None felt a sense of community either with the surrounding Chinese population or with the rest of the deeply fissured foreign groups in Shanghai. That most of them opted for a policy of accommodation rather than resistance may be regarded, in the circumstances, as a natural and unsurprising response to an impossible situation.

The cases of the 10,000 or so British and Commonwealth citizens and the smaller number of Americans who found themselves trapped in Shanghai by the Japanese occupation of the International Settlement on December 8, 1941, perhaps deserve to be judged by rather sterner standards. Unlike the Russians,

Jews and French, there could be little doubt in the case of the Anglo-Saxons as to where they owed their national loyalties according to law and accepted contemporary practice. Yet the wartime conduct of not a few of these "Shanghailanders" left them open to reproach—in some cases to post-war prosecution.

That collaboration was seen by the British authorities as a disturbingly widespread phenomenon among the British in Shanghai quite early in the occupation is evident from a telegram dispatched to London in May 1942 by General Wavell, British commander-in-chief in India. No doubt basing himself on intelligence reports, Wavell wrote:

> Reports from Shanghai indicate British subjects, many of military age, living more or less normal lives, although good prospects of escape exist if effort made. Reports also indicate some continue serve in Police and Municipal Administration. Fact that extremely few British civilians have so far escaped significant in view of these reports. . . . Our prestige will be still further lowered if British subjects continue serve puppet Municipal Council, and if British firms continue to operate by agreement with Japanese as appears to be the case.[11]

This report actually understated the extent to which, in the early phase of the occupation, Allied civilians adapted with seeming insouciance to the realities of the new order in Shanghai.

In fact, virtually the entire British and other Allied staffs of the Shanghai Municipal Police and the Shanghai Municipal Council (both of which were dominated, at senior levels, before the war by British citizens) remained at their posts for several weeks, in many cases for months, in some for more than a year, after the start of the occupation. In acting thus they facilitated the smooth handover and functioning of the administration of Shanghai with its port, its major industries and other strategic facilities under Japanese auspices. The 300 or so senior British officials of the Chinese Maritime Customs Service did not remain at their posts: all were dismissed in December 1941—although they contested the authority of the Nanking (puppet) government to dismiss them.[12]

An immediate caveat should be entered—one that illustrates the difficulty of any attempt at too rigorous a definition of "collaboration" and that illustrates the moral ambiguity of the behavior of these police and municipal employees, who, if judged simply by the results of their actions, must surely be said to have aided the Japanese war effort. Astonishing as it may seem, the British members of both the International Settlement police and the Municipal Council who remained at their posts after December 8, 1941, were acting in strict accordance with instructions received before the war from the British government.

These instructions, which were in line with similar guidance by the British government to the civil authorities in, for example, the German-occupied Channel Islands, were issued confidentially in 1941 to all British members of the Shanghai Municipal Police by the British commissioner of the force, K. M. Bourne. Responding to requests from some police officers to be released to join the British armed forces, Bourne wrote: "I can assure you that until this war is over our duty lies in Shanghai. . . . The greater the danger and the more trying the conditions to be faced *where we are needed* the greater the obligation to stick it out until British [*sic*] is victorious." A note appended to the copy of this document in the Public Record Office states: "After this had been issued Major K. M. Bourne obtained furlough and went to Canada where he joined H.M. Forces."[13] Sauce for the goose—but not for the goslings! (Bourne's apparent abandonment of his force was the result, of course, of orders from above. For much of the war he worked for the British Security Executive in New York. In February 1945 he was appointed to take charge of the Chinese Intelligence section of the Government of India's intelligence bureau.)

Immediately after the Japanese occupation of the International Settlement in December 1941, a Japanese officer assumed command of the Settlement police force. The British and other foreign members of the force continued to serve for the time being—"remembering [as a postwar report put it] that the first duty of this international force was to the community".[14] The question "*Which* community?" arose very quickly. In late December British police officers baulked when asked to assist the Japanese gendarmerie in arresting some foreign citizens, including British and Americans, accused of anti-Japanese activities. On advice from a senior British officer they declared that they would assist in arresting Chinese who were accused of such political crimes but not foreign subjects.[15] Police records over the ensuing weeks contain many instances of assistance by British policemen in arrests of Chinese accused of resistance activities.[16] At one level this may seem like a clear act of collaboration. On the other hand, these officers were doing no more than they had done in the period 1938 to 1941 when the SMP Special Branch (like their counterparts in the French Concession) had cooperated on a regular basis with the Japanese in suppressing Chinese resistance activities directed against the Japanese in Shanghai. This may perhaps be seen as one of many instances of appeasement merging into collaboration.[17] Some members of the force, including a few of the most senior officers, carried out such orders after December 1941 without qualms. Others became increasingly perplexed at what they felt was the false position in which they found themselves. In September 1942 some of the latter sent a request for guidance, through the Swiss consulate, to the British government.[18] They do not seem to have received any reply. Several British policemen were dismissed in February 1942 but the rest continued to serve and some were promoted by the Japanese commissioner as a reward for efficient service. Eventually they were all dismissed and most were interned.

In certain cases service in the force terminated with an abruptness in which dark comedy mingled with personal tragedy. A postwar statement by Superintendent J. A. McFarlane, former police quartermaster, describes with indignation how, on January 6, 1943, he had been standing in his office in uniform when

> about five or six male Japanese in plain clothes entered, and through the Japanese Superintendent who was supposed to be actually in charge of the Department but under my tuition [*sic*], I was informed that the gentlemen who had just entered were members of H.I.J.M. Gendarmerie and they were to ask me a few questions at Headquarters.

He was arrested in full uniform and taken away for questioning; later he was imprisoned and tortured.[19] Some of the replacements for the dismissed British police officers were Japanese, others Russians: "We have finally been given a chance to prove ourselves," said Chief Inspector B. Maklaevsky, the first Russian to attain that rank in the force, in January 1943.[20] By the last phase of the war most of the former British policemen in Shanghai had come to feel bitter resentment against their government. Their indignation was compounded, upon their release at the liberation, when they discovered that they had no jobs to return to, the International Settlement having been retroceded to China in 1943. The British government disclaimed responsibility for paying them pensions on the ground that, unlike the British police in, for example, Hong Kong, they had been employees of the Shanghai Municipal Council, not servants of the Crown.

The sequence of events in the case of officials of the Shanghai Municipal Council was similar. There too the American and other Allied governments appear to have given advice to their citizens similar to that given to the British: they should continue to work in order to maintain public order and local services. The result was, in effect, to place most of the officials concerned in an awkward predicament that can only be described as officially sanctioned collaboration. Against this background the behavior of those whom we might define as volunteer collaborators in Shanghai becomes more comprehensible. If such was the example offered publicly by the most prominent local quasi-official representatives of the British empire, is it any wonder that other British, American, and Australian citizens drew the conclusion that collaborationism of a more active sort could be squared in good conscience with patriotic duty?

What, then, were the motives that led to what might be termed full-blooded collaboration? The collaborators may be divided into three main groups: the first consists of "business collaborators", similar at some levels to the Chinese economic collaborators whom Parks Coble discusses in Chapter 5; their behavior can perhaps be interpreted as subservience to *force majeure*— physical force as applied by the Japanese occupiers and contending Chinese factions, and, perhaps even more, market forces in what had, after all, been (and remained to some degree even under occupation) the most anarchically liberal economic center in the Far East. The second group may be termed "anti-imperial" collaborators. Their motives were generally an amalgam of personal pique and ideological hostility to the British and other empires.

Finally, there were the straightforward opportunists: adventurers, criminals and gangland figures who emerged like sewer rats from the Shanghai underworld. From each of these three groups I have selected a few *cas témoins* to illustrate the theme. Of course, in many individual cases the ideal types merge in varying proportions; nevertheless, this taxonomy may be useful in analyzing some of the underlying motives for collaboration.

A form of business collaboration, not with the Japanese but with the Germans, was discernible at the very outbreak of the European war, when major British business enterprises received official guidance to apply the Trading with the Enemy regulations very flexibly in Shanghai "so as to give the Germans as little handle as possible for enlisting Japanese sympathy or support against us" (as a report for the major British trading firm Butterfield and Swire put it). The same report added:

> Our instructions are to complete all contracts already entered into with Germans, to pay debts due to them before the outbreak of war, to deliver cargo held in German names prior to the outbreak of war, and generally to round off all existing engagements but not to enter into new ones. One point of interest in this connection is that the German Embassy and Consulate, which occupies a part of the Glen Line Building, were instructed by us on the first day of the war to remove the flag which they fly above the building, but when they appealed for reconsideration of our ruling and we referred it to the Embassy, the Ambassador told us that he thought no great harm would be done, and that we might allow them to display the flag as they always have done.[21]

Against this background the drift into economic collaboration with the Japanese becomes a little more comprehensible. After the outbreak of the Pacific war some British-owned or managed enterprises functioned as if nothing had changed. The British staff of the Hankow Light and Power Company, for example, continued to operate that public utility under Japanese control. E. A. Nottingham, proprietor of the English-language *Shanghai Times*, continued to publish the paper in the Japanese propaganda interest after December 8, 1941. In both cases the Japanese war effort derived at least some demonstrable advantage from the actions of British citizens.

The most interesting case of this type was also perhaps the single most significant example of economic collaboration by a British-owned business enterprise in China during the war. The Kailan Mining Administration, whose headquarters were in Tientsin, employed 47,000 Chinese laborers in its mines, which produced over 6.5 million tons of coal in the financial year 1939–40. Of this, some 2 million tons were supplied to Shanghai, supplying about 40 percent of the city's entire coal needs. In 1941 these were the only mines in Japanese-occupied China that had not been taken over by the Japanese. The concern's chief manager, Edward J. Nathan, was a British businessman of the utmost respectability who had been awarded the Order of the British Empire before the war.

In view of the supreme importance of coking coal to the Japanese steel industry and therefore to Japan's war effort, the company had sought guidance from the Foreign Office before the war as to what attitude it should adopt in the event of war between Britain and Japan. But the government declined to offer any advice. In August 1941, therefore, Nathan gave the local Japanese authorities (who were already in control of the Tientsin area, having inflicted a humiliating diplomatic defeat on the local British Concession authorities[22]) an assurance that he "accepted responsibility for the continued functioning of the Mines until such time as the Japanese were able to assume this responsibility if, after war had broken out, they decided to do so."[23] Nathan did not at that time inform the British government of this undertaking—although, given the abjectly submissive posture of the British government in the face of Japanese provocation at Tientsin over the previous two years, he may have had good reason to believe that his promise was in accord with official British policy.

When war between Britain and Japan broke out in December 1941, Nathan kept his undertaking. He and all seventy-one senior British staff of the KMA remained at their posts, producing coal for the Japanese war effort under Japanese supervision and training Japanese managers to take over their own functions. Over the next few months Nathan repeatedly boasted to Japanese officials and to the Swiss consul in Tientsin that he had "completely discharged the responsibilities I assumed in virtue of the undertaking I gave to Generals Shiozawa and Tanabe in August 1941."[24] In February 1943 Nathan was replaced by a Japanese manager. Upon his resignation the Japanese embassy in Peking wrote to him:

> General Shiozawa appreciates your good faith in carrying out the obligations which you had undertaken and fully understands the army-controlled Kailan Mining Administration must attribute its present smooth operation to your great devotion which you have made [*sic*] since December 8th 1941.[25]

Unfortunately for Nathan, the British Foreign Office had a similar understanding of the value of his services to the Japanese war effort. In May 1942 the Foreign Secretary, Anthony Eden, issued a stern personal denunciation of Nathan's "reprehensible" conduct.[26] Both Nathan himself and the KMA's British parent company devoted strenuous efforts during and after the war to justifying his actions. The main burden of their apologia rested on an unabashed claim to the priority of their business interests over the national interest. They pointed out that any other course of action would have resulted in the transfer of the KMA to Japanese hands and, after the war, into Chinese control "with the result of the total loss of the Company's enterprise in China."[27] Following his resignation, Nathan was interned by the Japanese in Shanghai for the remainder of the war.

Although the Foreign Office refused to withdraw its criticism of his conduct, he was never prosecuted and later assumed control of the English parent company. The Foreign Office contemptuously rejected Nathan's offer in December 1946 to pay the government £934 15s 8d, representing "the total sums received by me from the Japanese Army-controlled Kailan Mining Administration as honorarium and living expenses . . . at the rate current at the outbreak of the war."[28] One of the many ironies of this case is that, whereas the British police and municipal officials in Shanghai might defend their conduct under the occupation on the basis of the official guidance they had received, Nathan could lodge, no less sincerely, a defence based on the exact opposite: *lack* of official guidance.

Recently opened papers of the British Special Operations Executive reveal another side of this affair which, while it in no way exonerates Nathan, places the attitude of the Foreign Office in a somewhat different light. In the autumn of 1941 the British authorities, aware that war in the Far East was imminent, had prepared plans for the destruction of key sections of the Kailan mines, with a view to preventing Japanese exploitation of the mines in time of war. The sabotage scheme was hatched on September 25 at a meeting at the Thatched House Club in London between Colonel P. C. Young, a director (and former general manager) of the company, and a Secret Intelligence Service officer. Young proposed that, with the help of British engineers at the mines, the central powerhouse could be blown up, rendering the entire mines unworkable for a year. Destruction of the mines had already been recognized as a priority by the British government and a secret agent had been dispatched the previous June to look over the target area. He stayed there for a month but "was so impressed by Japanese security measures and the Japanese contacts of Major Nathan that he dared not take the latter into his confidence."[29] Following the agent's report, an operational plan for the destruction of the mines was ordered to be prepared on November 22, 1941. Further meetings on the subject took place in London and Singapore over the next two weeks but by the outbreak of the Pacific war nothing had been done. In 1942 and 1943 there were renewed discussions of a possible guerrilla attack on the mines, and a US aerial bombing mission hit them in October 1942, killing a large number of Chinese workers—but without significantly hampering the mines' further operation.

The failure to take action before December 8, 1941 became the subject of angry post-mortems in London. The main impediment to action appears to have been the insistence of the Foreign Office

> that before approval of the operation could be given, destruction should not be attributable to the British, if that could be arranged, and that adequate steps should be taken to safeguard the lives and interests of the British and Belgian personnel of the Mines, at the same time insisting that the Chinese Government should not be informed of the project.[30]

As a Special Operations Executive memorandum in April 1942 put it, the Foreign Office had "considered and hesitated over our Appreciation for one month and then attached such qualifications to their approval that they rendered the formulation of any practicable scheme impossible."[31] The Foreign Office's stern rebuke to Nathan's employers, written in May 1942, shortly after SOE's criticism of the Foreign Office's dilatory handling the previous autumn of the sabotage scheme, was evidently born of a guilty conscience on the part of the Foreign Office itself.

Since Nathan, his entire British staff, and his business partners in London remained convinced in their own minds that they had not acted unpatriotically, their behavior may be classed as an instance of *unconscious* collaboration. Our next category consists, by contrast, of *conscious* collaborators who deliberately chose to support the Japanese war effort for ideological reasons. These were "anti-imperialists"—at least in the sense that most of them advanced, in one form or another, a justification of their actions based on hostility to British imperialism in the Far East.

The anti-imperialist collaborators in Shanghai may be further divided into three sub-groups. The first includes Indians (among them some Sikh constables of the Shanghai Municipal Police), Filipinos and other Asiatics who, with a greater or lesser degree of enthusiasm, embraced the Japanese argument that the new order in East Asia represented liberation from British, American, French, or Dutch imperial rule. Second, there were collaborators of mixed race, such as the Chinese-American Herbert Moy, who broadcast from Shanghai for the Japanese, or the half-Chinese, half-British Lawrence Kentwell, who published violently anti-British propaganda before the war and pro-Japanese propaganda during it. Finally, there were a few European-race "anti-imperialist" collaborators, mainly Australians and Irish.

In the case of Lawrence Kentwell, the psychological motives that led to collaboration are particularly well documented. Born in 1882 aboard a British sailing ship in Hong Kong harbor, the illegitimate son of the ship's captain and a Chinese woman, Kentwell had graduated from Columbia University, New York, and from Lincoln College, Oxford, where he earned a fourth-class degree in jurisprudence in 1913. While in the United States he became an American citizen, thereby losing his British citizenship. In 1915 he was renaturalized as a British citizen and in the following year was admitted to the Shanghai bar. Over the next few years he acquired an unsavory reputation for unprofessional conduct, alleged forgery of banknotes, and non-payment of rates. Already at this early stage the British and Indian authorities had taken a dislike to him: "he is a rotter," a Foreign Office official minuted.[32] Shortly afterwards he tore up his British passport in open court. From then until 1941 he bombarded the British judicial and political authorities in Shanghai and London with a stream of abusive letters complaining of persecution, denouncing British imperialism, and threatening retribution. He was disbarred by the British court in Shanghai, an action that provoked further protests and denunciations by Kentwell.

The *fons et origo* of Kentwell's half-crazed enmity to Britain appears to have been his experience of racial discrimination—first at Oxford, then in relation to service in the British army during the First World War, but above all in Shanghai. One of his bitter complaints was his exclusion, on the ground that he was of mixed race, from the Shanghai Club. "The arrogant Englishmen of the Shanghai Club regard me as an interloper and a step lower in the wrung [*sic*] of the social ladder. This I will never concede and will fight to the finish. I am a man and not an insect."[33]

Kentwell's anti-imperialist political activity began early. According to his own account (in a statement in 1945), he was a pupil of Sun Yat-sen at Mills School in Honolulu in 1901–3 and served as his secretary-interpreter in New York in 1905–6. In 1926 he founded the *China Courier*, an anti-British journal. In the following year Kentwell announced that he was applying for citizenship of China, "my motherland," and intended "to throw myself heartily into her fight for the recovery of her legitimate rights."[34] The Shanghai Club, he declared, must be pulled down, set on fire, or turned into a lodging house for rickshaw coolies. (Oddly, this was almost prophetic: after 1949 the club became a Chinese seamen's rest home.) Around this time he was said to be working as an adviser to Chiang Kai-shek. By 1928 the Foreign Office had concluded that he was "mentally unbalanced and violent."[35]

In 1929 Kentwell adopted a Chinese name, Kan Teh-yun, and founded a "Chinese Patriotic League", based in Macao, devoted to the cause of expelling British imperialism from all its outposts in Asia. He established another magazine, *The China Truth*, published at Canton, whose main purpose was to call for the end of foreign extraterritoriality in China. British officials, growing more and more irritated by Kentwell's raving effusions, almost matched his capacity for personal abuse: "the obnoxious 'British object'" was how a Home Office official referred to him.[36] But Kentwell would not shut up. "The snobbery of Englishmen in the Far East [he informed the British consul-general in Canton], particularly noticeable in the Shanghai Club, spells the downfall of England."[37] In 1931 he was denaturalized by the Home Secretary—a decision that Kentwell declared "very ridiculous indeed."[38] Over the next decade Kentwell poured forth a stream of anti-British propaganda. By 1932 he was writing on notepaper with the letterhead "Headquarters of the Retrocession Commissioner for the International Settlement of Shanghai and for Hong Kong and Kowloon."[39]

In 1939 Kentwell received a subsidy from the Japanese in support of a new magazine, *The Voice of New China*, which continued to appear at least until 1942 when one issue carried a portrait of Adolf Hitler on the cover. Claiming authority from the Nanking (puppet) regime, he wrote to Prime Ministers Chamberlain and Churchill demanding rendition of the British concessions in China. In normal times Kentwell's bombastic letters and publications might have been consigned to the "cranks" file. But in time of war he became an irritation, then a nuisance, and finally placed himself in the category of traitor—paradoxically not to Britain but to his "motherland" China. The Nanking government appointed him a member of its Legislative Yuan. He attended a few meetings but since he knew only the Cantonese dialect found that he "could not understand the discussions."[40] In 1942 he returned to

Shanghai, intending (as he later claimed) to engage in "secret work against the Japanese and the Wang Ching Wei regime."[41] He moved into the Foreign YMCA on the Bubbling Well Road. In spite of his later claims to the contrary, however, he continued his pro-Japanese propaganda.

Kentwell was, in fact, more than a crackpot. His publications, even if self-serving, bizarre, and crude in both conception and expression, were often lively, readable and effective as anti-imperialist propaganda. British officials might laugh and sneer at him, but the Japanese and their Chinese clients evidently found him useful at a certain level.

Finally in this anti-imperialist group we have the European-race collaborators. A representative case is the Australian Alan Raymond, who broadcast from Shanghai for the Japanese through the greater part of the war. Raymond had had a dubious prewar career as a salesman in Shanghai, in the course of which he accumulated unpaid debts and attracted the attention of the Shanghai police.[42] In early 1942 he emerged as the moving spirit in an "Independent Australia League" in Shanghai in which a handful of other local Australian residents participated. He wrote anti-British articles in the local English-language press and broadcast regular commentaries to Australia, supporting the Japanese and calling upon his countrymen to sever the British connection and withdraw from the war. Raymond's main partner in these activities was another Australian, John Joseph Holland, an unsuccessful journalist and arms salesman who, according to a French police report, had been involved with various international swindlers in the Shanghai rackets.[43] Together with Holland, Raymond was placed on an Allied list of war criminals to be pursued at the end of the war. Holland was arrested in September 1945 in the Grand Hotel in Sapporo (Hokkaido) while enjoying a shave by a girl barber and a simultaneous manicure.[44] In the cases of both Raymond and Holland, the genuineness of their anti-imperialist sentiments is open to question. They stand somewhere on the borderline between the second category and the third—that of the pure opportunists.

These include some of the politically and psychologically most interesting of the collaborators. A few were people on the fringes of respectability who drifted into collaboration not so much out of conviction but because it seemed the easiest way out of financial difficulties or other personal problems. One such was the American journalist Don Chisholm, who broadcast over the Japanese-controlled XMHA radio station in Shanghai in 1942. Another was the British sailor J. K. Gracie, who broadcast for the Japanese under the pseudonym "Sergeant Allan McIntosh". In a postwar statement, Gracie outlined candidly the motives that had led him to collaborate. Down and out in Shanghai at the outbreak of the war, he had appealed for help to the British Residents' Association, which sent him to the Salvation Army hostel. But he felt (or so he later claimed) that he was "being discriminated against because my wife was of Japanese descent, so refused to go to the Hostel in Wayside and consequently found myself without help of any sort." At that point he was offered a job on the powerful German radio station in Shanghai, XGRS, and accepted it, receiving payment in Reichsmarks. In March 1942 he renounced his British citizenship—though the British authorities later refused to recognize this. Later that year he was nevertheless arrested and interned by the Japanese as a British citizen. He was released after agreeing to go back to broadcasting. When he returned to his house he discovered that his wife and daughter had been sent away to Japan. He continued to broadcast political commentaries on the Japanese station XGOO until the end of the war.[45]

Several of the opportunist collaborators were criminals who used their special expertise on behalf of the occupation authorities. Some were adventurers of the kind for which Shanghai was notorious. Among these we may class the American Hilaire du Berrier, born in Flasher, North Dakota, of partly French extraction. An aviator who had flown for the Spanish Republicans and had sought to buy aircraft for them in Britain, he had moved to the Far East and operated a squalid extortion racket in Shanghai before the war. According to a report by the Shanghai Municipal Police Special Branch in April 1941, he had worked as an agent for the Japanese intelligence service. Whether he continued to do so after the outbreak of the Pacific war is unclear. During the occupation he found time to contribute to the English-language intellectual monthly published in Shanghai, *XXth Century*, which was financed by Goebbels's Propaganda Ministry. According to his own account, Du Berrier was arrested by the Japanese in 1943 and tortured. After the war he wrote reports for American counter-intelligence in Shanghai. Later he worked as a correspondent for *Newsweek* magazine and (again according to his own account) as an adviser on Vietnam at the Geneva conference in 1955.[46] Du Berrier is one of many examples in wartime Shanghai of cosmopolitan gangsters who hovered on the fringes of the political and criminal underworlds, ready to offer their services to virtually any cause willing to pay.

Surprisingly few of the collaborators mentioned above faced postwar criminal charges. Gracie was sentenced in 1947 by a British court in Hong Kong to eight years' imprisonment. Kentwell was sentenced to seven years in prison by a Chinese court. (His attempt to disclaim the Chinese citizenship of which he had in earlier days boasted was not taken seriously.) Moy committed suicide in August 1945 after listening to the Japanese emperor's rescript over the radio. Nottingham, Nathan, Chisholm, and Du Berrier all walked free. It is difficult to avoid the conclusion that race and class form the primary explanations for these differential outcomes.

The impression should not be left that collaboration was the norm or that it completely blotted out resistance in European Shanghai. As in the Channel Islands, the Allied civilians in Shanghai did not, for the most part, behave very differently from other civilian populations under enemy occupation. Most simply carried on with their everyday lives as best they could. Limited forms of British resistance were active briefly in the city. The potentially most important organized resistance group, a six-man British Special Operations Executive team headed by W. J. Gande, was captured soon after the start of the occupation, imprisoned and tortured. Thereafter the British intelligence agencies, like the Americans, had to work in Shanghai through Chinese surrogates, since they were unable to reestablish effective underground organization of their own in the city. On the individual level there is the case of Petty Officer James Cuming, radio operator of the British gunboat *Peterel*, sunk in the Whangpoo by the Japanese on the first day of the war, who happened to be on shore leave at the time of the Japanese attack. In response to Japanese pressure the civilian head of the British Residents' Association in Shanghai, Hugh Collar, a director of Imperial Chemical Industries in the city, sent word to Cuming that, if he surrendered, Collar would "accept responsibility towards His Majesty's Government."[47] Cuming ignored the appeal and remained at large underground in Shanghai throughout the war. For part of this period he worked for a clandestine Chinese Nationalist group in the city.[48]

This short survey nevertheless shows, first, that foreign collaboration in Shanghai, sometimes officially sanctioned, sometimes not, sometimes conscious, sometimes not, sometimes ideologically inspired, sometimes opportunist, was quite widespread. Second, the various cases surveyed illustrate the general thesis that resistance and collaboration in World War II, theoretically contrary and antithetical positions, nevertheless in the real world often lived in a strangely symbiotic relationship and occasionally marched together arm-in-arm.

How can all this be explained? Beyond the reasons specific to each of the categories of collaborator, at least one more general explanation may be summed up in the phrase: "the Shanghai mind." That was the pregnant (and to the British ruling class in Shanghai deeply offensive) coinage of Arthur Ransome in an article written from Shanghai for the *Manchester Guardian* in 1927 in which he denounced those British who "look round on their magnificent buildings and are surprised that China is not grateful to them for these gifts." The complex of attitudes that Ransome pinned down with cruel precision was a classic example of the colonialist mentality—it lacked only a Kipling or Maugham to capture its supremely philistine cultural parochialism and the snootiness of its social pretensions. (J. G. Ballard conjures up some occasional glimpses in his semi-autobiographical novel *Empire of the Sun*.)

The "Shanghai mind" was also something more than the local variant of the colonialist mentality—and Ransome was perceptive enough to notice it: the British in Shanghai regarded their own economic interests not merely as synonymous with but as *the* defining criterion of British national interests in the Far East. "Unless British policy coincides with their own," wrote Ransome, "they are prepared at any moment to be the Ulster of the East."[49] The unique constitutional status of Shanghai, a colony in fact that was not a colony in name, had given its British ruling class delusions of grandeur and a collective self-importance that accorded ill with the diminishing power that Britain could muster, militarily, diplomatically, and politically, in the city and in East Asia in general.

Symptomatic of the "Shanghai mind" was Hugh Collar's explanation in his postwar memoir of his cooperation with local German businessmen in a price control committee set up by the Shanghai Municipal Council early in the (European) war: "If it sounds a little queer that we should contemplate working with our enemies, it must be remembered that we were working for the International Settlement ... for the common good."[50] What was the commonality of interest that lay behind such a statement? Interestingly, the Germans in Shanghai too at this period behaved on occasion as if they believed in such a shared economic weal. In December 1940, Sir Frederick Maze, Inspector General of the the Chinese Maritime Customs Service, reported that he had

> had occasion recently to approach indirectly Dr Fischer, the German Consul General, in connection with pulling strings to enable Stanley Wright [a customs official] to return to China, and, while promising to do what he could privately to assist in the matter, he at the same time asked my intermediary to tell me "to remain here and not 'pull out' now".[51]

What such statements seem to reveal is a certain community of understanding, even, on occasion, of perceived interests, between Europeans, albeit citizens of powers that were at war with one another. The Germans' relations with their Japanese ally were almost as difficult throughout the war as those of the British and Americans with the Chinese—in each case reinforcing attitudes of racial contempt. The conventional racial attitudes of the period undoubtedly help explain many of the points of friction in these wartime alliances—and at the individual level the occasional collapse into collaborationism. Was the preposterous Kentwell, then, altogether off the mark in his philippics against the color bar at the Long Bar of the Shanghai Club? For many of the collaborationist minority the unique ambience of European Shanghai—its hierarchical cosmopolitanism, its marriage of glamor and squalor, its indeterminate constitutional status, its savage economic inequities, and perhaps above all its animating political idea—racial inequality— helped distort loyalties, weaken the links tying individuals to political communities, and thus open a pathway for the descent into treason.

NOTES

1 H. R. Kedward, *Resistance in Vichy France* (Oxford, 1978); Paul Jankowski, *Communism and Collaboration: Simon Sabiani and Politics in Marseille, 1919–1944* (London, 1989); Isaiah Trunk, *Judenrat: The Jewish Councils in Eastern Europe under Nazi Control* (New York, 1972); Poshek Fu, *Passivity, Resistance and Collaboration: Intellectual Choices in Occupied Shanghai, 1937–1945* (Stanford, 1993).

2 Unsigned report dated October 20, 1945, U[nited] S[tates] N[ational] A[rchives] RG 226, entry 182, box 14, folder 87.

3 See, *inter alia*, French Concession monthly police report for July 1941, A[rchives] du] M[inistère des] A[ffaires] E[trangères], Nantes, Shanghai consulate Rep.

Num. 333; Japanese Consul-general T. Horiuchi to Foreign Minister, January 17, 1942, Japanese Foreign Ministry Archives, microfilm UD 47; S[hanghai] M[unicipal] P[olice] records, USNA RG 263, report dated April 22, 1941, file D8157–F2; and reports in SMP D8149.

4   US counter-intelligence report, October 24, 1945, USNA RG 226, entry 182, box 2, folder 8.
5   Memorandum, December 16, 1942, A[uswärtiges] A[mt] archives, Bonn, Botschaft China Prot 2a1.
6   *Shanghai Times*, July 23, 1942.
7   See R. L. Speaight to H. Somerville-Smith, December 3, 1940, P[ublic] R[ecord] O[ffice] FO 371/24361 leaf 175; *Shanghai Times*, January 4, 8 and 16, 1941; British intelligence report April 1–30, 1941, PRO WO 208/296.
8   Le Rougetel, Shanghai, to Foreign Office, September 4, 1941, I[ndia] O[ffice] R[ecords], London, L/P&S/12/499.
9   *Bulletin d'Information Economique*, French consulate, Shanghai, April 10, 1945.
10   Jacques Guillermaz, *Une Vie pour la Chine: mémoires, 1937–1989* (Paris, 1989), p. 136.
11   Wavell to Chief of Imperial General Staff, May 14, 1942, PRO WO 208/378A.
12   Memorandum by R. M. Talbot, Commissioner of Customs, December 28, 1942, Maze papers, vol. XV, fols. 238–40, S[chool of] O[riental and] A[frican] S[tudies], London.
13   Undated memorandum, PRO FO 371/69562.
14   Undated, unsigned memorandum, "The Outline Activities of the Foreign Affairs Section, Police Headquarters, during the Period of Japanese Occupation of Shanghai", USNA RG 226, entry 182, box 12, folder 77.
15   "Assistance to Foreign Section of Japanese Gendarmerie Headquarters", December 20, 1941, SMP D8299/364.
16   See, e.g., "Assistance to Japanese Gendarmerie", December 30, 1941, SMP D8299/374.
17   On this issue, see Frederic Wakeman, Jr., *The Shanghai Badlands: Wartime Terrorism and Urban Crime, 1937–1941* (Cambridge, 1996), esp. pp. 25, 27 ff., 41, 74, and 156.
18   R. M. Moin *et al.* to Swiss Consulate-general, September 7, 1942, PRO FO 371/53592.
19   Statement dated August 30, 1945, USNA RG 226, box 57, entry 140, folder 463.
20   *Shanghai Times*, January 30, 1943.
21   Butterfield and Swire, Shanghai, to John Swire and Sons, London, September 15, 1939, Swire papers, JSSII, 2/17, box 53, SOAS.
22   On the background see Aaron Shai, *Origins of the War in the East: Britain, China and Japan, 1937–1939* (London, 1976).
23   "Memorandum of conversation with General Shiosawa [*sic*]", head of China Affairs Board, Peking, August 8, 1941, Nathan papers, Bodleian Library, Oxford, MSS Eng. Hist. c. 452 ff. 19–23.
24   Nathan to Consul-general Joerg, March 10, 1943, ibid., ff. 87–9.
25   Japanese embassy, Peking, to Nathan, March 12, 1943, ibid., ff. 91–2.
26   Foreign Office to Chinese Engineering and Mining Company, May 13, 1942, ibid., f. 207.
27   Chinese Engineering and Mining Company to Foreign Office, June 1, 1942, ibid., c. 453 ff. 2–4.
28   Nathan to Foreign Office, December 23, 1946, ibid., f. 196.
29   Undated [1942] SOE memorandum, PRO HS1/175.
30   Ibid.
31   SOE memorandum, April 23, 1942, ibid.
32   Minute signed "G.M.", April 14, 1927, PRO FO 372/2387/276.

33 Kentwell to British Consul-general, Canton, October 2, 1931, PRO FO 676/90.
34 Kentwell to Registrar of British supreme court, Shanghai, January 22, 1927, PRO FO 372/2486/25.
35 Minute dated August 8, 1928, PRO FO 372/2486/20.
36 Whitelegge (Home Office) to Forbes (Foreign Office), December 24, 1928, PRO FO 372/2486.
37 Letter dated October 2, 1931, PRO FO 676/90.
38 Kentwell to Home Office, July 23, 1931, PRO FO 676/90.
39 See Kentwell to Prime Minister, October 19, 1932, PRO FO 371/16237/306.
40 Statement by Kentwell, n.d. [1945], USNA RG 226, entry 182, box 2, folder 12.
41 Ibid.
42 See SMP file N 163 (C).
43 Report by French Political Police, Shanghai, March 5, 1941, SMP file D9532 (C).
44 *Sydney Morning Herald*, September 28, 1945.
45 Gracie's statement dated February 5, 1946, and related documents, PRO FO 369/3791.
46 Foreign Office file, October 1936, PRO FO 371/20580/W13429/9549/41; SMP reports on Du Berrier 1937-41, N 765 (C), D8000; Du Berrier's *curriculum vitae*, N. F. Allman papers, Hoover Institution Archives, Stanford, Calif., box 12, file 45; OSS reports by Du Berrier, October 13, 1945, USNA RG 226, entry 182A, box 8, folder 64; and sim., ibid., entry 140, box 57, folder 464.
47 Hugh Collar, *Captive in Shanghai* (Hong Kong, 1980), pp. 25–8.
48 See Desmond Wettern, *The Lonely Battle* (London, 1960); also Peter Oldham, *Lieutenant Stephen Polkinghorn, DSC, RNR* (Auckland, N.Z., 1984), pp. 3–6.
49 Quoted in Nicholas R. Clifford, *Spoilt Children of Empire: Westerners in Shanghai and the Chinese Revolution of the 1920s* (Hanover, N.H., 1991), p. 240.
50 Collar, *Captive in Shanghai*, pp. 11–12.
51 Maze to J. H. Cubbon, December 30, 1940, Maze Papers III, PP MS 2, SOAS.

4 The other Japanese community
Leftwing Japanese activities in wartime Shanghai

Joshua A. Fogel

To speak of *the* Japanese community of wartime Shanghai as a monolith would be to misrepresent its internal complexity. To the extent that we know of the Japanese in Shanghai in the 1930s and 1940s, we understand them to be a group closely self-protective and dependent on the home government and military for its security. The great majority of the Japanese in Shanghai in those tense years were most concerned with ensuring their government's active involvement in protecting their community and its interests against the Chinese.

There were, however, less well known voices among the Japanese who called for peace and urged their compatriots and government to take Chinese interests into account. Their stories come together about 1930 and overlap in the decade of the 1930s. Their range of successes and failures is broad. Their legacy, while debatable, has still played an important role in the revitalization of Sino-Japanese amity since 1972. After setting in context the modern Japanese experience in Shanghai, this chapter will examine a number of often linked events and Japanese personages whose commitment was to make things turn out much differently from the way they did.

BACKGROUND: THE JAPANESE COMMUNITY OF SHANGHAI

In Shanghai, as elsewhere in mainland China, the Japanese were the last of the foreign powers to become deeply involved in China with local affairs. By the 1930s, however, they had become by far the largest presence. From a population of less than fifty in 1873, just two years after the first Sino-Japanese Treaty of Commerce, the number of Japanese in Shanghai rose steadily. In 1935 there were 26,208 Japanese in Shanghai of a total of 76,931 throughout China proper.[1] This proportion made the Japanese community of Shanghai the largest concentration of any city in China proper. From before the first Sino-Japanese War, the Japanese in Shanghai had been moving into the Hongkew (Hongkou) quarter of the city. Though they had won the right to establish their own exclusive concession area as a result of the Treaty of Shimonoseki, the Japanese never did claim such a right in Shanghai, as they did in Tianjin and Hankou. Instead the great majority remained in the

International Settlement. Of the 26,208 in 1935, 19,651 resided there; only 1,450 were in the French Concession and some 5,107 in the Chinese quarters of the city.

Many of those in the International Settlement lived in the area of North Sichuan Road, near the center of the concession. Along North Sichuan Road alone were several Japanese schools. Japanese-operated shops were principally on Wusong Road and Wenjianshi Road. This region was informally known as the "Japanese Concession" or "Japantown," though there was no such formal designation. It was not located at the heart of Shanghai's major thoroughfares.[2]

The Japanese established a consulate in Shanghai in 1872, and it was elevated to consulate-general status in 1891. With the Treaty of Shimonoseki, Japan acquired most-favored-nation status, and soon thereafter its consul in Shanghai sat on the governing consular board within the settlement. In 1871 international telegraphy was made possible between Shanghai and Nagasaki, and that same year Reuters set up shop in Shanghai. Four years later, the Mitsubishi Company opened regular sea lanes between Yokohama and Shanghai, and a branch of Mitsui Bussan was established in 1877. The Yokohama Specie Bank established a Shanghai branch in 1893, and five years later the Ôsaka Shipping Company opened a Yangzi Line. It was not until 1907 that the Shanghai branch of the Japanese Residents' Association (JRA) was established, by which time these and many other banks and commercial establishments had branches in the city. Established first as a Japanese businessmen's association in 1911, the Japanese Chamber of Commerce came into existence in 1919 when there was a critical mass of Japanese commercial concerns.[3]

Of the fifteen Japanese schools in Shanghai in 1939, nine were run by the Shanghai JRA, which also operated a clinic, a cemetery, and a crematorium. The Higashi Honganji had set up a branch temple in Shanghai as early as 1874, and by the 1930s was managing several schools there. Other Japanese religious groups—Tenrikyô, Japanese Christians, and Shintô—had temples, shrines, and schools in Shanghai, too.

Shanghai was as well a center of Chinese and international journalism. In addition to a corps of correspondents from the major Japanese dailies and weeklies, a number of Japanese newspapers were based in Shanghai, such as the *Shanhai nippô* (founded in 1903), the *Shanhai nichinichi shinbun* (founded in 1914), and the *Shanhai mainichi shinbun* (founded in 1918). Also the *Jiangnan zhengbao* (founded in 1918), a Japanese-owned and operated newspaper published in Chinese, was run out of Shanghai.[4]

There were also Japanese clubs, bathhouses, restaurants and bars, beauty salons, and inns in Shanghai. Hongkew was filled with Japanese goods and stores, and in many of the local Chinese shops Japanese was frequently spoken. Indeed, one could live an almost entirely insulated Japanese existence in Shanghai. In this regard, the Japanese were much like their counterparts from Europe. As early as 1920, though, the Japanese outnumbered all other foreign nationalities in Shanghai. By 1930 there were three times as many Japanese as British subjects in the city.

In tandem with the growth and development of the Japanese community and business interests in Shanghai (and elsewhere on the mainland), there was an increasing Japanese police presence there. The largest force was the consular police, a group particularly feared by Japanese leftists active in China. There was as well the "higher police"; these were the "thought police" charged with rooting out subversion. The judicial police handled crimes committed within the Japanese community. Finally, the peace preservation police dealt with a variety of local health and welfare issues.[5]

The wide array of Japanese investments in Shanghai, more than elsewhere in China, represented interests worth protecting at great cost. As anti-Japanese boycotts and other outward demonstrations of Chinese ire at Japanese activities in China developed from the 1910s forward, the JRA in Shanghai and the Japanese community as a whole assumed an ever more bellicose stand. There were as well a number of Japanese military and paramilitary outfits at work in Shanghai: a Shanghai chapter of the Imperial Military Reserve Association, patriotic youth groups, and civilian (vigilante) groups. They all became extremely harsh in their denunciations of Chinese strikes and boycotts aimed at Japanese interests.[6]

Amid these loud calls for Japan to get tough and protect the Japanese and their concerns in Shanghai, there were other voices as well. After describing the background of the Japanese presence in the city, this chapter will look at several of the more remarkable instances of Japanese activists who risked considerable personal safety, to say nothing of their lives, in the interest of what they assumed would foil Japanese imperialism on the mainland. What drove Japanese at this time to strike out and devote themselves to Sino-Japanese amity in the face of heightening Sino-Japanese tensions? What was it about Shanghai that may have fostered this particular stance? In what ways did their experiences before coming to Shanghai, their reasons for making the trip, and the distinctive nature of their contacts in the city foster the political positions they adopted?

UCHIYAMO KANZÔ AND HIS SHANGHAI BOOKSTORE

In 1913 a recent Japanese convert to Christianity, Uchiyama Kanzô (1885–1959), followed his pastor's suggestion and set off for Shanghai to make his mark in life. Four years later he opened his own bookstore, the Uchiyama Shoten, in an alley off North Sichuan Road in Hongkew. He would continue to operate it for the next thirty years. Uchiyama stocked primarily Japanese volumes, mostly religious works at first, though later catering to the many and varied interests of his customers, both Japanese and the many Chinese who had studied in Japan. As his store expanded, its second storey, which he had converted into a tatami room, became the meeting site for discussions among Chinese and Japanese writers.

As the years passed, Uchiyama thus became a mediator of sorts between Chinese and visiting Japanese authors, and his bookstore became a "salon" for brokering Sino-Japanese literary contacts. He dubbed these intellectual interactions *mandankai* or "conversation groups." It was through his auspices, for example, that the great writer Tanizaki Jun'ichirô (1886–1965) was able to meet and interact with the likes of Tian Han (1898–1966), Guo Moruo (1892–1978), and Ouyang Yuqian (1887–1962). Later, Tanizaki introduced Uchiyama to the poet and novelist Satô Haruo (1892–1964), and through Uchiyama, Satô met many famous Chinese writers.[7]

Of all his Chinese contacts and associates, Uchiyama forged a special bond with China's most famous writer of the prewar era, Lu Xun (1881–1936). Lu Xun moved to Shanghai from Guangdong with his wife in early October of 1927, and two days later he visited the nearby Uchiyama Shoten for the first time.[8] Several days after that, as Uchiyama later recounted the story, Lu Xun returned, bought a large stock of books, and asked the proprietor "in impeccable Japanese" if they might be delivered to his home. Ready to oblige, Uchiyama asked for his customer's name and address.

"My name is Zhou Shuren," he said.

"Uh, you are Lu Xun? I certainly know your name well, and I knew as well that you had arrived from Guangdong, but I did not recognize your face. My apologies." It was from that time that my association with Lu Xun commenced.[9]

In late March of 1930, Lu Xun was compelled to leave his residence for fear of arrest, and for one month until the end of April hc hid out in thc Uchiyama Shoten. In early May he found a safer apartment.

As business prospered, Uchiyama moved his bookstore to North Sichuan Road in 1929. Its growth was fueled at least in part by the contemporaneous publication by the big publishing houses in Japan of huge multi-volume series of works, with each volume costing one yen. These series are the ancestors of today's ubiquitous *zenshû* (collected works) and *sôsho* (collections), although prices have increased a bit. Uchiyama marketed these editions of works in China, and because they made immense bodies of literature available at such reasonable prices he was able to forge close ties with many Chinese intellectuals. In addition to having the largest stock of Japanese books throughout China, he also sold 830 titles of Japanese books in Chinese translations.[10]

As many have since recalled, Uchiyama did his best to remain as apolitical as possible. Under the circumstances—with tensions between the Chinese and Japanese governments high, several recent localized Japanese military interventions in China, and the full-fledged invasion of the 1930s—being apolitical at this time meant being unwilling to accept the pronouncements of one's own government toward China. It also meant that Uchiyama steered clear of becoming entangled in the internecine political skirmishes on the Chinese left. Of course, the overwhelming inclination of his Chinese clientele was strongly left-wing, and many of them were or would soon become Communists, but he stayed out of that fray. It was exceedingly difficult during the 1930s and 1940s to hold to an avowed position of apoliticality when the entire surrounding world was becoming so politicized. This was, none the less, Uchiyama's stance.

Furthermore, because he was in China and not in Japan, Uchiyama was able to sell Japanese books in translation, such as the writings of Marx and Lenin, that by the 1930s would have been increasingly difficult, if not outright impossible, to put on sale back home. He also remained in Shanghai after the victory of the Chinese Communists in 1949 and has since been officially lionized as a *lao pengyou*. Needless to say, there was an unambiguous political stance in his remaining on the mainland and his longstanding sympathy for the left. For Uchiyama, that stance was less political than it was cultural and personal.

Many other Chinese writers in addition to Lu Xun spent time at the Uchiyama Shoten. There were other Japanese in Shanghai who also frequented the bookstore, both to buy books and to make contacts with radical Chinese. Shanghai was rapidly becoming a breeding ground for subversive types from both countries. Their joint meetings transpired at a small handful of sites, and the second floor of Uchiyama's shop was one of them.

Another was the second floor of the Gongfei Coffee Shop at the end of North Sichuan Road. The "salon" that formed here was a place where leftwing Chinese and Japanese writers and cultural types frequently congregated. Ozaki Hotsumi (1901–44), the reporter and spy *extraordinaire* in the ring surrounding Richard Sorge (1895–1944), was a regular from the late 1920s on, as was Xia Yan (Shen Duanxian, b. 1900) upon his return to China in May 1927 after seven years in Japan.

Xia supported himself principally by translating current Japanese literature—largely of the proletarian literary movement—into Chinese: Hirabayashi Taiko's story "Seryôshitsu ni te" (At the Free Clinic), Kaneko Yôbun's play *Jigoku* (Hell), Fujimori Seikichi's short story "Gisei" (The Sacrifice), Nakano Shigeharu's "Harusaki no kaze" (The Wind of Early Spring), Kobayashi Takiji's story "Kanikôsen" (Crab-canning Ship), and many others. He obtained most of these works from the Uchiyama Shoten, and it was actually Uchiyama himself who introduced Xia to Lu Xun in 1928. Around this time he joined the Chinese Communist Party (CCP), which, of course, Lu Xun never did, and their friendship was, needless to say, short-lived. In October of 1929 Lu Xun, Xia Yan, and others took part in the planning of what would eventually materialize as the League of Leftwing Writers. At a meeting at the Gongfei Coffee Shop on February 16, 1930, a planning committee to found the League came into existence. Xia Yan brought a copy of the League's founding manifesto to Nishizato Tatsuo (see below), and Nishizato translated it into Japanese and had it published in the cultural column of *Shanhai nippô*. This event brought Nishizato to the attention of the Japanese consular police.[11]

THE ROLE OF THE TÔ-A DÔBUN SHOIN

Another breeding ground for Japanese radicalism in Shanghai and a site of Sino-Japanese cultural and political interactions from the 1920s through the 1930s was the Tô-A dôbun shoin (East Asian Common Culture Academy), surely the most famous of all the Japanese schools in the city. A product of the imagination of mainland adventurer and reformer Arao Kiyoshi (1858–96) and the hard work of his disciple, Nezu Hajime (1860–1927), and Konoe Atsumaro (1863–1904), the school was founded in 1900. It was to be, for both Chinese and Japanese, dedicated to the long-term reform of China along Japanese lines and thus to long-term Sino-Japanese friendship. The curriculum at Tô-A dôbun shoin stressed contemporary subjects—business, political science, agriculture—and with a heavy dose of Chinese-language training. Before it dissolved in 1945, with Japan's defeat in the war, it graduated some 3,652 students.[12]

If it was hard enough to control Japanese students living in Tokyo who were separated from their families elsewhere in Japan, it was that much harder to do so in Shanghai. A number of Japanese students became deeply sympathetic to the Chinese labor movement in Shanghai, where they may have witnessed the May 30 Incident, Chinese workers' demonstrations, or organized activities of the young Chinese Communist Party. Some became so enamored of Chinese leftist politics that they abandoned their education and threw themselves into the movement, and their language training and familiarity with the local terrain served them well.

There were periodic incidents among the students, including strikes and walkouts spearheaded by the Chinese students. Despite the close scrutiny of the various Japanese police agencies, Chinese and Japanese students from the late 1920s became active in decidedly leftwing and anti-imperialist actions. There were socialist study groups set up by the students with which the school authorities did not interfere. These activities intensified into the early 1930s, when, as Chalmers Johnson has pointed out, "what amounted to a Japanese cell of the Chinese Communist Youth League had been established" at the Tô-A dôbun shoin.[13]

Among the subsequently more notorious students of these years were such well known Communists as Ozaki Shôtarô (b. 1906, class of 1930), Anzai Kuraji (b. 1905, class of 1931, postwar member of the central committee of the Japan Communist Party (JCP)), Nishizato Tatsuo (class of 1930), and Nakanishi Tsutomu (1910–73, class of 1933 though he never graduated, postwar JCP member of the Diet). They and others worked with Chinese and with other Japanese in and around Shanghai in the 1930s.[14]

FROM JOURNALISTS TO SPIES, FROM STUDY GROUPS TO PRACTICAL ACTION

One of the less well known Japanese activists in Shanghai at this time was Kawai Teikichi (1901–81). As a student at Meiji University, Kawai had come into contact with radical leftwing groups envigorated by the recent Bolshevik revolution. Through an acquaintance in China in the mid-1920s, he also began to hear about the revolutionary events on the mainland, and he resolved to go to China as soon as he could. To save sufficient funds for the trip, he worked for several weeks for the Seiyûkai, a rightwing political party. This insouciance, this lapse in his ability to distinguish clearly between the far left and the far right—what I dub his "political dyslexia"—plagued Kawai for his entire career and made him a favorite target for the more politically astute. Lacking the full genius of political hindsight, people like Kawai in the 1920s and even early 1930s viewed what we now see clearly as radical rightwing activity as simply radical, opposed to an oppressive government, and anti-capitalist. Kawai, for example, continued through his entire life to argue that Kita Ikki (1883–1937), an avowed fascist executed for his behind-the-scenes role in the February 26 Incident, was in fact a progressive revolutionary. Of course, many did see these left–right differences clearly at the time, but for others it was apparently still inchoate.

After a short first trip to China in 1928, Kawai returned in 1930, first to Beijing and in June to Shanghai. The friend who brought him there was Komatsu Shigeo. Komatsu had worked for the Japanese Home Office in Beijing as a translator, before leaving to work under Tachibana Shiraki (1881–1945), the journalist and expatriate scholar of Chinese affairs, in Shanghai. By 1930, he was in the employ of the South Manchurian Railway Company (SMR). Kawai took to Shanghai instantly. He felt he had finally arrived at the heart of the Chinese revolution, and he loved it.

Upon their arrival in Shanghai, Komatsu telephoned the Chinese translator, Wen Shengguang, and the private China scholar, Tanaka Tadao (1894–1964). Tanaka had earlier served as a translator of Japanese documents for Deng Yanda (1895–1931), and through him had made many acquaintances in the Chinese Communist movement—among them Liu Shaoqi (1898–1969), Xiang Zhongfa (1880–1931), and Li Lisan (1899–1967); he also knew Negishi Tadashi through contacts at the Tô-A dôbun shoin. He had worked as well for the Tokyo branch of the Research Department of the SMR, but by 1930 he was engaged in his own research on Chinese currency systems. He had come to Shanghai after Jiang Kai-shek (1887–1975) had brought down the Wuhan regime, and he was living with Wen Shengguang and Wen's Japanese wife, writing for the weekly *Shanhai shûhô*. Komatsu and Kawai joined Tanaka and Wen for dinner soon thereafter to discuss China-related issues.[15]

Their meetings soon became more regular, and they were joined in August by Soejima Tatsuoki and Tejima Hirotoshi, friends of Kawai's from Beijing whom he had summoned to Shanghai. In addition, several students from the Tô-A dôbun shoin participated in these meetings: Anzai Kuraji, Shirai Yukiyoshi (class of 1932), Mizuno Shigeru (class of 1933), and Nishizato Tatsuo. Funakoshi Hisao (1902–45), a journalist for the *Shanhai mainichi shinbun*, also attended.

They saw themselves as a study group—the Chinese Problems Study Group—and their recognized theoretical leader was Wen's friend, Wang Xuewen (1895–1985). Wang was a graduate of Kyoto University where he had studied economics under Kawakami Hajime (1879–1946), the leading Marxist economist in Japan. He was virtually bilingual in Japanese by virtue of having spent some fourteen years there. He had joined the Chinese Communist Youth League in Japan, before returning to Shanghai in 1927 and joining the CCP itself. Perhaps most important, he had been assigned the job by the party of rallying "antiwar, anti-imperialist" Japanese in Shanghai to active participation in the Communist cause. None of the Japanese with whom he had contact knew that Wang held positions of importance within the Chinese Communist Party at this time, though few of them would probably have been bothered by knowledge of that fact. Wang remained active in Shanghai until 1937, when he repaired to Yan'an, where he and Japanese Communist Nosaka Sanzô (1892–1993) organized and taught at the Japanese Peasants' and Workers' School for captured troops of the Japanese army.[16]

With Wang as their guide, the group discussed such topics as the developing Chinese Communist movement and the nature of Chinese society, both hot issues in leftist intellectual circles at the time in China. Through another connection, Nakanishi Tsutomu also heard Wang's analysis of the recent third party plenum of the sixth congress of the CCP (September 1930), the critique of the Li Lisan line, and was deeply impressed. The serial that Tanaka was working for, *Shanhai shûhô*, had been owned by a conservative reformist of the Kang Youwei school but by 1930 he had died, Kawai and Komatsu had soon thereafter joined the staff, and *Shanhai shûhô* had become pro-Communist.

In mid-October, a CCP member by the name of Yang Liuqing—originally from Taiwan, he had participated in the Hailufeng Soviet of 1927 and was active in the Japanese study group—suggested that the members go beyond studying Chinese society and get involved in action. Wang agreed. At Kawai's suggestion they named themselves the Nis-Shi tôsô dômei, or Sino-Japanese Struggle Alliance. Tanaka and Wen disagreed with this direction, fearing severe police reprisals, and did not join the Alliance, and Kawai criticized them for being too bookish. Many years later Kawai confessed that the Alliance had been established on a directive from the CCP to Yang, who was then operating under the pseudonym of Jiang.[17]

The first and most flamboyant act fomented by the Sino-Japanese Struggle Alliance was an antiwar propaganda stunt at the Japanese Naval Landing Party in Shanghai. The latter was a stark, visible symbol of Japanese military protection of Japanese nationals and their property in Shanghai. To commemorate the thirteenth anniversary of the Russian revolution, the young men printed up posters and bilingual leaflets in opposition to any hostilities between China and Japan. Their activities had already brought them under the scrutiny of Japanese consular police and the Kenpeitai (military police). On the evening of November 7, 1930, they used coal tar to write in immense characters on the wall of the Naval Landing Party building:

Down with Japanese imperialism!
Link hands with the Chinese Soviets!
Turn your guns around and bring down the capitalist-landlord state!
Long live the Chinese Communist Party!
Long live the soldiers, workers, and peasants!

The event was, needless to say, widely reported in the press.

In sympathy with these antiwar sentiments, a group of students in the Tô-A dôbun shoin joined the Alliance. Just before this event, a Chinese Communist Youth Group had formed within the student body, and a student strike was under way there. One Iwabashi Takeji, an activist in the Alliance, was responsible for handing out anti-war leaflets to Japanese officer candidates in port at Shanghai. On December 27, a number of students were arrested, and members of the Alliance turned to Wang for guidance, but before he could get back to them from party channels, most had fled the city for Beijing. These repressions of Alliance activities were exaggeratedly reported in the press as the "Japan Communist Party Incident." By early 1931, the arrested Tô-A dôbun students had been released and a number of them were expelled from school. Nishizato was arrested as a leader of this incident by the Higher Police in Tokyo in August 1931; he was imprisoned in Nagasaki and released in only December 1932. For a time such radical activities among the Japanese of Shanghai quieted down.[18]

SHANGHAI AND THE JAPANESE IN THE SORGE SPY RING

Another CCP directive passed to Yang in October of 1931 called on him to find Japanese to cooperate with the intelligence-gathering activities of Richard Sorge. Yang turned to Ozaki Hotsumi and Kawai Teikichi, and it was at Yang's home in Shanghai that these two Japanese first met in October 1931.[19] Ozaki told Kawai to meet him the very next day, and the two men repaired to a restaurant, accompanied by "a foreign woman," where they met a foreign man. The woman was Agnes Smedley (1892–1950), the man Richard Sorge. Kawai knew neither of them, but assumed they were Comintern agents. Sorge asked him if he could go to North China and Manchuria to collect data on Japanese army activities, and Kawai assented. Sorge had been charged by Red Army Intelligence with finding out if the Japanese planned to invade south into China proper or north into Siberia. Ozaki would provide Kawai with contacts. When Kawai, who was just thirty years of age, asked if this was a Comintern assignment, Ozaki laughed it off and asked Kawai to trust him.[20]

As he recounted in a volume of memoirs, Kawai assumed he was working on behalf of peace, anti-imperialism, socialism, and hence ultimately in the best interests of Japan. He traveled to Beijing first, where he was inundated by anti-Japanese slogans and banners everwhere. He describes the process by which he turned his entire being into a set of eyes and ears, amassing information on behalf of the international proletariat, and intent on discovering what Japan was up to in the region. As was his wont, he garnered much of his data from Japanese bar girls in establishments frequented by Japanese employees of the SMR, the Gaimushô, the local Japanese press, and later members of the Japanese armed forces. He soon made his way to Fengtian, where the information about the Manchurian Incident was coming fast and furious. He wrote up his impressions, which were dispatched through secret couriers back to Ozaki in Shanghai. Finally, a Chinese contact delivered to Kawai a letter in Ozaki's hand instructing him to return to Shanghai.

In early December, after two months on the job, Kawai arrived back in Shanghai. He had much to tell Ozaki, who promptly asked him to write it up immediately and append his own thoughts. He could clearly see that the mood in Shanghai had swung in a sharply anti-Japanese direction in those two months. The next day he and Ozaki went to Smedley's apartment in the French Concession, and Sorge soon arrived. Ozaki had already translated Kawai's report for him into English. Sorge shook his hand and began pelting him with specific questions about Japanese troop strengths and their aims. Kawai told him that the Guandong army wanted to sever Manchuria from the control of the Nanjing regime and establish a state under Japanese control. The fact that there were only 30,000 Japanese troops in the region, he surmised, probably meant that they would not invade Siberia any time too soon—not exactly a clairvoyant conclusion. The army had enlisted the support of two ultrarightist groups to these ends. After responding to Sorge's questions, Kawai was asked to go back to Manchuria, again traveling under cover of being a reporter for *Shanhai shûhô*.[21]

On January 18, 1932, a small group of Japanese monks walking the streets of Shanghai and intoning the Nichiren chant, for which they were greatly despised among the local populace, were set upon by angry Chinese. One was badly beaten, another killed. The incident outraged the Japanese community of Shanghai. Reprisals were meted out by some Japanese vigilantes, and the troubles escalated. The JRA requested military assistance and demonstrated in front of the Japanese consulate, demanding arms to defend themselves. Seventy pistols were distributed to them, which were quickly turned to offensive ends as they attacked Chinese merchants and rioted. By January 21, reports that a Japanese warship was on its way reached Shanghai; it arrived two days later. The Chinese responded by arming the local populace, and fighting erupted on January 29. That such a minor fracas could lead to what would be called the Shanghai Incident in which some 25,000 Chinese were killed or wounded is evidence of the heightened Sino-Japanese tensions in the city.

Kawai arrived back in Shanghai in the early morning hours of January 30. He somehow made his way amid the fighting to his newspaper office. Was he saddened by the fact that, for all his efforts to the contrary, China and Japan were at war? Was he distraught that the imperialist military forces of his native land had attacked and brutalized the Chinese? No, he was ecstatic, because the reverberations of bombs and gunfire were, in his estimation, the death throes of capitalism, for "the laws of history were straightforward." He made contact with Ozaki, and they later visited Sorge. After making his report, Kawai was again asked to return to Manchuria to continue his work.[22]

Sorge, though, needed another contact person in Shanghai, because Ozaki was planning to leave the *Asahi shinbun*. Ozaki recommended Yamagami Masayoshi (1896–1938), branch head of Rengô tsûshin, the Japanese news service, in Shanghai. Yamagami had initially come to Shanghai in 1925 as a reporter for the *Shanhai nippô*. His travels through China's major southern cities brought him into contact with such luminaries of the Creation Society as Yu Dafu (1896–1945), Cheng Fangwu (1897–1984), Wang Duqing (1898–1940), and Mu Mutian (1900–71) in Guangdong as well as with Lu Xun. In December of 1927 he filed a detailed report on the Canton commune. Two years later he wrote a play, *Shina o shinkan saseta mikkakan* (Three days that shook China), as a historical testament. After the collapse of the Canton commune, he returned to Shanghai and from there to Japan. In October 1929 he was back in Shanghai, where he bumped into Lu Xun on the street, an event recorded in Lu's diary. Yamagami was living on North Sichuan Road with a Japanese woman, the first Japanese beautician in Shanghai, who operated her own salon in the area.

In late 1928, shortly after he arrived in Shanghai, Ozaki went to visit the office of the Creation Society on North Sichuan Road. He met many leftwing writers there and even wrote under a pen name for their serial, *Dazhong wenyi* (Literature and art for the masses). One such writer, Tao Jingsun (1897–1952), who succeeded Yu Dafu as editor of *Dazhong wenyi*, recalled in his memoirs that Ozaki later introduced him there to Yamagami. Yamagami and Ozaki, both members of the Japanese fourth estate in Shanghai, had been friends for some period of time. Both men contributed, under pseudonyms, essays to Tao's journal, which translated a large number of pieces from the proletarian literature movement in Japan. Tao had studied medicine and lived in Japan for twenty-two years, where he had met Guo Moruo and founded the literary magazine *GREEN* in Kyûshû.[23]

Ultimately, Yamagami was too busy to devote the necessary time to helping Sorge, but he suggested that another journalist with good leftist credentials, Funakoshi Hisao, fill the needed slot. Funakoshi had already been involved in the Sino-Japanese Struggle Alliance and later in communicating Kawai Teikichi's reports to Ozaki, and hence to Sorge. He worked with Sorge and Kawai until Sorge left China in 1933 and subsequently for Sorge's replacement in Shanghai.

NISHIZATO TATSUO AND THE CHINESE COMMUNIST PARTY

Another manner in which one leftist Japanese with years of experience living in Shanghai accommodated himself to the changed circumstances and the heightened political atmosphere of the 1930s is typified by Nishizato Tatsuo. Released in late 1932 after sixteen months in prison, Nishizato found he had missed both the Manchurian Incident and the establishment of the "puppet" state of Manzhouguo (Manchukuo). In 1934 he was able to get back to Shanghai, where he found the main difference from several years before to be the shift toward a harsher Chinese attitude toward Japanese. With the help of friends he was able to secure a position with Rengô tsûshin in Shanghai, an indication that for every overt Japanese activist in China there were probably any number of sympathetic ones.

Nishizato also began to try to establish contact with the Chinese Communist Party. One day he met his former friend Wang Xuewen in Jessfield Park, and with Wang's help Nishizato began the process of entering the CCP. "My new life began," as he recalled many years later. As he would describe it, he was so opposed to the Japanese war of invasion against China and he so wanted to express his solidarity with the Chinese people that the best course he could pursue was to join the CCP. He wanted to fight shoulder-to-shoulder with the Chinese people against "world fascism."

He was assigned by the CCP the task of carrying on anti-war work among Japanese troops. Every week he met with a representative of the CCP in the French Concession in Shanghai. This contact was his lifeline to the Communist movement elsewhere in China; it was from this line of information that he learned, for instance, of the Fifth Encirclement Campaign being waged by Jiang Kai-shek's forces against the Communists in Jiangxi. He eventually took a position with the *Yomiuri* newpaper to support himself while continuing his political activities.[24]

LATER DEVELOPMENTS IN 1930s SHANGHAI

Japanese operatives and sub-operatives in the Sorge-Ozaki ring continued their work in China after the early 1930s, but mostly in cities other than Shanghai. Funakoshi moved on to Tianjin and Hankou, making occasional trips to the northeast, while Kawai, too, traveled mainly in Manchuria. That was where the action about which Sorge sought information was to be found. Sorge and Ozaki themselves remained in Tokyo. Other Japanese sympathetic to Chinese yearnings, though, remained in Shanghai.

As the political scene in Japan lurched sharply to the right, leftwing activists usually were compelled either to undergo a "reorientation" (*tenkô*) of their views and a concomitant embracing of the Japanese imperial institution, or effectively to go underground. As hundreds of their former fellows were willing, for an assortment of reasons, to compromise their socialist views and avoid prison terms, or worse, others among these leftists fled the home islands for China. It was, ironically, there that they frequently found work—which was by the mid- to late 1930s impossible for them to come by in Japan—with the largest Japanese colonial enterprise in history, the Research Department of the South Manchurian Railway Company. Their recruitment was made possible by the fact that the leaders of the immense research division, men such as Itô Takeo (1895–1985), shared their views on many issues, if not their overall world view. Itô himself employed several dozen such men—including such Communists as Ozaki Hotsumi and Ishidô Kiyotomo (b. 1904).[25]

Most of these Japanese leftists moved to Manchuria. Some, though, were hired to work in Shanghai, where Itô was head of the Research Department's branch office. Just at this moment in the late 1930s, as Japan was preparing for total war, the SMR was impelled to expand its research activities broadly. It needed capable men who knew how to conduct research, and Itô and others in the SMR knew where to get them. The irony of their position, leftists working for such a colonial enterprise in the middle of Japan's most egregious imperialist adventure, was not lost on these men.

This is how Itô described the situation in Shanghai:

> There were as well a fair number of leftists at the Shanghai office [of the SMR] where I was working. All sorts of people had come with introductions from acquaintances of mine from the Shinjinkai [New Man Society, a liberal–radical student organization of the late 1910s and early 1920s] days. Altogether our office had over three hundred employees and a budget of over three million yen.
>
> As the Research Department expanded, several large-scale research projects were carried out, and the Research Division of the Shanghai office bore its share of the responsibility. Shanghai played the most important role in three research projects: *Shina kôsenryoku chôsa* [Investigation of the resistance capacity of the Chinese], *Nichi-Man-Shi infure chôsa* [Investigation of Japanese–Manchurian–Chinese inflation], and *Sekai jôsei bunseki* [An analysis of international conditions]. The first of these occupied the Shanghai office for three calendar years, 1939–41. Most prominently active in the project was Nakanishi Tsutomu.[26]

Exceedingly few, probably not even Itô himself, knew that Nakanishi was a Japan Communist Party operative, a mole of sorts in the SMR. Itô certainly knew that Nakanishi held personal and scholarly views considerably to the left of center, and even had he known of Nakanishi's party affiliation it is entirely likely that he would have acted no differently.

Nakanishi had learned Chinese exceedingly well—so well, indeed, that he could pass as Chinese when circumstances demanded—while a student at the Tô-A dôbun shoin a decade earlier. In China he became deeply enamored of the Chinese revolution and was eventually expelled from school. He returned to China in 1934 and entered the SMR. Through the mid-1930s he wrote in SMR journals on the Chinese labor movement and general economic conditions in China and Manchuria. He served as one of the thirty-one researchers employed by Itô at the SMR's Tianjin office in 1935 to carry out the now legendary village investigations in the Jidong region. His many articles on Chinese agriculture repeatedly lacerated the "ruthless feudal exploitation" exercised by Chinese landlords over the peasant population.[27]

Undoubtedly because of his expertise in village investigation, his knowledge of Chinese, his wide travels in China, and his methodological acuity, Nakanishi, still a low-level functionary in the overall SMR machine, was given the lion's share of responsibility in the project designed to uncover the resistance capacity of the Chinese people. I have discussed this material elsewhere[28] and will not reproduce it here, except to note that the thrust of Nakanishi and his fellow workers' immense study was to encourage the Guandong Army, sponsor of the study, to seek an immediate political solution and get out of China quickly. A ground war on the Asian mainland, he warned, would be unwinnable.

CONCLUSIONS

Many of the Japanese who traveled to Shanghai for their tertiary education were looking for an altogether new experience, a way to make a contribution to Japan's future in the new, increasingly international world. What better place than the most cosmopolitan city in East Asia? From the late Meiji period through the early years of the Shôwa period, this outward-looking attitude was far more pronounced that it had been before. Similarly, journalists posted voluntarily or otherwise to China in these years sought out or found a world in Shanghai full of extraordinary excitement and experience unlike anything they could bring to it. A confluence of forces—including a proclivity to sympathize with the nascent Chinese student and labor movements, the new global perspective afforded by living in Shanghai, the intimate personal and cultural links forged with Chinese intellectuals and writers with a similar view of the contemporary world, and the proselytizing activities of Chinese Communist activists, among others—pushed many of them in a decidedly leftwing direction.

Through the 1930s and into the early 1940s, political and military tensions escalated between China and Japan, as well as within Japanese society. These tensions affected the nature of the activities of the small groups of Japanese leftist sympathizers in Shanghai. Initially literary contacts became increasingly political and resulted in activism—indeed, this was a route that many Chinese writers themselves had traveled. For some Japanese activists, this path led as far as to international espionage. The heightened tensions within Japan forced many Japanese to relatively brief careers as researchers in China.

Ultimately both of these groups—namely, the Japanese active in anti-militarist, anti-imperialist, and strongly leftwing politics in China and those who went to work for the largest colonial Japanese enterprise that has ever existed—were decimated by the Japanese military and government. Where the majority population of Japanese in Shanghai had once felt isolated and threatened, now with the Japanese military build-up on the mainland it was decidedly those opposed to Japanese pursuance of war against China who feared for their lives. Fot the Japanese leftist activists in Shanghai, the mushrooming of intelligence agencies represented an ominous threat and finally the end to their continued work. In a volume of his memoirs written after the war, Kawai Teikichi described the scene in this way:

> Shanghai was the international capital of espionage. Lines of intelligence linked some people there with Washington, others with London or Berlin, Moscow or Tokyo. Just among Japanese intelligence organs [in Shanghai], there were those of the army, the navy, the Tokyo Metropolitan Police, the Foreign Office, the Justice Ministry, the Taiwan Governor-General's Office, and the Korea Governor-General's Office. Each of these had independent agencies and competed with each other. Of course, the object of intelligence gathering was politics, military affairs, and thought. Furthermore, the Shanghai Municipal Council stood at the forefront in the inspection of all of Shanghai.[29]

Only the journalist-spy Ozaki was actually executed, but others died in prison or shortly after being released in late 1945 from malnutrition. From the early 1940s Japanese leftists and others even remotely sympathetic to them began to be arrested by the various Japanese police agencies in China and at home. Ozaki, Sorge, and their operatives were taken in 1941 and 1942. Nakanishi was seized in 1942, largely, it appears, because his report on the resistance capacity of Chinese had made the Japanese authorities suspicious of his true sympathies; Nishizato was taken in the same sweep of arrests. A large number of SMR researchers, including Itô, were hauled off to jail in 1942 and 1943. Many died of malnutrition or exposure in the wintry Manchurian climate.

None the less, a significant minority of these scholars and activists went on to brilliant postwar careers in government, leftwing politics, and academic life. They wore their wartime prison sentences on their lapels as a badge of honor. Uchiyama Kanzô, the remarkable man who has never been studied in English, was one of a tiny few able to bridge the Sino-Japanese gap at this savage historical juncture. His determinedly apolitical stance, but clear sympathy in the eyes of Chinese, enabled him to remain with his store through the harshest years of Sino-Japanese hostilities, the end of World War II in 1945 and the establishment of the People's Republic in 1949, until his death in 1959.

Of course, these leftwing activists were far from a majority of the Japanese resident in Shanghai or elsewhere in China in these years. Indeed, Japanese journalists were among the most severe denigrators of contemporary

Chinese society and politics of all Japanese visitors there in the entire prewar period. None the less, the handful of remarkable individuals discussed above did make a distinctive contribution to modern Chinese political history and Sino-Japanese relations, in spite of the fact that at a higher level Sino-Japanese relations were rapidly disintegrating. Given the way the war ultimately turned out, they probably are justified in the enormous postwar pride they have felt for their prewar and wartime activities. No history of the period is complete without their stories.

NOTES

1 Ten years earlier, the Japanese had numbered 47,246 in China proper, marking a mild but consistent increase. The Japanese population in Manchuria, by contrast, increased twentyfold between 1908 (58,433) and 1935 (1,156,646), much more rapidly than in the cities of China proper.

2 Katô Yûzô, "Shanhai ryakushi" [A brief history of Shanghai], appended to Matsumoto Shigeharu, *Shanhai jidai: jaanarisuto no kaisô* [The Shanghai years: memoirs of a journalist] (Tokyo: Chûô kôronsha, 1974), I, pp. 316–17. Mark Peattie offers slightly different figures for 1935 Shanghai; see Peattie, "Japanese Treaty Port Settlements in China, 1895–1937," in *The Japanese Informal Empire in China, 1895–1937*, ed. Peter Duus, Ramon H. Myers, and Mark R. Peattie (Princeton: Princeton University Press, 1989), p. 170. For information on Japanese travelers to Shanghai at the end of the Edo period, see Joshua A. Fogel, "The Voyage of the *Senzaimaru* to Shanghai: Early Sino-Japanese Contacts in the Modern Era," in *The Cultural Dimension of Sino-Japanese Relations* (Armonk, N.Y.: M.E. Sharpe, 1994); and Joshua A. Fogel, *The Literature of Travel in the Japanese Rediscovery of China, 1862–1945* (Stanford: Stanford University Press, 1996), chapter two. For more information of the earlier history of the Japanese at Shanghai, see Yonezawa Hideo, "Shanhai hôjin hatten shi" [A history of the growth of the Japanese in Shanghai], *Tô-A keizai kenkyû*, part 1, 22, 3 (July 1938), pp. 394–408; part 2, 23, 1 (January–February 1939), pp. 112–26.

3 Katô Yûzô, "Shanhai ryakushi," in Matsumoto Shigeharu, *Shanhai jidai*, pp. 318–19; and Mark R. Peattie, "Japanese Treaty Port Settlements in China," p. 183. Roughly one-fourth of all Japanese in Shanghai were directly tied to the cotton industry, and many more did business with it. See Peattie, p. 204; and Peter Duus, "Zaikabô: Japanese Cotton Mills in China, 1895–1937," in *The Japanese Informal Empire in China*, pp. 65–100.

4 Katô Yûzô, "Shanhai ryakushi," in Matsumoto Shigeharu, *Shanhai jidai*, pp. 319–20; Peattie, "Japanese Treaty Port Settlements in China," p. 196; and Ozaki Hotsuki, *Shanhai 1930 nen* [Shanghai 1930] (Tokyo: Iwanami shoten, 1990), p. 10.

5 Peattie, "Japanese Treaty Port Settlements in China," pp. 184, 192, 201–3.

6 Banno Junji, "Japanese Industrialists and Merchants and the Anti-Japanese Boycotts in China, 1919–1928," in *The Japanese Informal Empire in China*, pp. 314–29; Donald A. Jordan, *Chinese Boycotts versus Japanese Bombs: The Failure of China's "Revolutionary Diplomacy," 1931–32* (Ann Arbor: University of Michigan Press, 1991); and Peattie, "Japanese Treaty Port Settlements in China," pp. 206–7.

7 Ozawa Masamoto, *Uchiyama Kanzô den: Nit-Chû yûkô ni tsukushita idai na shomin* [Biography of Uchiyama Kanzô: a great commoner in the establishment of Sino-Japanese friendship] (Tokyo: Banchô shobô, 1972), p. 83; Uchiyama

Kanzô, *Kakôroku* [Diary] (Tokyo: Iwanami shoten, 1961), p. 122; Ozaki Hotsuki, pp. 26–33; and Paul Scott, "Uchiyama Kanzô: A Case Study in Sino-Japanese Interaction," *Sino-Japanese Studies* 2.1 (1990), pp. 49–52. Satô Haruo later translated Lu Xun's famous tale, "The True Story of A Q," into Japanese; see Ge Baoquan, *"A Q zhengzhuan" zai guowai* ["The True Story of A Q" overseas] (Beijing: Renmin chubanshe, 1981), pp. 57–64. I have described Tanizaki's 1926 visit to Shanghai in detail in my "Japanese Literary Travelers in Prewar China," *Harvard Journal of Asiatic Studies* 49, 2 (1989), pp. 575–602; and in *The Literature of Travel in the Japanese Rediscovery of China*, pp. 250–75.

8   I have referred here to Xu Guangping (1898–1968) as Lu Xun's wife, though they may not actually have been married at this point. They had met and fallen in love the previous year, when Lu was married to another woman. He was intent that she fully understand his work, and to that end he assumed a paternal role in her life. In a letter dated December 2, 1926, he had written to her: "I think you do not have as much knowledge of life as I have ... I feel that it would help you considerably to study something new ... You have another weak point as well in that you cannot read works in foreign languages. It would be very valuable for you to learn Japanese. I will see that you study [Japanese] hard next year." (See Lu Xun, *Lu Xun chuanji* [Collected works of Lu Xun] (Beijing: Renmin daxue chubanshe, 1987), XI, p. 478. My thanks to my student, Tanaka Rei, for locating this passage and bringing it to my attention.) Despite lessons he planned for her from a textbook he put together himself, Xu showed little aptitude for Japanese.

9   Uchiyama Kanzô, "Ro Jin sensei tsuioku" [Remembrances of Mr Lu Xun], in Uchiyama Kanzô, *Ro Jin no omoide* [Memories of Lu Xun] (Tokyo: Shakai shisôsha, 1979), p. 39. This article originally appeared in the journal *Kaizô* in 1936. The story has been retold many times, and were it not for Uchiyama's own memoir, we might have reason to doubt its veracity. See also NHK's "Dokyumento Shôwa," part 2, "Shanhai kyôdô sokai" [The International Settlement of Shanghai], an hour-long television documentary broadcast on Japanese educational television (NHK) in 1986.

10 Ozaki Hotsuki, *Shanhai 1930 nen*, pp. 41–2; and Scott, "Uchiyama Kanzô," pp. 52–4.

11 Ozaki Hotsuki, *Shanhai 1930 nen*, pp. 64–9; and Leo Ou-fan Lee, "Literary Trends: The Road to Revolution, 1927–1949," in *The Cambridge History of China* XIII, *Republican China, 1912–1949, Part 2* (Cambridge: Cambridge University Press, 1986), pp. 429, 443. Lu Xun studies in Japan are an industry in themselves. For highly abbreviated English-language introductions to Lu Xun's time in Japan and to Japanese studies of Lu Xun, see, respectively, William A. Lyell, Jr, *Lu Hsün's Vision of Reality* (Berkeley: University of California Press, 1976), pp. 52–102; Maruyama Noboru, "Lu Xun in Japan," in *Lu Xun and His Legacy*, ed. Leo Ou-fan Lee (Berkeley: University of California Press, 1985), pp. 216–41; and Nishizato Tatsuo, *Kakumei no Shanhai de, aru Nihonjin Chûgoku kyôsantôin no kiroku* [In revolutionary Shanghai: the chronicles of a Japanese member of the Chinese Communist Party] (Tokyo: Nit-Chû shuppan, 1977), p. 85. For data on Xia Yan, see Zhou Bin, *Xia Yan zhuanlüe* [Short biography of Xia Yan] (Shanghai: Shanghai wenyi chubanshe, 1994), especially pp. 39–64.

12 On the Tô-A dôbun shoin, see three pieces by Douglas R. Reynolds: "Training Young China Hands: Tôa Dôbun Shoin and its Precursors, 1886–1945," in *The Japanese Informal Empire in China, 1895–1945*, pp. 210–71; "China Area Studies in Prewar China: Japan's Tôa Dôbun Shoin in Shanghai, 1900–1945," *Journal of Asian Studies* 45, 5 (1987), pp. 945–70; "Recent Sourcebooks on Tô-A Dôbunkai and Tô-A Dôbun Shoin: A Review Article," *Sino-Japanese Studies* 1, 2 (1989), pp. 18–27.

13 Chalmers Johnson, *An Instance of Treason: Ozaki Hotsumi and the Sorge Spy Ring*, expanded edition (Stanford: Stanford University Press, 1990), p. 55.

14 Ozaki Hotsuki, *Shanhai 1930 nen*, pp. 114, 116–17; and Nishizato Tatsuo, *Kakumei no Shanhai de*, pp. 12, 26, 48–9, 74. Although Nishizato was willing to accept the fact that his *alma mater* played a role in Japanese imperialism, he clearly stated that none of the students were "running dogs."

15 Kawai Teikichi, *Harukanaru seinen no hibi ni: watakushi no hansei ki* [Days of my distant youth: a record of half my life] (Tokyo: Tanizawa shobô, 1979), pp. 48–9, 84, 176, 184, 191, 193, 207–11, 259, 262, 320, 339, 341–3; and Ozaki Hotsuki, *Shanhai 1930 nen*, pp. 119–25.

16 Peng Hao, "Chuanhe Zhanji de zuji" [The career of Kawai Teikichi], *Zhongguo Zhong-Ri guanxi shi yanjiuhui huikan* 14 (1988), pp. 28–9; Kawai Teikichi, *Harukanaru seinen no hibi ni*, pp. 368–9; Nakamura Shintarô, "Nosaka Sanzô to En'an dôkutsu no Nihonjin" [Nosaka Sanzô and the Japanese in the caves of Yan'an], in *Son Bun kara Ozaki Hotsumi e* [From Sun Yat-sen to Ozaki Hotsumi] (Tokyo, Nit-Chû shuppan, 1975), pp. 231–40; Ozaki Hotsuki, *Shanhai 1930 nen*, pp. 124–6; and Nishizato Tatsuo, *Kakumei no Shanhai de*, p. 89. There is an entry on Wang Xuewen in a recent Chinese historical dictionary which elides all mention of Wang's contacts among the Japanese in Shanghai: *Zhongguo minguo shi cidian* [Historical dictionary of the Republic of China], ed. Chen Xulu and Li Huaxing (Shanghai: Shanghai renmin chubanshe, 1991), p. 41.

17 Kawai Teikichi, *Harukanaru seinen no hibi ni*, pp. 371–4, 377; Kawai Teikichi, *Aru kakumeika no kaisô* [Memoirs of a revolutionary] (Tokyo: Shin jinbutsu ôraisha, 1973), pp. 12–13; Kawai Teikichi, *Zoruge jiken gokuchû ki* [Prison notes from the Sorge case] (Tokyo: Shin jinbutsu ôraisha, 1975), p. 2; Ozaki Hotsuki, *Shanhai 1930 nen*, pp. 126–9; and Chalmers Johnson, *An Instance of Treason*, p. 57. Nishizato Tatsuo explains in his memoirs, *Kakumei no Shanhai de* (p. 90), that the group opted for the "Shi" of Shina in their title, rather than Chûgoku, despite claims that the former denigrated the Chinese, because the latter would not have been familiar to most Japanese. On "Shina" and "Chûgoku," see Joshua A. Fogel, "The Sino-Japanese Controversy over *Shina* as a Toponym for China," in Fogel, *The Cultural Dimension of Sino-Japanese Relations*, pp. 66–76.

18 Kawai Teikichi, *Aru kakumeika no kaisô*, p. 11; Ozaki Hotsuki, *Shanhai 1930 nen*, pp. 130–35; NHK "Dokyumento Shôwa," part 2; and Chalmers Johnson, *An Instance of Treason*, pp. 57–8. Nishizato Tatsuo (*Kakumei no Shanhai de*, p. 92) contradicts Kawai's account of this event (and implicitly those of Ozaki and Johnson, which were based on Kawai's memory of the incident) in one pertinent detail. He claims that the line "Long live the Chinese Communist Party" was not one of the slogans plastered on the wall; it would have been, he claims, contrary to the nature of their movement. As a lifelong Communist, Nishizato found he had many similar bones to pick with Kawai; when describing events of those times in China, he frequently found himself agreeing with fellow comrade Nakanishi Tsutomu in opposition to Kawai. On Nishizato's arrest, see *Kakumei no Shanhai de*, pp. 100, 110–14.

19 Because much has been written about Ozaki's role in the Sorge spy ring, what follows will focus more directly on the role played by Kawai. For scholarship on Ozaki, see Chalmers Johnson, *An Instance of Treason*; F. W. Deakin and G. R. Storry, *The Case of Richard Sorge* (London: Chatto and Windus, 1966); Gordon Prange, *Target Tokyo: The Story of the Sorge Spy Ring* (New York: McGraw-Hill, 1984); and Julius Mader, *Dr.-Sorge-Report: Ein Dokumentarbericht über Kunderschafter des Friedens mit ausgewählten Artikeln von Richard Sorge* (Berlin: Militärverlag der Deutschen Demokratischen Republik, 1984). Kawai held the unique distinction of all those intimately involved in the spy ring of both surviving prison and World War II and being willing to speak and write about it

after the war. In addition to three volumes of memoirs, cited *inter alia*, he wrote fourteen popular volumes of Chinese and Japanese history. I have discussed his work as a non-academic scholar in "Senzen Nihon no minkan Chûgokugaku" [Non-academic genres of Sinology in prewar Japan], in *Kôsaku suru Ajia* [Asia entangled], ed. Mizoguchi Yûzô, Hamashita Takeshi, Hiraishi Naoaki, and Miyajima Hiroshi (Tokyo: Tokyo University Press, 1993), in the series *Ajia kara kangaeru* (Reconsiderations from Asia), 1, pp. 259–65. Kobayashi Fumio has almost fawningly written about Kawai's scholarship in several essays, such as "Kawai Teikichi no Chûgoku kan" [Kawai Teikichi's view of China], in his *Chûgoku gendai shi no danshô* [Fragments from the contemporary history of China] (Tokyo: Tanizawa shobô, 1986), pp. 108–32.

20 Kawai Teikichi, *Aru kakumeika no kaisô*, pp. 48–51.

21 Kawai Teikichi, *Aru kakumeika no kaisô*, pp. 53, 55, 61, 64, 71–5.

22 Kawai Teikichi, *Aru kakumeika no kaisô*, pp. 82–6; and Jordan, *Chinese Boycotts versus Japanese Bombs*, pp. 223–33, *passim*.

23 Ozaki Hotsuki, *Shanhai 1930 nen*, pp. 90–6, 142–3, 188–90; Chalmers Johnson, *An Instance of Treason*, pp. 51–2, 81, 266; and *Zhonghua minguo shi cidian*, p. 421. In early 1931, Yamagami, having earlier secured Lu Xun's permission, began to translate "The True Story of A Q" into Japanese. Just at that time the Longhua Incident erupted, in which five young leftist authors were arrested and murdered by the Guomindang. The translation was dedicated to these five "martyrs," and some of their writings were also translated and included in the final product, which appeared later that year, *Shina shôsetsu shû A Q seiden* [A collection of Chinese fiction: The True Story of A Q]. Yamagami used the pen name of Lin Shouren; Lu Xun proofed the translation for accuracy; and Ozaki, writing under the pseudonym of Shirakawa Jirô, contributed an introduction.

24 Nishizato Tatsuo, *Kakumei no Shanhai de*, pp. 115, 122–3, 125–8, 131–2, 167.

25 Itô Takeo, *Life along the South Manchurian Railway: The Memoirs of Itô Takeo*, trans. Joshua A. Fogel (Armonk, N.Y.: M.E. Sharpe, 1988), pp. xv–xvi, 173. See also Ishidô Kiyotomo's fascinating memoirs, *Waga itan no Shôwa shi* [My heretical history in the Shôwa period] (Tokyo: Keisô shobô, 1987), and *Zoku waga itan no Shôwa shi* [My heretical history in the Shôwa period, continued] (Tokyo: Keisô shobô, 1990). There are any number of works on the SMR and its Research Department. Among the better ones on the SMR are: Andô Hikotarô, *Mantetsu: Nihon teikokushugi to Chûgoku* [The SMR: Japanese imperialism and China] (Tokyo: Ochanomizu shobô, 1965); and Harada Katsumasa, *Mantetsu* [The SMR] (Tokyo: Iwanami shoten, 1984). The better works on the SMR's research activities would include: Hara Kakuten, *Gendai Ajia kenkyû seiritsu shiron: Mantetsu chôsabu, Tô-A kenkyûjo, IPR no kenkyû* [Historical analysis of the founding of modern Asian studies: studies of the Research Department of the SMR, the East Asian Research Institute, and the Institute of Pacific Relations] (Tokyo: Keisô shobô, 1984); Hara Kakuten, *Mantetsu chôsabu to Ajia* [The Research Department of the SMR and Asia] (Tokyo: Sekai shoin, 1986); Yamada Gôichi, *Mantetsu chôsabu, eikô to zasetsu no yonjûnen* [The Research Department of the SMR: forty years of glory and frustration] (Tokyo: Nihon keizai shinbunsha, 1977); and Kusayanagi Daizô, *Jitsuroku: Mantetsu chôsabu* [The true story of the Research Department of the SMR] (Tokyo: Asahi shinbunsha, 1979).

26 Itô Takeo, *Life along the South Manchurian Railway*, pp. 175–6. On the Shinjinkai, see Henry Dewitt Smith, *Japan's First Student Radicals* (Cambridge, Mass.: Harvard University Press, 1972).

27 Nakanishi Tsutomu, *Chûgoku kakumei no arashi no naka de* [In the tempest of the Chinese revolution] (Tokyo: Aoki shoten, 1974), pp. 35–7, 47–8, 77–8, 81–3, 96–101, 112–15, 142–5, 166, 177; Yamada Gôichi, *Mantetsu chôsabu*, pp. 139,

150–2; and Joshua A. Fogel, "Introduction: Itô Takeo and the Research Work of the South Manchurian Railway Company," in Itô Takeo, *Life along the South Manchurian Railway*, pp. xiv, xv, xvii–xviii.

28 See Fogel, "Introduction: Itô Takeo and the Research Work of the South Manchurian Railway Company," pp. xviii–xxii.

29 Kawai Teikichi, *Aru kakumeika no kaisô*, p. 114.

5 Chinese capitalists and the Japanese

Collaboration and resistance in the Shanghai area, 1937–45

Parks M. Coble

In the 1930s, the Shanghai area was the center of Chinese commerce, banking, and industry, possessing a substantial modern sector and capitalist elite. The Sino-Japanese War of 1937–45 dealt a devastating blow to Chinese business. The economic heartland of China was ravaged, and millions came under Japanese occupation for nearly eight years. Despite the importance of this period and the drama of these events, the experience of Chinese in the war era has attracted only limited scholarly attention. As Fu Po-shek has noted, "In contrast to the impressive scholarship devoted to the human condition in Nazi-occupied Europe, especially Vichy France, Chinese historians have yet to pay attention to the problem of human responses to occupation."[1]

Reasons for this neglect are rather obvious. The conflict was followed by the civil war and Communist revolution. Agonizing over which capitalists collaborated with the enemy, and thus became *hanjian* (traitors to China), quickly gave way to the categories of "class enemy" or even "enemy of the people." With these groups often expanding in the People's Republic to include millions—even those who had been close to the Chairman himself—the crimes of an earlier era were simply subsumed in the much larger total. By the Cultural Revolution, those who had served the Guomindang government or worked with the Allied powers were often considered just as guilty as those who had collaborated with Japanese-sponsored puppet organizations.

In the work which has been published on the war era, capitalists are often depicted in stereotypical terms. The greedy capitalist collaborator, eager to make profit by working with the enemy, has been a stock figure in descriptions of the war by Communist writers. Indeed, this stereotype was developed by leftists even before collaboration had occurred. Communist writer Pan Hannian warned in early September 1937, just one month into the fighting at Shanghai, that Chinese national capitalists were compradore in nature and would seek appeasement. "Some industrial and commercial businessmen, because the war had been prolonged and this has caused their business to stop ... are intimidated by bankruptcy. They fantasize about peace."[2]

At the other extreme, wartime propaganda from Chongqing, which sought to assure the world that China was prepared to fight to the finish, often portrayed the capitalist as patriotic hero, sacrificing profit and capital to serve

China's war needs.[3] The surprising factor about these stereotypical images is not that they exist, but that so little scholarly work has been done to produce a more nuanced portrait.

The war experience, I would argue, deserves careful scholarly treatment. Not only was the war one of the major events in modern history, it was the immediate background of the Communist revolution. This chapter is an initial attempt to analyze the behavior of Chinese capitalists in the lower Yangzi during the war era, and to determine the impact of the war on the capitalists and their relationship with the Japanese occupiers.

Industry and commerce in the lower Yangzi area suffered enormous destruction because of the intense fighting, although the degree of damage varied from one area to another. In Shanghai, the city government estimated damage to Chinese industry at over 560 million yuan. In the heavily industrialized Zhabei section destruction was almost total; in the Nanshi (south city) area, extensive. By contrast, in the foreign settlements the physical damage was much lighter, but Japanese occupied the portion of the International Settlement north of Suzhou Creek, including the important industrial and shipping centers of Hongkou and Yangshupu. These were sealed off until February 1938, when limited access was permitted to Chinese residents. Although Chinese factories in these areas were spared heavy damage, many fell under Japanese control. Overall, most estimates are that over half of all industrial property in the Shanghai area (Chinese and foreign-controlled) was destroyed in the fighting. Outside of Shanghai, according to one estimate, the destruction of industrial equipment and property (through 1943) ranged from 80 percent for Nanjing and 64 percent for Wuxi to much lower figures of 28 percent for Hangzhou and 12 percent for the Wuhan area.[4]

The Chinese government urged Chinese industrialists to move their plants westward to unoccupied China as a patriotic contribution to the war. Results of this undertaking were modest, although important to China's war effort. By 1940 an estimated 448 plants had been moved to the interior, mostly from Shanghai and Wuhan, only a minuscule portion of China's prewar industry. Why was not more done? The Guomindang government provided some assistance and coordination, but Nanjing's effort was not well planned. Virtually no preparations had been made prior to the war, and after the fighting began Japan came to dominate the Yangzi river on the water and in the air. Under these battlefield conditions, moving industrial facilities was difficult. Ships were sunk, docks and warehouses destroyed, and losses from Japanese bombing were heavy. Conditions worsened as the war progressed; many industrialists shipped equipment to Wuhan only to have it later lost when being taken up river to Chongqing. In allocating shipping, moreover, the government naturally gave priority to troop movements and then to shipping military arsenals and iron and steel plants.

China's private industrialists, whose plants produced principally textiles, flour, matches, and other consumer goods, were mostly left to fend for themselves. The combination of war conditions and government actions thus limited the effectiveness of the transfer program, even though some Chinese industrialists sincerely desired to contribute to the war effort and escape Japanese control. Perhaps the miracle is that any made it to Sichuan at all.[5]

In fact, most Chinese capitalists who could, chose to relocate in the nearby unoccupied foreign concessions in Shanghai. This "solitary island" (*gudao*), as it was called, became a center of frenzied economic activity in 1938 and 1939. Although little industry had been situated in the International Settlement south of the Suzhou Creek or French Concession prior to August 1937, factories of all types were established in the settlement and western roads area, including cotton-spinning and weaving mills, silk filatures (which had previously been dispersed in the interior), paper mills, enameling plants, tanneries, and cigarette factories. Chinese writers refer to this era as the "flourishing" period of Shanghai's economy, a sharp contrast to conditions in the occupied areas. Production levels in Shanghai in 1939 were equal to or greater than in 1936 for cotton weaving, silk weaving, and flour milling. Wool weaving, paper manufacture, and dyestuff production actually experienced substantial increases.[6]

The rush by Chinese industrialists to move plants from the interior to the settlements, the abundant supply of cheap labor due to the refugee populations, the access to raw materials through the international markets, and the accumulation of liquid capital in Shanghai banks, created the economic conditions for the "flourishing solitary island." Even the arrival of refugees from Europe after the eruption of war there contributed to the boom, since many were highly skilled. Only the outbreak of the Pacific war, which led Japan to occupy the International Settlement completely, terminated Shanghai's special economy.[7]

Some Chinese capitalists could adapt to the conditions of war more readily than others. Bankers, for instance, with their limited physical facilities, could move into the International Settlement most easily. Indeed, the Settlement had been the center for Chinese and foreign banking before the outbreak of war. Most banks simply consolidated in Shanghai the activities of their branches in such cities as Jiading, Hangzhou, and Nanjing, as the outer locations came under Japanese military control. The Nanjing Bankers' Association, for instance, set up an office in the building of the Shanghai Bankers' Association. Of course, relocating in Shanghai could not compensate for lost business opportunities in the occupied areas.[8] For industrial manufacturers, relocating to the foreign concessions was far more difficult. Plants which survived the battlefield came under Japanese occupation unless the industrialists had been able to move equipment swiftly. Occupied factories and commercial property were often directly confiscated by the Japanese military and turned over to Japanese management. Many Japanese companies with plants in China—such as Toyoda or Kanegafuchi—suffered heavy losses in the fighting. Japanese authorities attempted to compensate them by awarding confiscated Chinese-owned properties. If Chinese manufacturers were per-mitted any role, they were forced to accept Sino-Japanese "cooperative management," which meant becoming a junior partner to a Japanese firm. Economic agencies established by the Japanese military and later run by the Wang Jingwei puppet government, such as the Cotton and the Wheat Commissions, controlled access to raw materials and markets.[9]

Chinese businessmen did not relish losing control of their enterprises to Japanese and tried numerous tactics to regain their businesses in the occupied areas. One approach attempted early in the war was simply to register one's company as a protected foreign enterprise or to employ a foreign merchant as a front so as to enjoy the protection of a foreign flag. The San Bei Steam Navigation Company, owned by Yu Xiaqing, who was one of the most venerable of Shanghai capitalists, suffered enormous losses during the battle of Shanghai. Of 90,000 tons of shipping it possessed when the war started, nearly 30,000 was commandeered by the Guomindang government and largely sunk. Another twenty ships of about 20,000 tons were disabled by the war or trapped in Japanese blockades. To overcome these problems, Yu bought two Norwegian transport ships of about 20,000 tons in 1938 which flew the flags of Norway and Panama. This protection allowed the vessels to make regular runs to Saigon and Rangoon to purchase rice, garnering Yu handsome profits. The rice sold for much higher prices in the refugee-swollen foreign concessions of Shanghai than the purchase cost in Southeast Asia. To counter public criticism of profiteering, Yu donated substantial amounts of rice to refugee relief.[10]

Yu still had nearly 40,000 tons of shipping which belonged to the San Bei company. He drew upon some long-standing connections with the Italian consul in Shanghai to reorganize these San Bei assets as a joint enterprise, the Sino-Italian Steamship Navigation Company. The old San Bei ships began to fly the Italian flag, whose protection was substantial, since Tokyo had relatively good relations with Rome. Yu's ships thus continued to carry passengers, while those of its arch-rival, the China Merchants' Steam Navigation Company, were largely confiscated or confined by blockade.[11]

This type of foreign protection rarely worked so effectively. The Japanese were wary of recognizing "foreign" ownership if they thought it was only a ruse. The Dasheng mills in Nantong, for instance, attempted to hide under a foreign flag when the city fell in August 1938. By dint of a mortgage arrangement with a German bank, Dasheng reinvented itself as a foreign enterprise, using a German name and displaying swastikas on factory buildings. This German tie delayed but did not prevent a Japanese takeover of the enterprise.[12] Japanese special services doubted the connection yet first offered Dasheng management a collaborative arrangement as a junior partner with the Japanese Kanegafuchi Company. When Dasheng management rejected this plan, Japanese military forces finally occupied the mills in March 1939, and turned them over to Kanegafuchi. Under Japanese control, the output of the plant was geared toward production of cloth for use by the

Japanese army. Clearly, Chinese businessmen whose enterprises were located in the occupied zone had few options. If foreign flag protection failed, the best that they could hope for was to continue as junior partners to the Japanese.

Perhaps the surprising thing is that Chinese owners of industries in the occupied zone had any room for maneuver at all. Indeed, many Japanese hardliners in the special services of the military sought to bring the entire modern sector in China under total Japanese control. Their failure to eliminate completely the involvement of Chinese capitalists in the occupied areas was due more to circumstances than to desire. When Tokyo's presumption of a short war in China proved incorrect, the military adopted a strategy of "using the war to feed the war" (*yizhan yangzhan*). In other words, the economy of the occupied areas had to be revived in order to supply the needs of the Japanese military in China.[13]

Naturally, Japanese military leaders would have preferred to achieve this economic revival in China under the complete control of Japanese capital. Plans were made to do just that. In north China the Xingzhong company, which was capitalized by the South Manchurian Railway, had earlier been given responsibility for management of key industries, including coal, iron ore, and electric power production. This was to be undertaken with the cooperation of Japanese firms such as Mitsui and Mitsubishi. In April 1938 Tokyo assigned Xingzhong's functions to the newly created North China Development Company (Kita Shina kaihatsu kabushiki kaisha), which was capitalized at 350 million yen.[14]

Japanese planners had long sought to control and develop the resources of north China; indeed, the Japanese military's insistence on "separating" north China had been a major cause of the war. By contrast, fewer Japanese planners had anticipated the spread of the war into central China and less preparation had been made. None the less, a companion firm for the North China Development Company, the Central China Development Company (Naka Shina shinkō kabushiki kaisha), was given similar responsibilities. By contrast with the northern firm, whose capital was 350 million yen, however, the central China company's capital was set at only 100 million yen.[15]

Japanese planners were thus inclined to favor projects in north China over those in the center and south. When the unexpected scale of the China war further strained Japanese finances, scarce resources were first pumped into the better-planned projects in north China. In 1938, total Japanese investment in China was 1.7 billion yen, of which 60 percent was invested in north China and only 37 percent in central China.[16]

The Japanese drive for economic control in central and south China was thus not as complete or well financed as efforts in the north. Conditions and policies often varied from time to time and place to place, reflecting changes in the wartime situation and disagreements among Japanese groups. Particularly after the start of the Pacific war, the Japanese made greater efforts to gain the economic and political participation of Chinese elites in the occupied area. As Akira Iriye has noted,

Japanese policy toward China was forced to change because of setbacks in the southwestern Pacific in 1942. Destruction of Japanese shipping meant that not enough supplies and foodstuffs from the south seas were available to the Japanese forces in China. Moreover, increasing numbers of troops stationed in China had to be diverted to the Solomons.

It was against this backdrop, Iriye notes, that Tokyo adopted a new China policy in December 1942, one designed to lend credibility to the puppet regime in Nanjing.[17] Tokyo's new plan for China called for, among other things, extracting more raw materials, promoting a revival of China's economy, and increasing the strength of the Wang government. To demonstrate the political viability of Nanjing, it was to establish new economic control agencies with the active participation of Chinese capitalists.[18]

These circumstances afforded Chinese industrialists who found their factories under Japanese control, with only slight room for maneuver. Any Chinese industrialist who sought to participate in operating a factory in the occupied zone was forced into some type of partnership with either Japanese elements or Chinese puppet agencies. The degree of compromise varied with time and place, but compromise (or collaboration) was required.[19]

Chinese capitalists thus found themselves in a wide range of circumstances during the war era. The easy generalizations often made about businessmen—patriotic capitalist sacrificing for the national good, scheming collaborator aiding the Japanese invader, or tool of foreign imperialists—are simply wrong. Few fit easily into one category. Examination of individual capitalists and enterprises reveals a complex mosaic of motives and actions in almost every case.

Take, for example, the Central Chemical Glass Works (Zhongyang huaxue boli chang), a small enterprise which had been established in the Yangshupu district of Shanghai in July 1934. The firm manufactured high-quality, specialty glass implements and instruments. It was the first Chinese company, for instance, to produce glass beakers of sufficient strength to withstand the high temperatures of chemical and medical work. Its founder, Wang Xinsheng, had been born in Kobe, Japan, of a Japanese mother and a Chinese father and had been educated in both countries. Despite his mixed background, Wang's first reaction when war erupted was to move the factory to Chinese-held territory, first to Changsha and later to Chongqing. Unfortunately, Wang lost virtually all of the material and equipment shipped. Sixty tons went down to Japanese bombing in transit from Shanghai, and a second shipment was lost in a shipwreck *en route* to Chongqing.[20]

Having failed to establish production in the interior, Wang tried to reopen in Shanghai. The Japanese authorities, however, confiscated the plant and placed it under military management, using the pretext that the name "Zhongyang" (Central) denoted Guomindang ownership. Production was shifted to meet military needs. At this point Wang utilized his Japanese ties. He had his mother, whose Japanese name was Kinoshita, write the Japanese consulate in Shanghai, claiming that the factory was Japanese property and that it be protected. The company then reopened with the name Kinoshita Works.

Despite Wang's seeming cooperation with the occupying force, current biographers of Wang writing in the People's Republic note certain patriotic actions by the industrialist. The plant sold materials to unoccupied China, despite the risks involved. Flasks and beakers from the plant, for instance, were used at universities in Kunming. Perhaps because of this, Japanese and puppet authorities suspected that the plant promoted anti-Japanese activity. In May 1943, when Wang had prepared seventy boxes of glass instruments for transshipment through Wenzhou to unoccupied areas, puppet authorities visited the plant, and Wang fell under increased scrutiny. Japanese consular officials routinely monitored shipments from the plant.

When the war ended, Wang's plant was temporarily confiscated by Guomindang agents as enemy property. Classified as a traitor by a Shanghai court, Wang departed for Hong Kong, where he established a new company. Wang's experience represents a variety of responses to the Japanese invasion. Had he had better luck in transporting his materials, he might well have established his factory in the interior and avoided contact with puppet authorities altogether, despite his mixed heritage. When that approach failed, he used his mother's citizenship to secure the plant, while at the same time maintaining trading links with the interior. Whether the latter was done for patriotic or simply commercial reasons is unclear. Wang's current Chinese biographers, on whose research this account is based, argue that he was patriotic and that he helped to develop Chinese industry. No easy generalization can be made to describe Wang's strategy except that he strove to keep his enterprise operating during the war.

A somewhat different set of circumstances befell the Zhengtai Rubber Works of Shanghai. This company, which had been established in 1927 with Japanese technical assistance, principally manufactured rubber shoes. Despite its early Japanese connections, the firm directly benefited from the anti-Japanese boycotts which occurred after the Jinan and Manchurian Incidents. Its total work force reached about 1,000 in the early 1930s. Although the firm suffered a setback in 1933 when an industrial accident claimed the lives of eighty workers, its sales soared in 1934 when the Chinese tariff on imported rubber shoes, mostly from Japan, was raised to 30 percent.[21]

When the war erupted, the Zhengtai plant, located in the Hongkou section of Shanghai, was directly in the line of battle. Management fled to the French Concession. In early September 1937, two leaders of the firm, Hong Fumei and Yang Shaozhen, made contact with a Japanese businessman, Fujimura Ichinori, who visited the plant site on their behalf. He found the buildings heavily damaged, the remaining materials plundered by Japanese soldiers. Fujimura had signs placed on the site proclaiming that it was a branch of his Japanese firm and arranged for two Japanese to stand watch over the facility. When Zhengtai managers received 370,000 yuan in insurance claims in 1938, they began to repair the plant, reopening in July. As an added protection, the Chinese registered the firm under the Japanese name at the German consulate. In exchange for providing this cover, Fujimura received fourteen fen for every dozen pairs of rubber shoes Zhengtai produced, as well as monopoly rights for his firm to supply the Chinese partner with raw materials.[22]

During the "flourishing period" of Shanghai's economy, the Zhengtai company became profitable once again. By 1940 it had increased its capital from 550,000 to 800,000 yuan. Zhengtai management purchased an old textile mill on Wuding Road and converted it into a second factory for producing rubber shoes. This activity, of course, required the permission of the Japanese. Zhengtai lost its cover in 1939 when Fujimura's firm was reorganized and he was dismissed. His replacement demanded that Zhengtai make greater concessions, giving his firm ownership of 51 percent of the stock in the enterprise. Yang Shaozhen refused, countering temporarily by using an American adviser as cover. This refusal placed Zhengtai in a precarious position, for the Japanese controlled the sources of raw materials for rubber manufacturing. Most other Chinese firms such as Hongda and Shijie had been forced into these cooperative arrangements with Japanese firms under which they became junior partners.

Although Zhengtai maintained its separate identity as a company, in the long run only Japanese connections could enable it to operate in the occupied areas. The company began dealing with the Japanese military, supplying thousands of pairs of shoes for Japanese soldiers in the Shanghai area. Later in the war, Zhengtai expanded to produce bicycle and car tires as well as electric wires. Zhengtai's management also had to work with puppet organizations established by the Japanese and the Wang Jingwei government. Yang Shaozhen joined the board of directors of the rubber production control association of the Shanghai puppet government. This organization controlled raw products for rubber production which became increasingly scarce as the Pacific war continued. Zhengtai thus persisted as an independent entity but made considerable compromises with the Japanese, behavior that might be labeled collaborationist. Following Japanese surrender, Guomindang authorities confiscated Zhengtai facilities on the grounds that the firm had served the enemy.[23] Hong and Yang certainly did not reopen their plant with the goal of assisting the Japanese occupation, yet, denied any chance of evacuating their plant to the interior, they chose to operate under conditions which required collaboration.

The difficult choices facing Chinese industrialists are particularly evident when examining their fate in nearby Wuxi. After Shanghai, Wuxi was the most important industrial center of the lower Yangzi. Six major family groups—Rong, Tang, Xue, Yang, Cai, and Cheng—dominated the important cotton, flour-milling, and silk industries there, controlling about 70 percent of all industrial and commercial capital in the city. In 1934 the capital of the Rong family enterprises in Wuxi was 5.64 million yuan, the Tang-Cai family group's was 3.21 million, the Xues' 2.57 million, the Tang-Cheng group's

2.04 million, and the Yangs' 1.76 million.²⁴ The battle of Wuxi was intense and most Chinese factories sustained major damage during the fighting. Wuxi industrialists who survived pursued a variety of strategies. Their responses illustrate the full range from resistance to collaboration or something in between.

The Yang family turned to collaboration to survive during the war. One of China's oldest industrial families, the Yangs traced their industrial beginnings back to two brothers, Yang Yifang and Yang Oufang, who had ties to Li Hongzhang's *mufu* and who created the Yeqin enterprise group. Although descendants of the founders were active in both industry and banking, by the 1930s the key industrial leader of the Yang clan was Yifang's son, Yang Hanxi. The Yeqin textile mill was profitable in the early 1920s, but then went into bankruptcy and reorganization on several occasions after 1927, when economic conditions were less favorable for Chinese industrialists. In 1936, however, Yeqin had resumed production. Yang Hanxi had also established a second mill, the Guangqin plant, which had 23,040 spindles in 1930. In 1937, Yang Hanxi also managed to expand into flour production, creating the Guangfeng Flour Mill.²⁵

When war erupted, the Yang clan was hard hit. Its two major textile mills, the Yeqing and Guangqin, were both completely destroyed, but the Guangfeng flour mill suffered only limited damage. Yang Hanxi was eager to reopen the flour mill after the Japanese gained control of Wuxi in order to preserve some income, but this required actions which led to his arrest as a traitor after the war, namely cooperation with Japanese and puppet authorities. Yang assisted Japanese efforts to gain control of the economy, agreeing that his son, Yang Jingrong, participate in the Nanjing's government's Wheat Flour Control Commission, later heading its Wuxi office. Through these contacts, the Guangfeng mill supplied the Japanese military with flour and remained quite profitable, particularly through 1941. Although Guangfeng's output and size expanded little during the war, profits from speculation were significant.²⁶

So successful was Yang that he organized a new textile enterprise in Shanghai, the Zhaoxin mill, funded by investments from the Yang group and associated capitalists. The new enterprise grew rapidly, incorporating 17,000 spindles and 126 weaving machines. Yang's willingness to cooperate with the Japanese brought his family fortunes back, despite the disastrous losses of the early war period. The price was collaboration with the Japanese occupier. After the war the Yangs' business declined because of Hanxi's problems.²⁷

The Xue family suffered similar losses during the battle of Wuxi. Another prominent family in that city, they traced their origins to Zeng Guofan's *mufu*. Xue Nanming, the family leader, established or purchased several silk filatures, such as the Yongtai company, with a total of over 1,700 silk-reeling machines. He sent his youngest son, Xue Shouxuan, to the University of Illinois, and later entrusted him with the leadership of the family's industrial base. The younger Xue solidified his ties to the industrial community by marrying the daughter of Rong Zongjing (discussed below), perhaps the pre-eminent Chinese industrialist. Xue Shouxuan also established a reputation for using advanced technology and for the training of workers, a relatively novel concept in China. He added to the family's holdings, creating the Huaxin filature in 1931. By 1934, the Xue group included the Yongtai, Jinji, and Huaxin plants, had 2,400 silk-reeling machines, 20 percent of the total in Wuxi.

Although China produced much of its silk for export, traditionally foreign merchant houses in China handled the overseas marketing. Xue Shouxuan felt this practice limited Chinese profits, because producers were unable to benefit easily from changing conditions in foreign markets. Determined to break this foreign monopoly, he dispatched Xue Zukang to America to set up a branch of the Yongtai company in New York City in 1934. The Xues then marketed their silk output directly to the US market. While many other silk producers suffered during the economically troubled 1930s, the Xue group kept profits high through direct marketing.[28]

The Xues' success was derailed by the war. Many of their factories were completely destroyed, including the Jinji and Longchang filatures, while others, Yongtai and Huaxin, were heavily damaged. After the war, only one of their mills, the Yongtai, could be immediately reopened, and that with only seventy reeling machines at first. In 1949, the Xues possessed only one-fifth of their industrial capacity of 1937. In the face of these overwhelming losses, the strategy of Xue Shouxuan was simply to flee. After the Marco Polo Bridge Incident, Xue used available cash in the firm to purchase US currency and stock. He shipped both the current stock of silk and his family to America, where he established a silk stocking factory in New York. Xue's strategy was available to him because of his American education and ties and because Yongtai already had an American office. Xue thus avoided collaboration, but he never returned to China, dying in the United States in 1972.[29]

The Zhou family was a smaller group involved in silk production which was allied with the Xues. The great patriarch of the clan, Zhou Shunqing, had founded the Yuchang mill, which had 330 reeling machines in 1930. His son, Zhou Zhaofu, founded a second mill, the Dingchang, in 1929, with 256 machines. The total capital of the Zhous' enterprises was 434,0000 yuan in 1934, but by that date their property was heavily mortgaged and much of its control lost to bankers. The woes of the Zhou clan were compounded by the war, which left the Yuchang mill in ruins.

The Zhous' junior partner in the Dingchang mill, Qian Fenggao, salvaged the plant by collaborating with the Japanese. They had established the Central China Silk Reeling Company (Huazhong cansi gongsi), as one of the subsidiaries of the Central China Development Company. Qian's cooperation enabled him to gain Japanese capital to rehabilitate the Dingchang mill, which further benefited from the reduced competition in the area following the destruction of rival factories. At its peak the mill had 512 reeling machines. When the war ended, Qian was charged with being a traitor so the mill was turned over to his younger brother. The much reduced Zhou family had only a token share in the firm.[30]

Two other prominent families in Wuxi, the Tangs and the Cais, had long formed joint industrial ventures. Tang Baoqian and Cai Jiansan had co-founded the Jiufeng flour mill in 1909. During the boom period in the wake of World War I, the two men decided to move into cotton textile production, establishing the Qingfeng mill in 1922, using capital mostly from their respective families. The mill began with 14,800 spindles and 250 looms. The company benefited heavily from the anti-foreign boycott movement which occurred during the May 30 Movement of 1925. When Tang Baoqian's son, Tang Xinghai, returned from America in 1927, where he obtained a master's degree in textile management, he took over day-to-day direction of the mill. Under his leadership the Qingfeng company modernized and added a second plant. He purchased 50,000 spindles and 400 looms direct from England, bringing the total of spindles for Qingfeng to 64,768 and of looms to 720 in 1937. From 1930 to 1936, the annual value of production of Qingfeng increased from 5.14 million yuan to 11.43 million yuan, profits from 310,000 yuan to 1.1 million yuan.[31]

When war reached Wuxi, both the Qingfeng textile mill and the Jiufeng flour mill suffered heavy losses. Although Tang Xinghai, anticipating the fall of Wuxi, had moved 6,120 spindles to Shanghai before the Japanese arrival, the Tang and Cai properties were caught in Japanese bombardment. In all, Qingfeng lost 28,448 spindles, 277 looms, and its dyeing equipment. Together with electric generators and raw materials, the losses totaled more than 5 million yuan. The Japanese military occupied the textile plant and then turned over management to the Japanese Daikō Textile Company, which rehabilitated the mill, reopening it in May 1939. The new plant had only 28,000 spindles and 300 looms, yet even these were not fully utilized because of shortages of raw materials and poor worker relations.[32]

The Tangs meanwhile had set up a new mill in Shanghai, the Baofeng (also called the Qingfeng No. 2), using equipment and funds salvaged from the Qingfeng mill, together with investments from the National Commercial Bank (Zhejiang Xingye yinhang). In the "flourishing" conditions of wartime Shanghai, this enterprise did well, increasing to 27,140 spindles and 768 looms. After Pearl Harbor, when the Japanese began to stress salvaging the economy of occupied China, they began to press Tang Xinghai to collaborate, urging him to return to Wuxi (he was living in Shanghai) to resume a role in Qingfeng. The Daikō Company offered a joint management agreement with Tang and the original Qingfeng shareholders. Feeling that the Japanese "partners" would completely control the situation, Tang and the directors rejected the offer.[33]

Still, with Shanghai no longer a haven after December 1941, the Tangs ultimately engaged in some collaboration with the Wang Jingwei puppet government. Tang Xinghai served on Nanjing's Cotton Control Commission, and the family resumed a role in the management of Qingfeng. In 1942

Wang's government proclaimed its policy of returning nominal control of seized factories to their original Chinese owners (provided that Japanese firms like Daikō were compensated). The puppet government's Ministry of Industry required Qingfeng stockholders to pay Daikō 6.2 million yuan to regain their firm. Tang Xinghai then spent over a year trying to restart Qingfeng, resuming limited production in 1944. After the war, he was able to restore Qingfeng to a level of 62,728 spindles and 364 looms by 1947. Xingfeng relocated to Hong Kong in 1949, establishing the Nanhai Textile Mill. The Tangs thus tried to avoid collaboration for as long as possible, preferring to operate in unoccupied Shanghai at first, and then refusing the initial terms of accepting a joint management agreement under Japanese control.[34]

Another branch of the Tang family, related but financially separate from the Qingfeng Tangs, had invested with the Chengs. In 1918, Tang Xiangting, a cousin of Tang Baoqian, and Cheng Jingtang established the Lihua Cloth Company, which by 1934 had three mills in Wuxi. In 1920 they invested in new technology, creating the Lixin Cloth Printing and Dyeing Company. After a shaky start, Lixin prospered when the May 30 Movement led many Chinese consumers to boycott rival Japanese products. Perhaps the most daring investment by the Tang–Cheng pair was in 1934 when they established the first woolen mill in Wuxi. On the eve of the war the Tang–Cheng group was one of the most successful in Wuxi, with total capital of 4.8 million yuan, 40,000 spindles, and 1,200 looms.[35]

War devastated their enterprises. The Lihua No. 1 and No. 2 mills were completely destroyed. Lihua No. 3 and the Lixin printing and dyeing plant were heavily damaged. The buildings were occupied by the Japanese; the woolen mill was in ruins. The strategy of the Tangs and Chengs was to move to Shanghai. They took the remaining capital from Lixin and set up the Changxing textile printing mill, which had separate facilities for weaving, spinning, and dyeing. By the end of the war the plant had 14,760 spindles and 280 looms. They also opened a woolen mill in Shanghai to replace the one lost in Wuxi. Lixin did not resume operations in Wuxi until after the war, recovering to a level of 30,000 spindles and 700 looms by 1947. Despite the decision to move to Shanghai, some cooperation with the Japanese was required to continue operations through the war. Cheng Jingtang joined the puppet government's Cotton Control Commission.[36]

The industrialists of Wuxi thus exhibited a wide range of responses to the war. All suffered heavily because of the intensity of the fighting. Yang Hanxi chose to work with the Japanese to salvage his enterprises and was labeled a traitor after the war. Xue Shouxuan chose to leave for America and had the necessary connections to do so. The Zhou clan, financially weak on the eve of the war, was forced out by a partner who gained control by collaborating with the Japanese. The Tangs and Cais and the Tangs and Chengs all relocated in Shanghai to enjoy the "flourishing of the Solitary Island." After Pearl Harbor, they too faced the necessity of dealing with the occupiers.

Of all of the industrial capitalists in China, the Rong family group was in the best position to survive under wartime conditions because of its size and diversity. Founded by Rong Zongjing and his brother Rong Desheng, their industrial empire included the Maoxin and Fuxin flour mills (sixteen in all) and the Shenxin textile mills (ten in all). Their base spread from their native Wuxi to Shanghai, Hankou, and beyond. By the mid-1930s, the Rongs held 20 percent of all spindles in Chinese-owned textile mills and produced one-sixth of the milled flour.[37]

The war dealt a sharp blow to the Rong fortunes. One-third of their spindles, over half of their looms, and over one-tenth of their flour grinders were destroyed in the fighting, and much of the remainder was seized by the Japanese. Despite these losses, the Rongs were able to emerge from the war as a major industrial group through the pursuit of a variety of tactics. None the less, the strain of wartime conditions and the death of the senior figure, Rong Zongjing, broke up the unity of the clan. The elder brother had departed Shanghai for Hong Kong after the war erupted and died there on February 10, 1938, at the age of sixty-six. His brother, Desheng, was unable to maintain complete control over his nephews, and the Rongs began to disagree over the strategy to pursue in wartime.[38]

When war erupted the Rongs lost control of five of their seven textile mills in Shanghai. Two were destroyed—the Shenxin No. 1, founded in 1915 and having 72,800 spindles at the time, and the Shenxin No. 8, founded in 1930, with 50,000 spindles. Both were located in the western roads section of Shanghai and were bombed by the Japanese on October 27, 1937, heavily damaging the mills and killing over 200 workers. The sites of these two mills were occupied by the Japanese military, which turned them over to the Japanese Toyoda Textile Company for rehabilitation.[39]

Three other Shenxin mills, No. 5, No. 6, and No. 7, escaped with limited damage but were in areas occupied by the Japanese. The Shenxin No. 5, purchased by the Rongs in 1935, had 49,000 spindles. No. 6, located in the Yangshupu section, had 73,000 spindles and 900 looms in 1937. It lost several thousand spindles and 200-300 looms in the fighting. Shenxin No. 7, also in Yangshupu, had 53,844 spindles and 455 looms. Japanese military authorities entrusted the management and rehabilitation of these properties to Japanese firms. Shenxin No. 5 went to the Yuho Textile Company (Yūhō bōseki kabushiki kaisha); Shenxin No. 6 went to the Shanghai Textile Company (Shanhai bōseki kabushiki kaisha), and No. 7 went to the Kanegafuchi Company.[40] The Rongs thus retained control in Shanghai only of their Shenxin No. 2 and Shenxin No. 9 mills, which were located in the International Settlement and were not occupied until December 1941. The No. 2 mill had been founded in 1919 and had 41,000 spindles. The Rongs purchased Shenxin No. 9 in 1931, and by 1937 it had nearly 90,000 spindles and 569 looms. For political protection these mills were in theory "leased" to foreign owners, so as to provide registration and cover. The Shenxin No. 2, for instance, was ostensibly rented to an American company, Associated

American Industries, for a five-year period beginning on April 16, 1938. The American firm in turn obtained funds for this transaction from banks which then appointed a joint committee to operate the plant. This committee was composed, quite naturally, of the original management. Shenxin No. 9 underwent a similar transformation in May 1938 but used British cover and also was registered in Hong Kong.[41]

The Rongs actually did rather well in the war, at least compared with many other industrialists. Although Shenxin No. 2's capacity remained unchanged, its output of yarn increased after 1937. With the production of that year as an index of 100, output increased as follows: 1938, 126.5; 1939, 139.6; 1940, 143.4; 1941, 117.0. The Rongs expanded the capacity of Shenxin No. 9, increasing the number of looms to 763 and of spindles to 136,108, making it the largest mill in China. Shenxin No. 9's index of cotton yarn production was: 1937, 100; 1938, 127.2; 1939, 151.1; 1940, 152.0; 1941, 64.4. For cotton cloth: 1937, 100; 1938, 151.9; 1939, 164.8; 1940, 137.2; 1941, 41.6. The Rongs not only sold textiles in China, but greatly increased exports to Southeast Asia. The large communities of overseas Chinese began to boycott Japanese products and turned to the Rong brand.

The profits of the Rong family thus mounted. Shenxin's earnings, measured in fabi, increased from 543,300 yuan in 1937 to over 3 million in 1939 and 6.5 million in 1941. Shenxin No. 9's profits were 2.25 million in 1937, increasing to over 10 million for 1939 and 12.3 million in 1941. These figures are somewhat misleading because of inflation, however. When compared with the equivalent value in gold liang, the figures for profits show a remarkable rise in 1938 and 1939 and then a decline. Thus although the Rongs lost much of their industrial empire in the war, that which remained was very profitable.[42]

Even the wartime inflation worked to the Rongs' benefit. It allowed them to settle the heavy debt load which had burdened Shenxin throughout the 1930s. The effects of the world depression, the suspension of business in early 1932 when fighting had erupted in Shanghai, and the adverse impact of American silver purchase policy, had created rather unfavorable economic conditions for Shenxin in the mid-1930s. The company had, in fact, teetered on the verge of bankruptcy for a time before conditions improved in 1936 and 1937. With wartime inflation, old loans were rapidly repaid and by May of 1942 the company was debt-free.[43]

When the Pacific war erupted, the sanctity of the International Settlement and French Concession evaporated. Shenxin No. 2 and No. 9 textile mills and the Fuxin flour mills in Shanghai all came under Japanese control. By that point, however, Japan was ready to restore property to Chinese industrialists who were prepared to work with the Japanese and the puppet authorities. Prior to this the Rongs had tried to minimize their collaboration and contact with the Japanese.

This had not been purely a matter of patriotism, but partially of self-preservation. Some business leaders who collaborated were targeted for assassination by Guomindang agents. This appears to have been one factor in Rong Zongjing's earlier decision to depart Shanghai for Hong Kong.[44] Rong Desheng, however, had seemed genuinely determined to avoid collaboration as much as possible. He rejected earlier attempts by the Japanese to gain his participation in puppet organizations in exchange for possible restoration of Rong property. Conditions changed after Pearl Harbor, of course. The "solitary island" was no more. In December 1941, when Japan seized Shenxin No. 2 and No. 9, Desheng had to cooperate if he were to have any hope of surviving as an industrialist. He thus made overtures to the Japanese but did so in as discreet a manner as possible.[45]

By mid-1942, Rong had negotiated the return of control of Shenxin No. 2 and No. 9, although under the guise of a Japanese adviser, Ogawa Gorō. As the Japanese became more interested in restoring a role to Chinese capitalists, the Rongs were even able to regain control over properties lost since 1937, including the old Shenxin No. 5, No. 6, and No. 7 as well as the rebuilt No. 1 and No. 8, and three of their Fuxin flour mills. In July 1943, Japanese and puppet authorities formally returned control to the Rongs. Not all of these properties were in good shape. Shenxin No. 5 had lost about one-half of its spindles, No. 6 was partially gutted, and No. 7 had only 30,000 of the earlier 54,000 spindles remaining.[46] Regaining their enterprises in 1942 was not, therefore, an unbridled success for the family. Still, losses in production could be offset partially by hoarding of commodities and currency speculation. In sum, the Rongs seem to have had the resources and skills to survive in wartime.[47]

In return for restoration of the textile and flour mills, the Japanese required a *quid pro quo* from the Rongs—cooperation with the Wang Jingwei regime. Rong Desheng attempted to minimize the family's involvement as much as possible. Plant managers, most often not of the Rong surname, joined the control organizations of the puppet government. Shenxin assistant manager Tong Luqing, for instance, joined Nanjing's Cotton Control Commission; Fuxin's Shi Fuhou joined the Flour Control Commission.[48]

Despite this cooperation with the Japanese, Rong Desheng strove to keep good relations with Chongqing. He did not want to jeopardize the Rongs' future following an Allied victory in the war. He sent his son, Rong Er'ren, to Chongqing with a large sum for investment. Er'ren also registered all of the Rongs' property with the Guomindang government in September 1944 to avoid being labeled a traitor. Through early use of foreign registry and later substantial cooperation with puppet authorities, the Rong enterprises in Shanghai thus survived the war and even profited, especially before December 1941.[49]

The Rongs fared less well in Wuxi, their native place. The Shenxin No. 3 textile mill was the largest factory in the city, with 71,000 spindles, 1,478 looms, and three electric generators. The mill was a total loss, with only the steel-and-concrete structure left standing. When Japanese authorities restored title to the family in June 1943, little was left to build upon.[50]

The losses in Wuxi were partially compensated by added profits of the Wuhan plants. The Rongs had two mills in Wuhan, the Fuxin No. 5 flour mill and the Shenxin No. 4 textile mill. The flour mill had opened in 1919 and remained steadily profitable; the textile mill had been established in 1922, in large part to manufacture flourbags, and had experienced considerable financial difficulties. When war erupted, the immediate result was a sharp increase in profits for the textile firm. Shenxin No. 4, although posting only a modest increase in output, saw profits increase to 1.85 million yuan from less than 500,000 the previous year. The key factors were the cutoff of competition from the mills of Shanghai, the large needs of the Chinese military, which led to a rise in prices, and a good supply of raw cotton at modest prices in the immediate Wuhan area. The plant succeeded in paying off earlier debts which had accumulated.[51]

This favorable situation came to a rather sudden end in 1938 as Japanese forces began to close in on Wuhan. At that time the textile plant had 50,000 spindles and 875 looms; the flour mill had the capacity to produce 13,500 bags a day. Li Guowei, son-in-law of Rong Desheng, planned to move the factories to the Chongqing area, but many of the Shanghai-based stockholders objected. Since their continued operations in Shanghai were vulnerable to Japanese pressure, they feared actions which might anger the Japanese. At that point the evacuation of factory equipment to the interior would have required cooperating with the Guomindang's Industry and Mining Regulation Office. The Shanghai group proposed instead operating the Wuhan plants under Japanese occupation, using American registry.[52]

Li ultimately ignored these concerns of the Shanghai group and attempted to move the Wuhan plants to Chongqing. Li's decision may not have been entirely voluntary. When the Guomindang authorities had difficulty persuading some of the industrialists to move, they apparently hinted that the army's scorched-earth policy would require the destruction of remaining factories, if they were not evacuated. In order to protect the Shanghai counterparts, Li did agree to use the name Qingxin, not Fuxin or Shenxin, for the Chongqing mills. They could at least maintain the fiction that it was a separate company. Because of the delay which these disagreements entailed, only a part of the equipment could be moved. Exclusive of factory buildings and raw materials, only 60 percent of the Shenxin No. 4 materials and 30 percent of Fuxin No. 5 were evacuated.[53]

Despite these problems, Li Guowei established two small textile mills in the interior, one in Chongqing and one in Baoji, Shaanxi. Conditions in the interior were hardly ideal, with a lack of electricity and the threat of Japanese bombing. After the textile mill in Baoji was hit several times, facilities were moved into caves. Li Guowei also erected plants further inland—in Chengdu and Tiansui—to escape Japanese bombs. Still, because of high demand and the lack of competition in the interior, these industries were very profitable. The company also benefited from currency manipulation and commodity hoarding to maximize its advantage. As Sherman Cochran has noted, "Once

Shenxin's equipment was reassembled in Chongqing and Baoji, its management continued through the war to bribe officials, falsify financial records, maintain bank accounts under various names, exaggerate war damages, and hide caches of hoarded goods and raw materials."[54] This approach enabled the Rong enterprises to evade the taxes and controls of the Chongqing government. When the war was over, Li bragged to Rong Er'ren that he had US$ 1 million in foreign exchange.[55]

Peace did not entirely heal the breach between the Shanghai and Chongqing branches of the Rong clan, nor that between Zongjing's children and Desheng's. The Rong empire divided into segments. Still, despite the lack of unity, the Rong family emerged from the conflict as a major force in China. By 1947 they had 465,000 spindles in operation (compared with about 620,000 before the war). Even today the Rong family name remains prominent both within the People's Republic of China and without. Rong Zongjing's son Hongqing and son-in-law Wang Yuncheng became major textile industrialists in Hong Kong; Hongyuan relocated to Brazil, Hongsan to the United States. Rong Desheng's son Er'ren moved to America, while Hongren moved to Australia. Perhaps the most famous of Desheng's sons was Rong Yirin, who remained in China and went on to a prominent (if somewhat volatile) career in industry and politics. His son, Larry Yung, heads the Hong Kong-based CITIC Pacific.[56]

This has been but a brief sample of the activities of Chinese capitalists during the Sino-Japanese War, yet I would advance several hypotheses. First, the experiences among the capitalists varied dramatically. The degree of destruction to facilities of businessmen and industrialists differed sharply from one location to another. The unusual nature of the conflict, which was an undeclared war until December 1941, contributed to this mix. Because foreign powers enjoyed substantial rights in China, including the foreign concessions in Shanghai and the British Crown colony in Hong Kong, and because the Japanese continued to recognize many of these rights until December 1941, some Chinese businessmen were able to cloak themselves in these privileges, either by locating in the foreign settlements or using the cover of foreign registration, or both.

Few capitalists showed any enthusiasm for collaboration. There was no equivalent of a pro-Nazi movement as sometimes happened in Europe. Few of the Chinese capitalists, I would argue, took Japanese pan-Asianist ideology as anything more than propaganda. Most felt that they would be at best junior partners in a Japanese-controlled economy. At the same time, few Chinese really fit the stereotypical model of the heroic patriot. Faced with the choice of losing their firms or dealing with the Japanese, many followed the path of the Zhengtai Rubber Company or Yang Hanxi's flour concern in Wuxi. Yet neither did many capitalists evacuate their holdings to unoccupied China. This was not entirely due to a lack of patriotism; the removal of factory and business equipment to the interior was a difficult matter.

Most capitalists discussed in this chapter, in fact, reached compromises with the Japanese and the puppets. Perhaps they did so reluctantly, perhaps they delayed for a time, but few remained totally aloof. The existence of Shanghai as a "solitary island" was a key factor. In 1937, when the battle raged in eastern China, foreign Shanghai offered an outlet for the business-men, one more accessible than the interior. Once there, the initial months proved profitable. As the Japanese tightened and finally closed the noose on island Shanghai, the capitalists were thus trapped. By December 1941, in turn, the Japanese and puppet authorities were more interested in securing the participation of Chinese capitalists than they had been in 1937. The lure of retaining at least some control over and income from their factories and businesses in exchange for public support for the Wang Jingwei government was more than most could resist.

The major barrier to collaboration was probably not the patriotism of Chinese capitalists but lack of opportunity. Early on, the Japanese sought direct control over the economy of China; they opened the door to Chinese businesses only reluctantly and later in the war. Unlike the pattern in much of occupied Europe, where those in the lower strata of society could sometimes make rapid economic gains by working with the Nazis, opportun-ities in China were much more limited. Occasionally a junior partner such as Qian Fenggao outmaneuvered his former seniors—the Zhous of Wuxi—through collaboration, but such opportunities were rare. This study has also said little of smaller capitalists—shopkeepers, native bankers, small traders. The Japanese were too intent on controlling the economy and extracting income from it to support their war machine to allow any substantial opportunities for these elements. Big capitalists were eventually approached because they had capital, expertise, and social standing which the Japanese perceived as useful.

The strongest impression one gets from this sample is that the over-whelming motivation for capitalists was neither patriotism nor collaboration-ism but survival—to find some method of keeping their enterprises in operation. The inventiveness and tenacity of these entrepreneurs was quite remarkable. Perhaps this reflects the history of capitalist enterprises in China. Businesses in the twentieth century had always faced a difficult situation—foreign competition, a shortage of capital, lack of a sound legal structure, and a frequently unstable and hostile political environment. Most entrepreneurs learned to move quickly to gain profit from the smallest opening. A brief anti-Japanese boycott in the 1920s or early 1930s, for instance, was the salvation of companies such as the Zhengtai Rubber Company. Many businessmen thus came to think in short-range speculative terms.

Survival in wartime was obviously more difficult than in the situation businessmen faced in the 1920s and 1930s, but the difference was really more of degree than of kind. The same scrambling, risk-taking style continued. The same heavy reliance on family connections remained. Many businessmen also devised a strategy of splitting risks, operating enterprises in both unoccupied China and Shanghai. Many of these capitalists continued to follow this strategy in later struggles. In 1949, for instance, the Rong family kept some money in China, moved some to Hong Kong, and moved some overseas. As Wong Siu-lun noted in his study of the migration of Shanghai capitalists to Hong Kong, "In terms of their acquiring experience in relocating their enterprises, the war was a rehearsal for the exodus of the Shanghai capitalists to Hong Kong."[57] Even today, many Hong Kong capitalists are pursuing a similar strategy, keeping some capital in Hong Kong, investing some in China, and moving much of it overseas. This strategy of dividing risks in the face of uncertainty is similar to patterns that emerged during the war years.

Ultimately the war gravely weakened the capitalists. Although some, like the Rongs, earned substantial profits in the "solitary island," the level of physical destruction was great, and business conditions deteriorated steadily after 1941. Perhaps the greatest blow dealt to the capitalists, however, was the stigma of collaboration. Many emerged from the war only to be labeled as traitors by the returning Guomindang government. This chapter has not dealt with the post-1945 years, but, in brief, I would argue that this legacy of the war alienated the capitalists from the Guomindang regime, fed into the corruption and bureaucratic capitalism of the Nanjing government, and inhibited any economy recovery in post-war China. When the Communists swept to victory in 1949, they did not triumph over a strong capitalist class. The latter was a crippled force. Many capitalists survived the war with their enterprises still functioning, but they lost the "peace."

NOTES

1   Fu Poshek, *Passivity, Resistance, and Collaboration: Intellectual Choices in Occupied Shanghai, 1937–1945* (Stanford: Stanford University Press, 1993), p. xi.
2   *Dikang sanri kan* [War of resistance published every three days], No. 8, September 13, 1937, p. 3.
3   See, for example, *China at War* 2, 6 (June–July 1939), p. 71.
4   These figures are from Han Qitong, *Zhongguo dui Ri zhanshi sunshi zhi guji* [An estimate of China's losses in the war against Japan] (Shanghai: Zhonghua shuju, 1946), p. 32; see also Robert W. Barnett, *Economic Shanghai: Hostage to Politics, 1937–1941* (New York: Institute of Pacific Relations, 1941), p. 80; Usui Katsumi, "The Politics of War, 1937–1941," in James W. Morley, ed., *The China Quagmire: Japan's Expansion on the Asian Continent, 1933–1941* (New York: Columbia University Press, 1983), p. 314; *Yinhang zhoubao* [Bankers' weekly] 23, 43 (October 31, 1939), pp. 4–5.
5   Sun Guoda, "Kangzhan qijian da houfang minzu gongye fazhan yuanyin chutan" [A preliminary investigation of the causes of the development of national industry in the rear areas during the War of Resistance period], *Dang'an yu lishi* [Archives and history] 2 (1986), pp. 60–5; Tang Zhenchang, ed., *Shanghai shi* [A history of Shanghai] (Shanghai: Shanghai renmin chubanshe, 1989), pp. 786–90; Huang Liren and Zhang Yougao, "KangRi zhanzheng shiqi Zhongguo bingqi gongye neiqian chulun" [A first discussion of the movement to the interior of China's weapons industry during the anti-Japanese war of resistance period], *Lishi dang'an* [Historical archives], 2 (1991), pp. 118–25; William Kirby, "The Chinese War Economy," in James Hsiung and Steven Levine, eds, *China's Bitter*

Victory: The War with Japan, 1937–1945 (Armonk, N.Y.: Sharpe, 1992), p. 190.

6 *Yinhang zhoubao* 22, 23 (June 14, 1938), p. 4; 22, 39 (October 4, 1938), p. 3; Tang Zhengchang, *A History of Shanghai*, pp. 800–3; Jiang Duo, "Shanghai lunxian qianqi de 'gudao fanrong'" [The 'flourishing solitary island' of the first period of occupied Shanghai], *Jingji xueshu ziliao* [Materials for economic studies] 10 (1983), pp. 25–31; D. K. Lieu, *The Silk Industry of China* (Shanghai: Kelly and Walsh, 1940), pp. 259.

7 Barnett, *Economic Shanghai*, pp. 84–6; Jiang Duo, "The flourishing solitary island," pp. 25–31.

8 *Yinhang zhoubao* 22, 13 (April 5, 1938), p. 5; *Chugoku nenkan, 1939* [China yearbook] (Shanghai), pp. 184–6.

9 Douglas R. Reynolds, "Training Young China Hands: Tōa Dōbun Shoin and its Precursors, 1886-1945," in Peter Duus, Ramon Myers, and Mark Peattie, eds, *The Japanese Informal Empire in China, 1895–1937* (Princeton: Princeton University Press, 1989), pp. 265–7; Chen Zhen and Yao Luo, eds, *Zhongguo jindai gongye shi ziliao* [Historical materials on industry in modern China] (Beijing: San-lian, 1957) I, pp. 78-81; Zhang Xichang *et al.*, *Zhanshi de Zhongguo jingji* [China's wartime economy] (Guilin: Kexue shudian, 1943), pp. 172–3.

10 Sun Choucheng *et al.*, "Yu Xiaqing shilue" [A biographical sketch of Yu Xiaqing], in *Zhejiang wenshi ziliao xuanji* [Selections from literary and historical materials, Zhejiang province] 32, p. 127; Wang Renze, "Jindai hangyun ye jubo Yu Xiaqing" [Modern shipping authority Yu Xiaqing] in Xu Dixin, ed., *Zhongguo qiye jia liezhuan* [Biographies of China's entrepreneurs] II (Beijing: Jingji ribao chubanshe, 1988), pp. 42–3.

11 Sun Choucheng, "Yu Xiaqing," p. 127; Rhodes Farmer, *Shanghai Harvest: A Diary of Three Years in the China War* (London: Museum Press, 1945), p. 254.

12 This account is based on Yan Xuexi, "Riben dui Nantong Dasheng qiye de lueduo" [Japan's plundering of the Dasheng enterprises of Nantong], in Jiangsu sheng shixue hui, ed., *KangRi zhanzheng shishi tansuo* [Explorations in the history of the anti-Japanese war of resistance] (Shanghai: Shanghai shehui kexue yuan chubanshe, 1988), pp. 206–12. For background on Dasheng, see Samuel C. Chu, *Reformer in Modern China: Chang Chien, 1853–1926* (New York: Columbia University Press, 1965), pp. 21–31; Lu Yangyuan, "Jindai Zhongguo di yige da shiye jia—ji Zhang Jian de nanku chuangye" [Modern China's first big industrialist—remembering Zhang Jian's hard work to begin an undertaking], *Jiangsu wenshi ziliao* [Selections from literary and historical materials, Jiangsu province] 34, pp. 2–17; and Zhu Ronghua, "Zhang Jian yu Nantong Dasheng shachang" [Zhang Jian and the Nantong Dasheng textile mill], *Jiangsu wenshi ziliao* 31, pp. 60–75.

13 Zhongguo di'er lishi dang'an guan, ed., "Riben dui Huazhong lunxian qu jingji qinlue shiliao yizu" [A group of historical materials on Japan's economic invasion of the occupied district of central China], *Minguo dang'an* [Republican archives], 1 (1991), pp. 21–3.

14 Usui Katsumi, "The Politics of War," pp. 325–6; Sherman Cochran, "Business, Governments, and War in China, 1931–1949," in Akira Iriye and Warren Cohen, eds, *American, Chinese, and Japanese Perspectives on Wartime Asia, 1931–1949* (Wilmington, Del.: Scholarly Resources, 1990), pp. 128–31.

15 Utsui Katsumi, "The Politics of War," pp. 325–7; John H. Boyle, *China and Japan at War, 1937-1945: The Politics of Collaboration* (Stanford: Stanford University Press, 1972), pp. 116–17.

16 Tōa kenkyūjo, ed., *Shina senryō chi keizai no hatten* [The development of the economy of the occupied areas of China] (Tokyo: Tōa kenkyūjo, 1944), p. 77.

17 Akira Iriye, *Power and Culture: The Japanese American War, 1941–1945* (Cambridge, Mass.: Harvard University Press, 1981), pp. 98–9.

18   Yuan Yuquan, "Rikou jiaqiang lueduo Huazhong zhanlue wuzi paozhi 'Shang-tong hui' jingguo" [The Japanese bandits enhance their plundering of central China's strategic material: the development of the Commerce Control Commission], *Dang'an yu lishi* 1, 4 (1986), p. 82. This new approach was adopted at a liaison conference on December 18, 1942, and an imperial conference on December 21, 1942. See also Masuda Yoneji, *Shina sensō keizai no kenkyū* [Research on China's wartime economy] (Tokyo: Diamondō, 1944); Zhongguo di'er lishi dang'an guan, "A group of historical materials on Japanese economic invasion," pp. 21–3; Boyle, *China and Japan at War,* pp. 308–9, and *Gendaishi shiryō* [Source materials on contemporary history] XXXVIII (Tokyo: Misuzu shobō, 1972), pp. 66–90, for material on the conferences.

19   "Kangzhan zhong de Zhongguo jingji" [China's economy during the War of Resistance], in Wei Hongyun, ed., *Zhongguo xiandai shi ziliao xuanji* [A selection of materials on contemporary Chinese history] (Harbin: Heilongjiang chubanshe, 1981) IV, pp. 174–5; Boyle, *China and Japan at War*, p. 116–18; Usui Katsumi, "The Politics of War," pp. 325–7.

20   This account is based on Zhang Jinsheng and Hu Xinsheng, "Zhongguo huaxue boli gongye xianqu—Wang Xinsheng" [China's vanguard in the chemical glass industry—Wang Xingsheng], *Renwu* [Personalities] 3 (1989), pp. 119–26.

21   Yang Shaozhen and Hong Furong, "Zhengtai xiangjiao chang ershi er nian de jingli" [The experience of twenty-two years of the Zhengtai rubber factory], in (*Shanghai*) *wenshi ziliao xuanji* [Selections from literary and historical materials, Shanghai] 32, pp. 148–67; Shanghai shi gongshang xingzheng guanli ju *et al.,* eds, *Shanghai minzu xiangjiao gongye* [Shanghai's national rubber industry] (Beijing: Zhonghua shuju, 1979), pp. 17–19; 51–3; Meng Caiyi, "Kangzhan qianhou de Shanghai xiangjiao shiye" [The Shanghai rubber industry before and during the War of Resistance], *Shangye zazhi* [Commercial magazine] 1, 4 (December 1940), pp. 39–40.

22   Yang Shaozhen and Hong Furong, "The experience of twenty-two years," pp. 153–4; Shanghai shi gongshang xingzheng guanli ju *et al., Shanghai's national rubber industry*, pp. 51–3.

23   Yang Shaozhen and Hong Furong, "The experience of twenty-two years," pp. 155–8.

24   Qian Zhonghan, "Wuxi wuge zhuyao chanye ziben xitong de xingcheng yu fazhan" [The formation and development of Wuxi's five most important industrial capitalist systems] in *Wenshi ziliao xuanji* [Selections from literary and historical materials] 24, p. 140; Wang Gengtang, Feng Ju, and Gu Yiqun, "Wuxi jiefang qian zhuming de liujia minzu gongshang ye ziben" [The six well known commercial and industrial capitalist families in Wuxi before the liberation], *Jiangsu wenshi ziliao xuanji* 31, p. 1.

25   Qian Zhonghan, "The formation and development of Wuxi's five most important industrial capitalist systems," pp. 101–7; Yang Tongyi, "Wuxi Yangshi yu Zhongguo mianfang ye de guanxi" [The relationship of Wuxi's Yang family and China's cotton textile industry], in Zhongguo renmin zhengzhi xieshang huiyi quanguo weiyuan hui, wenshi ziliao yanjiu weiyuan hui, ed., *Gongshang shiliao* [Historical materials on industry and commerce] II (Beijing: Wenshi ziliao chubanshe, 1981), pp. 54–6.

26   Qian Zhonghan, "The formation and development of Wuxi's five most important capitalist systems," pp. 104–7; Yang Tongyi, "The relationship of Wuxi's Yang family," p. 62; Wang Gengtang *et al.*, "The six well known industrial and commercial capitalist families," pp. 4–6.

27   Qian Zhonghan, "The formation and development of Wuxi's five most important industrial capitalist systems," pp. 104–7; Yang Tongyi, "The relationship of Wuxi's Yang family," p. 68.

28 Qian Zhonghan, "The formation and development of Wuxi's five most important industrial capitalist systems," pp. 123–8; Wang He, "Wei fazhan Zhongguo siye er xiangji fendou" [The development of the Chinese silk industry and its continued struggle], *Jiangsu wenshi ziliao* 34, pp. 184–6; Wang Gengtang *et al.*, "The six well known commercial and industrial capitalist families," pp. 19–23; Lynda S. Bell, "From Comprador to Country Magnate: Bourgeois Practice in the Wuxi Country Silk Industry," in Joseph Esherick and Mary Backus Rankin, eds, *Chinese Local Elites and Patterns of Dominance* (Berkeley: University of California Press, 1990), pp. 134–8.

29 Qian Zhonghan, "The formation and development of Wuxi's five most important industrial capitalist systems," pp. 123–9; Wang Gengtang *et al.*, "The six well-known commercial and industrial capitalist families," p. 23.

30 Qian Zhonghan, "The formation and development of Wuxi's five most important industrial capitalist systems," pp. 125–6, 140; Wang Gengtang *et al.*, "The six well known commercial and industrial capitalist families," pp. 14–17; Bell, "From Comprador to Country Magnate," p. 126.

31 Qian Zhonghan, "The formation and development of Wuxi's five most important industrial capitalist systems," pp. 130–2, Xue Wenshi, "Ji jiefang qian Wuxi Qingfeng mian fangzhi chang" [On the Qingfeng cotton textile plant in Wuxi before liberation], *Jiangsu wenshi ziliao* 31, pp. 76–88.

32 Qian Zhonghan, "The formation and development of Wuxi's five most important industrial capitalist systems," pp. 132–3; Xue Wenshi, "On the Qingfeng cotton textile plant," pp. 86–8; Wang Gengtang, *et al.*, "The six well known commercial and industrial families," pp. 23–6.

33 Qian Zhonghan, "The formation and development of Wuxi's five most important industrial capitalist systems," pp. 132–3; Xue Wenshi, "On the Qingfeng cotton textile plant in Wuxi before liberation," pp. 86–8.

34 Qian Zhonghan, "The formation and development of Wuxi's five most important industrial capitalist systems," pp. 132–3; Xue Wenshi, "On the Qingfeng cotton textile plant in Wuxi before liberation," pp. 86–8; Wang Gengtang *et al.*, "The six well known commercial and industrial capitalist families," pp. 26–7.

35 Wang Gengtang *et al.*, "The six well known commercial and industrial capitalist families," pp. 27–9.

36 Qian Zhonghan, "The formation and development of Wuxi's five most important industrial capitalist systems," pp. 133–7: Wang Gengtang, "The six well known capitalist families," pp. 29–30.

37 Shang Fanmin, "Jindai shiye jia Rongshi xiongdi jingying zhi daoxi" [Modern industrialists, the Rong brothers and their style of management], *Minguo dang'an* 2 (1992), pp. 86-91; Huang Hanmin, "Rongjia qiye dizao zhe—Rong Zongjing, Rong Desheng" [The founders of the Rong industries—Rong Zhongjing, Rong Desheng], in Xu Dixin, *Biographies of China's Entrepreneurs* I, pp. 97–109; Wan Lin, "Wuxi Rongshi jiazu baofa shi" [The history of the sudden rise of the Rong family enterprises], *Jingji daobao* [Economic report] 50 (December 14, 1947), p. 1.

38 Qian Zhonghan, "Minzu ziben jia Rong Zongjing, Rong Desheng" [National capitalists—Rong Zongjing, Rong Desheng], *Jiangsu wenshi ziliao xuanji* 2 pp. 131–9; Qian Zhonghan, "The formation and development of Wuxi's five most important industrial capitalist systems," p. 109; Huang Hanmin, "The founders of the Rong industries," p. 109; Rong Shuren, "Wojia jingying mianfen gongye de huiyi" [Memoirs of management of the flour milling industry by my family], *Gongshang shiliao* II, pp. 52–3; Gong Tingtai, "Rongshi jiazu de shiye juzi—ji Rong Zongjing, Rong Desheng xiongdi" [The Rong family, industrial leaders— remembering Rong Zongjing and Rong Desheng], *Jiangsu wenshi ziliao* 34, pp. 111–38.

39   Shanghai shehui kexue yuan, jingji yanjiu suo, ed., *Rongjia qiye shiliao* [Historical materials on the Rong family enterprises] (Shanghai: Shanghai renmin chubanshe, 1962) II, pp. 3-4; M. C. Bergère, "Zhongguo de minzu qiye yu ZhongRi zhanzheng: Rongjia Shenxin fangzhi chang" [China's national industry and the Sino-Japanese War: the Rong family's Shenxin textile company], in Zhang Xianwen *et al.*, eds., *Minguo dang'an yu minguo shixue shu taolun hui lunwen ji* [A collection of essays on the study of Republican history and the Republican archives] (Beijing: Dang'an chubanshe, 1988), pp. 533–4; Chen Zhen and Yao Luo, *Historical materials on industry in modern China* I, p. 384.

40   Shanghai shehui kexue yuan, jingji yanjiu suo, ed., *Historical materials on the Rong family enterprises* II, pp. 326–7; Chen Zhen and Yao Luo, *Historical Materials on Industry in Modern China* I, pp. 391, 394; M. C. Bergère, "China's national industry," pp. 533–4.

41   Shanghai shehui kexue yuan, jingji yanjiu suo, *Historical materials on the Rong family enterprises* II, pp. 43–6; Chen Zhen and Yao Luo, *Historical materials on industry in modern China*, p. 394.

42   Shanghai shehui kexue yuan, jingji yanjiu suo, *Historical materials on the Rong family enterprises* II, pp. 68, 73–4. For Shenxin No. 2, profits measured in gold liang were: 1937, 4,737; 1938, 16,923; 1939, 10,439; 1940, 6,279; 1941, 7,932. Equivalent figures for Shenxin No. 9 were: 1937, 19,626; 1938, 42,882; 1939, 35,997; 1940, 20,142; 1941, 14,869.

43   Gong Tingtai, "The Rong family, industrial leaders," pp. 125–32.

44   Shanghai shehui kexue yuan, jingji yanjiu suo, *Historical materials on the Rong family enterprises* II, pp. 18–23.

45   Qian Zhonghan, "The formation and development of Wuxi's five most important industrial capitalist systems," p. 118; Huang Hanmin, "The founders of the Rong industries," p. 109.

46   Qian Zhonghan, "The formation and development of Wuxi's five most important industrial capitalist systems," p. 118; Cochran, "Business, Governments, and War in China," p. 124; Chen Zhen and Yao Kuo, *Historical materials on industry in modern China* I, pp. 391–5.

47   Bergère, "China's national industry," p. 539.

48   Qian Zhonghan, "The formation and development of Wuxi's five most important industrial capitalist systems," p. 118; Tang Zhenchang, *A history of Shanghai*, p. 803.

49   Qian Zhonghan, "The formation and development of Wuxi's five most important industrial capitalist systems," p. 118; Cochran, "Business, Governments, and War in China," p. 125.

50   Qian Zhonghan, "The formation and development of Wuxi's five most important industrial capitalist systems," pp. 117–18; Chen Zhen and Yao Luo, *Historical materials on industry in modern China* I, p. 392; Shanghai shehui kexue yuan, jingji yanjiu suo, *Historical materials on the Rong family enterprises* II, pp. 11–12, 47; Wang Gengtang *et al.*, "The six well known commercial and industrial capitalist families," pp. 9–13.

51   Zhou Zhengang, "Wuhan de Rongjia qiye" [The Rong family enterprises in Wuhan], *Dang'an yu lishi* 3 (1986), pp. 75–80; Li Guowei, "Rongjia jingying fangzhi he zhifen qiye liushi nian" [Sixty years of managing the Rong family textile and flour enterprises], *Gongshang shiliao* I, pp. 14; Tang Yongzhang and Gong Peiqing, "Hankou Fuxin diwu mianfen chang he Shenxin disi fangzhi chang" [Hankou's Fuxin No. 5 flour mill and Shenxin No. 4 textile mill], *Wuhan wenshi ziliao*, 33, pp. 5, 14–15; Shanghai shehui kexue yuan, jingji yanjiu suo, *Historical materials on the Rong family enterprises*, II, pp. 48–52.

52   Qian Zhonghan, "The formation and development of Wuxi's five most important

industrial capitalist systems," pp. 118–19; Zhou Zhengang, "The Rong family enterprises in Wuhan," pp. 75–80.

53 Rhodes Farmer, *Shanghai Harvest: A Diary of Three Years in the China War* (London: Museum Press, 1945), p. 177; Cochran, "Business, Governments, and War in China," p. 124; Shanghai shehui kexue yuan, jingji yanjiu suo, *Historical materials on the Rong family enterprises* II, p. 61; Zhou Zhengang, "The Rong family enterprises of Wuhan," pp. 75–80. After Pearl Harbor the Qingxin mills resumed use of the Shenxin and Fuxin names.

54 Cochran, "Business, Governments, and War in China," p. 124; Tang Yongzhang and Gong Peiqing, "Hankou's Fuxin No. 5 flour mills," p. 5; and Shanghai shehui kexue yuan, jingji yanjiu suo, *Historical materials on the Rong family enterprises* II, pp. 66–7.

55 Zhou Zhengang, "The Rong family enterprises in Wuhan," pp. 75–80; Qian Zhonghan, "The formation and development of Wuxi's five most important industrial capitalist systems," pp. 118–19.

56 Wan Lin, "A history of the sudden rise," pp. 1–5; Zhou Zhengang, "The Rong family enterprises of Wuhan," pp. 75–80; Wong Siu-lun, *Emigrant Entrepreneurs: Shanghai Industrialists in Hong Kong* (Hong Kong: Oxford University Press, 1988), pp. 28; 30–1; *Far Eastern Economic Review*, February 6, 1997, p. 43.

57 Wong Siu-lun, *Emigrant Entrepreneurs*, p. 18.

ACKNOWLEDGMENTS

The larger study of which this chapter is a part has benefited from grants from the Committee on Scholarly Communications with the People's Republic of China for Research at the Shanghai Academy of Social Sciences, from a faculty development leave from the University of Nebraska, and from a travel grant from the Stanford East Asia National Resource Center. Earlier versions of the chapter were presented at the Fairbank Center seminar at Harvard University, the Midwest Conference on Asian Affairs at the University of Iowa, the American Historical Association annual meeting, and the Luce Cornell seminar. The author thanks the Shanghai Academy of Social Sciences, Institute of History, Institute of Literature, and Institute of Economics; the Harvard–Yenching Library; the Fairbank Center for East Asian Research at Harvard; the East Asian Collection at the Hoover Institute; and the University of Nebraska–Love Library for access to collections. The author also thanks Sherman Cochran, Joshua Fogel, Fu Poshek, Takeshi Hamashita, William Kirby, Sophia Lee, Bernard Wasserstein, Wei Peh-t'i, Yeh Wen-hsin and the late Lloyd E. Eastman for their assistance.

6 Projecting ambivalence

Chinese cinema in semi-occupied Shanghai, 1937–41

Poshek Fu

Nation is both real and imagined. As an imagined political community, in Benedict Anderson's familiar phrase, nation is projected as a unified, undifferentiated collectivity. But, as recent scholarship shows, it is in fact a site of disparate and contesting discourses of national identity. These discourses are invariably structured in a context of unequal power relations. Hence, who constitutes and what defines a nation shifts in different historical circumstances and among people and groups in different political positions.[1] Herein lies the ambivalence of the question of loyalty. Who determined the meanings of nation and thus loyalty? This ambivalence brings into question the dichotomies of good vs. evil and loyalty vs. treason that have framed the dominant discourses in China both during the War of Resistance and historical scholarship on the wartime Chinese experiences.[2]

In this chapter I want to bring into focus the ambivalence of political loyalty in the cultural politics of Shanghai cinema during the War of Resistance. In the first four years of the war (1937–41), China had lost over ten provinces and all major cities along the coast (including Beijing, Guangzhou and Shanghai) to Japan. Unlike other cities, Shanghai's foreign section became a "solitary island" (*gudao*) of neutrality. It was a semi-occupied city. Operating out of the unoccupied foreign areas, the cinema of Shanghai, known in the Republican period as the "Hollywood of the East," remained a vital center for commercial film production despite the hardships and uncertainities. It had produced over 200 feature films during these difficult times, some of which were enduring works of art. Also, many new talents joined the film industry and went on to become major figures in the postwar cinema of China and Hong Kong; included among them are directors Yue Feng and Fang Peilin, and actors Chen Yunshang, Li Lihua, and Yan Jun. Yet the Chinese cinema of semi-occupied Shanghai has been little studied. This neglect has been perpetuated by the dominant discourse in Chinese scholarship that writes off the Shanghai cinema as "traitorous" (*hanjian*). Exemplified by Cheng Jihua's masterful and semi-official history, *A History of Chinese Cinema*, *gudao* was a period in which all studio owners, filmmakers and artists were "money-grubbers" (*shikuai*) who cared little about the national interest and secretly collaborated with the enemy. It was thus the "other" of the canonized cinema which was both nationalistic and socially progressive.[3]

Just as film historians are beginning to challenge academic stereotypes of the "Vichy cinema" by emphasizing its artistic innovations and political ambiguity,[4] this chapter aims to retrieve the neglected history of *gudao* Shanghai cinema. It combines an archival reconstitution of the multiple cultural–political forces that shaped the cinema industry with a close reading of an immensely popular film, *Mulan congjun* (Hua Mulan Joins the Army) in order to highlight the shifting and constantly transgressed boundary between loyalty and treason in the everyday life of semi-occupied Shanghai.

Film history is a difficult field because of the paucity of archival materials. Most of the films in history were lost to nitrate erosion or fire destruction. This problem is especially acute when we try to reconstruct the Shanghai cinema during the Occupation. Not only were many of the Occupation films destroyed, those that survived have been neglected by the archival institutions in China. Owing to their "traitorous themes," these films were not on the top of the long "waiting to be restored" list, nor were they considered fit for screening. Since film history is a relatively new sub-field in Chinese studies, moreover, film publications of the wartime are scattered and scarce. Fortunately, since the late 1980s, the laxity of ideological control and increasing contact with film critics and conservationists of the region, the Beijing Film Archive has begun to allow limited access to its rich Occupation collection. Some of these newly available materials enable me to rewrite the history of *gudao* Shanghai cinema.

I

Shanghai fell to Japan on November 12, 1937. But until the eruption of the Pacific War in December 1942, the city existed in a semi-occupied condition. Known as the period of *gudao*, the foreign areas of Shanghai—the International Settlement and the French Concession—maintained their neutrality. It was like a privileged island remaining outside Japanese rule, which was established in the surrounding environs (Nandao, Jiangwan, Pudong, Zhabei, and Wosong).

The war threatened to devastate the cinema in Shanghai. Since all of the major film companies, including the two giants, Star Studio (Mingxing dianying gongsi) and United China Productions (Lianhua dianying gongsi), were located in the war zone, they had to close down because of destruction after the end of the fighting. Unemployed, many directors and actors joined the exodus of such leftist artists as Zhao Dan and Yuan Muzhi, who organized themselves into dramatic troupes to "mobilize resistance" in the interior. Others with private means, like the "movie queen" Hu Die, sailed to Hong Kong for "temporary refuge." And a fortunate few who had worked for the Nationalist Central Studio (Zhongyang dianyingchang) were relocated on government funding to Wuhan and, later, to Chongqing.[5] The majority of studio employees, however, found themselves for one reason or another stranded in Shanghai, anxious about how to survive the uncertain times ahead.

In November 1937, as the war was shifting away from *gudao* Shangahi, the owner of Xinhua yingye gongsi (New China Movie Company) Zhang Shankun (1905–56), who had just moved to the safety of the Solitary Island, decided to resume production. Concerned for his livelihood as well as those of his employees, he tried to test the water by renting (since his own studio in the Chinese suburb had been destroyed) a small studio near Huxi, the "badlands," to shoot two low-budget melodramas—Yang Xiaozong's comedy *Feilai fu* (Unexpected Fortunes) and Bu Wancang's costume tragedy *Qigai qianjin* (Beggar Girl). Released in early 1938, both films turned out to be box-office successes. This "unexpected fortune" convinced Zhang to rebuild his business. In April 1938, he announced the full-scale reentry of Xinhua into the city's entertainment world by stunning the audience with the opening of a big-budget period piece, *Diaochan*, directed by Bu Wancang. The film, which had begun shooting in mid-1937 as a part of Xinhua's production plan, was only 80 percent complete when the war started in Shanghai. To complete the film now, Zhang rented a larger studio in Hong Kong where elaborate historical sets could be staged, and flew stars Jin Shan and Gu Eryi there from Wuhan, while shipping the remaining crew (including the female lead, Gu Lanjun) and all kinds of shooting equipment from Shanghai. This adventurous, costly move, which became the hallmark of Zhang's show-biz style, was made into a publicity stunt: big stars, big budget, and great style. To further publicize its product, Xinhua invested thousands of dollars in putting up advertisements for *Diaochan* on every Chinese-language newspaper in Shanghai, and posters of it were found all over the downtown area. Zhang also managed to show *Diaochan* at the Grand Theatre on Nanjing Road, the city's largest and plushest cinema, which had been devoted to first-run Hollywood films. The stylishly constructed film became an instant hit.[6]

The commercial success of both *Beggars' Girl* and *Diaochan* demonstrated to Zhang that the Occupation did not mean the end of filmmaking as everyone feared. In fact, from 1938 onwards, the entertainment business of *gudao* Shanghai did very well as the economy moved into a stage of what contemporary observers called the "anomalous boom." The huge influx of war refugees from the lower Yangzi delta region (that increased the total population of *gudao* to about 5 million in 1938) brought with it not only "cheap laborers" to fuel the manufacturing machine but also rich landlords and small-town merchants who swelled the ranks of avid consumers as the Occupation wore on. As a filmmaker remembered, all kinds of restaurants and night clubs were full every night despite extended hours, and cinemas had full houses although only old movies were shown. As in wartime London or Paris, it seemed that the Shanghai public flocked to the darkened theaters where they could find a refuge from the frustrations and uncertainities of everyday life. In this situation, exhibitors were anxious to get new supplies while, at the same time, film distributors representing Southeast Asian markets in Shanghai also were eager to resume buying movies.[7] Thus Zhang decided to fulfil his dream of building a movie empire, which began the story of Chinese cinema in semi-occupied Shanghai.

It is indeed difficult to overestimate the impact of Zhang on the cinema industry of semi-occupied Shanghai: they have in fact become synonymous in historical memory. Arguably he was the most visionary and controversial film producer China has ever known. A native of Nanxun, Zhejiang, Zhang was the only college graduate among his colleagues in the industry. After graduation from Nanyang College (later Jiaotong University), he was hired by the entrepreneur Huang Chujiu to head the advertisement department of his tobacco company. He soon proved himself to be a business prodigy able to successfully launch several of Huang Chujiu's new products. But the profits were not enough to save his debt-ridden business. In 1931, after Huang's bankruptcy, Zhang was appointed by the new management to take over the jewel of his empire, the Great World Amusement Palace (established in 1917).[8]

In a year, Zhang succeeded with a few publicity campaigns to turn Great World once again into a profit-making business. Then, with the support of the underworld boss Huang Jinrong, he bought the Gongwutai theater, which was formerly part of the amusement hall. Zhang stunned the audience by applying movie techniques to the Beijing Opera. The successful experiment not only brought him huge profits but also raised his interests in the new art form of filmmaking. In 1934, with his wife, the Beijing opera star Tong Yuejuan, he started Xinhua, hoping to capitalize on the expanding film business. Overshadowed by the powerful Mingxing and Lianhua studios, Xinhua remained an insignificant independent company until the immense success of Maxu Weibang's *Banye gesheng* (Songs at Midnight), an artistically adventurous horror released in mid-1937, that catapulted Zhang into the role of a major player in the crowded Shanghai show business. He then approached financiers with an ambitious plan for building Xinhua into a movie empire. The war shattered his dream, but only temporarily.[9]

Following the commercial success of *Diaochan*, Zhang secured support from the city's financial circles and started recruiting all the creative talents remaining in *gudao* Shanghai, now unbound by their former contracts and desperately seeking employment to survive. He was able to sign, for example, superstars Yuan Meiyun and Chen Yanyan, and veteran directors Bu Wancang and Zhu Shilin. To expand Xinhua's production capacity so as to avoid dependence on the inconvenient Hong Kong studios, Zhang signed a long-term lease of Dingxiang Park in the International Settlement bordering Huxi which could hold five stages at the same time. He was able to turn this move into a money-making and publicity stunt at the same time when he built a West Lake (Hangzhou) in the park which was opened for public visits for two weeks. Unable to go outside the crowded, distressing Solitary Island since the Occupation, people flocked to the exhibition to relive a world that existed only in their nostalgia. The profits enabled Zhang to increase his investment in Xinhua. The company now boasted a capital of over Ch$500,000 and a staff of top-notch artists and technicans. It was approaching a movie empire in Shanghai, announcing plans to make two movies every month from 1939 onward.[10]

Zhang's ambitious and aggressive move to the top of Shanghai's movie business was not unchallenged. The success of his early low-budget pictures had attracted many competitors. Around late 1938, unable to resume operations owing to financial insolvency, Mingxing Studio's Zhang Shichuan teamed up with the city's major exhibitors, Liu Zonghao and Liu Zonliang, to form Guohua dianying gongsi (China Productions), which employed everyone from the former Mingxing production crew (not yet signed up with Xinhua). Among its few top stars were "Golden Voice" Zhou Xuan and Bai Yun. Soon afterward the underworld boss Yan Chuntang's Yihua dianying gongsi (Chinese Arts Movie Company), which was founded in 1932, reopened with capital of Ch$300,000. Because almost all its former stars fled to Xinhua, it had to fill its ranks with starlets and be on constant lookout for new talent (its most successful discovery was actress Li Lihua) to keep the company competitive. Besides these two companies, all other independent producers were minuscule in both capitalization (with average of Ch$40,000) and production capacity. Most of these companies had no actors and directors under contract, but borrowed stars and rented studio facilities from the three majors after collecting enough money to start a project. For example, Bian Yuying started Yuandong yingpian gongsi (Far East Movie Company) in late 1938, which contracted out production work to Mingxing and invested in adding soundtracks to some of its silent classics (e.g. the martial arts series *Burning of Hongnian Temple*, or *Huoshao Hongnian xi*). Guangming yingye gongsi (Brightness Production), on the other hand, was founded in February by Shen Tianyin, a well connected production manager of prewar Yihua who, in order to survive, secured loans of Ch$50,000 from businessmen of various backgrounds and brought together a film crew consisting entirely of his former Yihua colleagues. And their film was shot at a studio rented from Yihua.[11]

II

This plethora of production companies led to an "anomalous boom" in *gudao* Shanghai's cinema business. Between 1938 and 1941 there were altogether over twenty movie companies at different times, while seven new cinemas were opened in 1939 alone, bringing the total number of movie theaters to twenty-eight (compared with about forty before the war, when Shanghai included the large areas north of Suzhou Creek). They were spread all over the city.[12] But *gudao* was too small a market for the survival of this many companies. To begin with, it continued to be dominated, as before the war, by Hollywood movies which displaced Chinese productions to the periphery of the market. While Hollywood fantasies were standard entertainment for the westernized elites, professionals, and white-collar workers in the modern sector, local productions appealed largely to the economically disadvantaged and semi-traditional *xiao shimin* or petty urbanites (e.g. shopkeepers, apprentices, schoolteachers and teahouse waiters). Corresponding to this cultural division of spectatorship was a strict hierarchy of exhibition practice. The city's four most prestigous cinemas (Grand, Roxy, Cathay, and Nanking), all located in the prime areas of Nanjing Road and Avenue Joffre, were devoted to first-run Hollywood movies and charged $1. 40 to $3.20 per show. Next in the hierarchy were the four to five second-run Hollywood venues (e.g. Rialto, Capitol, and Paris) which catered mainly to men of letters and employees of foreign companies. Less prestigous than them were three first-run Chinese theaters (Lyric, Huguang, and Strand; in late 1940, the Metropolis was added) whose charge was $0.70 to $1.10. At the bottom of this exhibition hierarchy were cinemas featuring third and fourth-run foreign (alternating with second-run Chinese) films which cost about $0.30 to $0.50.[13] Moreover, the Shanghai film industry remained dependent on the Western market for film stock, chemicals and equipment parts. The war disrupted the trade (e.g. Agfa film stopped coming in 1938, leaving Kodak the sole supplier), making production costs soar upward by 300 percent in 1940.[14]

Owing to the ambiguous status of *gudao*, however, both the vast interior under Nationalist rule and the occupied territories were largely inaccessible for film distribution, for both political and transport reasons. For example, in early 1938 Xinhua had sent its senior manager, Li Dashen, as far as Sichuan and Guizhou to open a market. The result was not encouraging. Although the exhibitors there were eager to show Shanghai films, which had a proven box-office record, the arduous transport system (and the stringent state censorship) made Free China an insignificant market. As a consequence, the overseas Chinese community in Southeast Asia (especially in Singapore, Thailand, Vietnam and the Philippines) became particularly important outlets for Shanghai production. The local market had been dominated by the Cantonese films from Hong Kong. Steeped in the operatic tradition and nostalgia of their homeland, the Chinese diasporas were generally more conservative in aesthetic expectations (and accompanying moral values) than the Shanghai audience. They preferred movies set in historical times, filled with songs and martial arts spectacles.[15] This shifting emphasis of film distribution, as we shall see, had a significant impact on the production policy of the film industry.

To survive the difficult and uncertain times of war and occupation, the Shanghai film industry tried to reach the largest possible audience and find financial support whererever possible in order to stay, if not profitable, at least solvent while struggling to maintain its allegiance to the cause of national resistance. How to balance commercial imperatives with political demands? In *gudao* Shanghai, pressures for continuing loyalty to the nation-state of China (that is, the Guomindang) were as intense and violent as the pressures for cooperation with the Japanese. Most studio owners and film-makers, who for one reason or another did not flee with the Nationalist government to the interior, were not heroes, choosing between two moral absolutes—resistance and collaboration. Rather, they sought a space in between the polarized field of good vs. evil, and loyalty vs. treason.

In fact, between 1938 and 1941, Shanghai was in the grip of political terrorism (assassinations and bombings). It was a terrorist war fought between the pro-Nationalist resisters, led mainly by Dai Li's Military Statistics Bureau (Juntong), and the Japanese Special Services agents and their Chinese collaborators (e.g. the Yellow Way Association and the Jessfeld Road "No. 76" operations). In 1938 and 1939, the Nationalist assassins got the upper hand in the war of terrorism by killing a number of high-ranking collaborators (especially the assassination of Reformed Government Foreign Minister Chen Lu and Mayor Fu Xiaoan) as a way to "exterminate traitors" (*chujian*). Threatening letters that included bullets or decayed hands were also sent by both sides to victims to encourage or discourage collaboration.[16]

At the same time, Japan began as early as 1938 to infiltrate Shanghai's film industry. Although the Japanese appeared to make little headway in influencing the industry up till 1940, rumors of who had collaborated and which film company was controlled by the Japanese agents terrorized the film community. In 1938, Toho Productions sent its senior producer, Matsuzaki Keiji, to Shanghai to look for partners to develop the market, while the director of the Manchukuo-based International Newsreels Company (Kokusai eiga shinbun sha), Ishigawa Aya, sought to expand his production network there. Despite support from the Reformed Government, Ishigawa was able to enlist only a few minor actors for his film studio and distribute his newsreels to a few Japanese theaters in Hongkou. Frustrated by the failure to create a "new Asian cinema," he soon left Shanghai.[17]

Matsuzaki Keiji was a little more successful, partly because he was politically less ambitious. Through the office of the Japanese Army Press Bureau, Matsuzaki recruited Liu Naou to help him establish a "link" with the Shanghai cinema. Liu was a half-Taiwanese, half-Japanese writer who was well known in the early 1930s for pioneering a modernist writing style before joining the Nationalist film studio as a writer-director. Liu brought with him his long-time associates, filmmakers Huang Tianshi and Huang Tianzuo, both of whom had been out of work since the fall of Shanghai. Liu and Matsuzaki tried to approach Zhang Shankun, owner of the largest film company in the Solitary Island. In a secret meeting, according to Huang Tianshi, they expressed interest in investing in Xinhua. Since accepting Japanese capital carried the risk of political compromise, and thus exposing himself to Nationalist terrorism, Zhang refused the offer but, fearing retaliation by the Japanese secret services, went into hiding for two weeks. After this, Liu and Matsuzaki turned their attention to small film companies which were in financial trouble. They were able to fund Shen Tianyin's Guangming Studio in its premier production, *Chahua nu* (*La Dame aux camélias*, d. Li Pingqian) in the disguise of "overseas Chinese money." They then shipped a copy of the film secretly to show in Japan in Novemeber 1938, which became an instant scandal back home, forcing Shen repeatedly to explain his innocence and apologize and, finally, under public pressure, to close his new company.[18]

These political threats, coupled with financial pressure, help explain the preponderance of unambitious, low-budget movies produced in Shanghai in 1938. Short of capital, most independent producers could afford only to follow the commercial trend set by the three majors—Xinhua, Guohua, and Yihua. Among them, both Yan Chuntang and the Liu brothers were interested mainly in what they thought would sell easily and cheaply: domestic melodrama, tragic romances and other popular genres. Only Zhang Shankun had the reputation and energy to shoot big, ambitious projects. Yet among the thirteen movies Xinhua produced in 1938, judging from movie synopses, all except *Diaochan* and Cao Yu's *Leiyu* (Thunderstorm), were uncomplicated entertainment features.[19]

In restrospect, the avoidance of politically and artistically adventurous projects seems understandable, given the uncertainties of wartime production. And *gudao* Shanghai cinema was in its tentative inception, still searching for the appropriate mode of filmic expression under the menace of Occupation. Yet throughout 1938 and early 1939, parallel to the political terrorism, critics of both the right and left violently attacked the film industry for failing to rally the Shanghai public to the cause of national resistance. It was thus complicitous with the invaders. As fifty-one literary supplement editors (including such Communists as Yu Ling and A Ying) complained in an open letter to the industry, for example:

> The Shanghai cinema had a tradition of remarakable achievement and lofty ideals before the war. Unfortunately, it has degenerated since the emergence of *gudao* into a pitiable situation in which all sorts of monsters and ghosts and immortals (*yaoshen guiguai*) run wild on the screen. Some of these new films feature such idiocies as romantic love between humans and ghosts. Filmmakers justify themselves by claiming that the films are aimed at fighting feudalism … In fact, all these filmmakers are, perhaps unconsciously, serving the interests of the enemy by poisoning [*mazui*] our compatriots.[20]

The binary structure, exaggerated images, and moralizing language of this open letter articulated succinctly the prevalent nationalist discourse which has framed the dominant narrative of wartime Shanghai filmmaking ever since.

III

In response to these terrorist and ideological pressures, and to search for a fresh cinematic style so as to have an edge on the market, Zhang found in historical drama a medium which could project loyalty on the Shanghai screen. The discovery was a matter of coincidence. On a business trip to Hong

Kong in 1938 he met Ouyang Yuqian, a former Xinhua creation consultant and famous dramatist involved in the movement to politicize the Beijing Opera, who had fled to the colony to avoid Japanese harassment. Zhang commissioned him to write a script. He also tried to persuade Hu Die to return with him to Shanghai, but she preferred to live out her semi-retirement in the colony. So Zhang instead recruited a rising Cantonese star named Chen Yunshang (Nancy Chan), whose charm and charisma, "Western" look, studied elegance, and robust, attractive physique marked her out as the next possible "movie queen."[21]

Before Chen Yunshang's arrival, Zhang had already launched a massive publicity campaign on her behalf. Like *Diaochan*, lovely pictures of her were printed in every major newspaper, tabloid, and fan magazine, and prominently displayed in all major department stores along Nanjing Road. At the same time, Xinhua publicists reported that Hollywood studios were overawed by Chen's fluent English, feminine charm, and exquisite elegance, and were competing to sign her. But, thanks to Zhang's persistence, Chen agreed to come to Shanghai to make a Chinese film before leaving for the United States. When Chen arrived in December 1938, her name was already familiar to the Shanghai viewing public, which was curious to see what made her so appealing to Hollywood.[22]

Chen brought with her Ouyang Yuqian's new script, *Mulan congjun* (Hua Mulan Joins the Army). This was a filial story about the semi-mythical woman warrior Hua Mulan, who, disguised as a man, served in the army in her frail father's stead to fight off foreign invasion. The script was carefully and elegantly crafted, and its portrayal of Hua Mulan was warm, spirited, compellingly entertaining, yet at the same time imbued with patriotic fervor. It was indeed a skillful conflation of political commentary with a conventional narrative mixing boy-and-girl romance and light comedy, clearly addressed to an audience of petty urbanites. This narrative strategy was an apparent attempt to resolve the dilemma between commercial considerations and ideological imperative. With a fine script by a patriotic "exile," and a promising star, Chen Yunshang, fresh from Hong Kong, Zhang became ambitious about the project. He brought in a remarakable supporting cast (including the male lead Mei Xi and famous buffoon Han Langen) and assigned Bu Wancang, who had a prewar reputation in making historical drama, to direct the film. As it turned out, *Hua Mulan Joins the Army* disappointed no one; it became a landmark Occupation film.

On Lunar New Year's Day 1939, *Hua Mulan Joins the Army* was premiered at the Astor Theater on Avenue Edouard, a first-run Mandarin cinema which opened that same day. For the next eighty-five days the film ran to full houses, a box-office smash hit that broke all records in the industry. It also received enthusiastic reviews from critics all over the city. This immense popularity was due in part to Zhang's successful publicity campaign and in part to the forceful projection of political loyalty through the figure of Hua Mulan.[23]

The publicity campaign for *Hua Mulan Joins the Army* centered around two themes: the star Chen Yunshang and the concept of newness. Besides publicity reports and pictures, a glossy fan photo of Chen was offered with every ticket purchased, while a gigantic portrait of the woman warrior in military costume was mounted at the busiest intersection between Nanjing and Tibet Roads. Both aimed to draw mass attention to the charisma of the star. At the same time, Zhang privileged the motif of newness in his promotion of the film: Chen was a *new* face, costume drama a *new* subject in *gudao* Shanghai cinema, it was exhibited at a *new* venue on *New* Year's Day—a day that the Chinese associate wishfully and spiritually with the dawning of a more fulfilling time. The publicity strategy (formulated by Zhang) was effective to the extent that there was in fact a popular desire to get over the uncertainties and hardships (especially the claustrophobic pressures of overcrowded conditions, an inflationary spiral, and deteriorating social order) brought by the war.[24]

Hua Mulan Joins the Army was not, however, an artistically adventurous film. Perhaps under pressure to finish in time for New Year release (production time was limited to less than two months from the time Chen Yunshang arrived), and restricted by the lack of location shooting in the city, there is something unsophisticated and extemporaneous about the film. Camera work is for the most part clumsy and flat, and all fighting scenes lack realism. Bu Wancang follows the Hollywood continuity style of presenting a coherent, clearly defined space in which human figures and their actions take the center stage (with all the film techniques that include eyeline matches framing, shooting angles and figure placement),[25] and demonstrates his skill in producing a clear flow of dramatic situations which are spiced up with much comic relief and memorable romantic expressions.

But what seized the Shanghai audiences' imagination was the magnetic presence of Chen Yunshang, who succeeds in projecting both the force and the idealism of a heroine with whom they could identify. The opening scene, in which the camera follows in mid-frame the attractive, self-assured Chen Yunshang hunting on horseback, and the way she cleverly defeats a throng of local hooligans trying to harass her, solidly identify the star with the heroine as well as providing the audience with a persuasive sketch of Hua Mulan's physical prowess and intelligence. The next scene comes with Mulan being scolded by her father for failing to act properly as a girl. Becoming tender and affectedly sweet, she protests that she went hunting for the sake of his health. Her filial piety then conflates into political loyalty when she changes to military uniform, handsome and dignified, and performs a series of sword movements in order to convince her reluctant parents to let her replace her father to fight off the invading nomads. This moment of commitment is valorized as the camera pans to a close-up of Mulan pleading, "Dad, you have taught me martial arts since I was a little girl. There's no use of it if I only stay home; I would rather go to the front in your place. Thus I can dedicate myself to the ideal of political loyalty [*jinzhong*] on the one hand, and to the virtue of filial piety [*jinxiao*] on the other hand."

Why project loyalty through the figure of Hua Mulan? As the famous critic-dramatist A Ying pointed out: "Whenever the Chinese race finds itself in the midst of a crisis, we are prone to think of this great heroine."[26] Indeed, Hua Mulan was only one of the many heroines (e.g. Qin Liangyu and Mu Guiying) whose legends ran through Chinese popular culture. In imperial China, contrary to the Confucian elaboration of effete beauty and virtue, they were represented as an alternate model of female power and physical prowess. But while these women had the honor of becoming saviors of the state, they remained submissive to the patriarchy and their behavior served as an exemplum of social morality.[27] With the rise of modern nationalism at the turn of the century, women were reconfigured for new significations. In resistance literature during the war, women were represented (mostly by male writers) as prostitutes or raped victims, whose violated bodies signified the defiled purity and sufferings of China under Japanese domination, or as heroines whose traditional feminine virtues (filial piety and chastity) were now reappropriated to fuse with the cause of sovereign nationhood. The heroine was a powerful trope for the indomitable spirit and inexhaustible strength of China. Indeed, in a national crisis, every one of its people, man and woman, would fight to save the nation. As a critic noted: "*Hua Mulan Joins the Army* makes it clear that at a time when the nation-state is in distress, not only men but also women should dedicate themselves to defend their homeland."[28] (Thus Hua Mulan joins the army when her elder brother is killed in war, and her father and young brother are unfit for frontline action.) At the same time, in nationalist discourse, as Partha Chatterjee notes, women remained a marginal figure in the "new patriarchy," where their specific experiences and desires were often displaced, or denied, by the dictates of nationalism.[29]

This fusion of patriotic heroism and social marginality in the construction of the woman warrior in nationalist disourse framed the representative ideology of *Hua Mulan Joins the Army*. In a sequence of long takes depicting soldiers traveling (rather than marching) to the front, Mulan is teased and harassed by several draftees, all pitiful characters either overweight or underweight (played by such buffoons as Han Langen and Liu Jiqun), who are reluctant to leave home and vent their anger and frustration on this attractive, "girl-like" recruit. Before Mulan beats them all to the ground, the camera cuts in to a medium close-up of her admonishing: "Now the front is in crisis, all of us join the army because we want to serve our country; there is no reason for us to harass each other." This scene was read by some critics as a critique of the Chongqing regime's disingenuous alliance with the Communists. The idea makes sense to the extent that Ouyang Yuqian was a liberal nationalist passionately concerned with national unity.[30] But if we read the screen images closely, rather than just the statement itself, and place them in the context of the cultural politics of Shanghai cinema, there emerges an alternative reading that reveals the ambivalence of Occupation filmmaking.

Unlike the script, the projected images of all the draftees, who were widely believed to be representing Chongqing resisters (as was later also recognized by critics in the interior), are overly negative, and with a nervously vindictive overtone. These projections emerged at a time when the city's film community was troubled by both terrorism and rumors. Zhang Shankun and the director Bu Wancang, among other filmmakers, were accused as *hanjian* by pro-Chongqing agents for their alleged deal-making and cooperation with the Japanese in order to continue making films in semi-occupied Shanghai.[31] Indeed, Shanghai was displaced by the war to the margin of the National Resistance. It had become a suspicious other in the nationalist discourse: the anti-Japanese press in unoccupied areas was filled with lamentations at the decentering of cultural Shanghai and with veiled accusations of people there who, by choosing not to exile to the interior, were seen as mostly weak-minded, selfish, hedonistic, and complicitous with the enemy.[32]

People in *gudao* Shanghai were aware of this marginalization, and it was an awareness accompanied by pain and guilt. Thus Hua Mulan's admonition may actually have aimed to dispel the disparaging stereotype, and with a vengeance. It amounts to a plea for recognition that, no matter whether they lived in anguish under occupation or in the freedom of the unoccupied zones, the Chinese should stand and fight together in defence of their country.

The film unfolds a Manichean drama of moral absolutes: good vs. evil, hero vs. villain. In a series of thinly disguised political allegories, the courageous Mulan discovers the military intelligence of the invading nomads and condemns the treachery and appeasement of the evil-looking army advisor (collaborator). She soon rises to become the military governor and defeats the marauders. The war is now over, she no longer needs to suppress her feminity and desires. Echoing a popular theme of Ming-Qing "beauty-scholar romances," in which talented, outgoing women often find lesser mates, Mulan falls in love with her lieutenant, Liu Yuandu (Mei Xi) and eventually marries him.[33] In a memorable romantic scene in which the lovers sing a lovely ditty, "Where is the moon?" to each other, the audience reveled in the director's graceful handling of the narrative twist. The song became an instant hit in Shanghai, and later in Southeast Asia.[34]

After the victory, the emperor grants Hua Mulan an audience in which he awards her a top position at court. But how can a woman enter officialdom in the Confucian patriarchy? How can a woman who has transgressed the moral order be rewarded? Indeed, Mulan declines the offer and asks to return home to serve her parents instead. At home, she surprises all her former colleagues in the army when she resumes her feminine sweetness. The filial daughter asks for her parents' blessing, and the film ends in the wedding ceremony in which Mulan throws herself into the arms of Liu Yundu— whereupon she returns to the "inner quarters" of the social order. This Hollywood-style ending (the utter failure to confront the "woman question" in a patriarchal society) led a critic to question: "If Mulan's elder brother is still alive, is there any need for our heroine to serve the country?"[35]

The magnetic appeal of Chen Yunshang, the skillful narrative, combining patriotic loyalty and patriarchal morality, and Zhang Shankun's impressive star-making strategy combined to make *Hua Mulan Joins the Army* an immense success in Shanghai. The film was widely lauded as "giving voice to the anger and passion of the Chinese here and now" (read: the Solitary Island) and thereby "marking a new departure in *gudao* filmmaking."[36]

IV

Following the critical and popular success of *Hua Mulan Joins the Army* came a flurry of historical films, or "patriotic drama." Almost all loyal officials, military heroes, filial sons and chaste wives from the historical pantheon were brought to the screen. Xinhua released Bu Wancang's *Qin Liangyu* (Chen Yunshang and Mei Xi), Zhang Shankun's *Xi Shi* (Yuan Meiyun and Liu Qiong), and Wu Yonggang's *Yue Fei* (Liu Qiong) in late 1939, for example, while Guohua made *Luanshi yingxiong* (A Hero in Turbulent Times) by Zhou Menhua, and Yihua produced *Jing Ke ci Qin wang* (Jing Ke's Assassination of Qin Emperor), starring Wang Yuanlong and Lu Ming. Small independents also joined in the competition. In early 1940, the well respected Fei Mu directed the critically acclaimed *Kong Fuzi* (Confucius) for Hezhong Pictures, and Jinxing Motion Pictures adapted the stage hit *Li Xiangjun*, starring Gu Lanjun.

This burst of historical productions stemmed actually from an intersection of political demand and commercial imperative. As the leftist director Wu Yonggang testified, the past represented a textualized site in which patriotic dissent could be discreetly articulated and expressed. In fact, using the past as allegory to comment on the present was a long-cherished tradition in Chinese culture. In order to evade Japanese terrorism and censorship by foreign settlement police, filmmakers, like dramatists, in *gudao* Shanghai found it necessary to create a narrative strategy of deploying historical language and symbolism to speak out against the Occupation. In addition, *Hua Mulan Joins the Army* not only proved that there was a market for patriotic drama in Shanghai, but Southeast Asian audiences also relished costume film filled with folk tunes, acrobatic elements and traditional aesthetics.[37]

By early 1940, however, the patriotic drama fever began to subside. After the box-office failure of big-budget *Yue Fei* and *Si Xi*, the industry leaders decided that it was time to give audiences something new. In any case, grand acts of heroism, inspiring as they might be, were rarely possible or practical in everyday life in *gudao* Shanghai. They turned to popular novels, folklore and local opera. Actually, the decision was determined as much by the filmmakers' image of audiences' shifting tastes as by political and financial pressures. Since September 1939, the Shanghai Municipal Police had begun to cooperate with the Japanese to further tighten its control over patriotic expressions while the puppet secret agents (the No. 76) terrorized *gudao*.[38]

Projecting loyalty in heroes and heroines became dangerous. Moreover, making patriotic drama was expensive because it involved elaborate sets and costumes and larger studio space. For example, a historical drama in 1939 cost twice as much as an average film (Ch$30,000). The disruption of foreign trade following the outbreak of the European war gave rise to inflation that brought filmstock prices up from Ch$0.30 in late 1937 to over Ch$1 in early 1940, and average production costs soared 400 percent over 1938.[39]

Minjian gushi (folktales and popular story) productions were however innocuous entertainment that was both politically and financially safe. They also found a ready market in Southeast Asia, which remained captivated by historical drama. In fact, in order to satisfy the Southeast Asian audiences, who loved Mandarin songs as well as martial arts fighting, Shanghai studio heads made sure that fighting and singing scenes were added to every one of their projects.[40] *Minjian gushi* film required little creativity (mainly adaptation) and used less lavish sets and props than movies on military heroes or heroines); it resulted in a rat race in the industry. To compete for early release, overlap of production was as common as sloppy craftsmanship. For example, in May 1940 the majors Guohua and Yihua jockeyed to be the first to finish the famous folk story *San xiao* (Three Smiles). The result: Yihua (starring the new stars Li Lihua and Yan Hua) finished it in six days while Guohua (starring Zhou Xuan) did so in six and a half days. In order to maintain its predominance in the business, Zhang Shankun likewise set new records in putting all his studio employees to work, producing a total of ten pictures in forty-five days.[41]

This rat race brought out the worst in Shanghai filmmaking. To add respectability, moreover, not a few of these folk dramas (mainly those from Xinhua) had tacked on narratively unmotivated patriotic endings or sub-themes, which some critics contemptuously called *guangming weiba* (tails of brightness) that further alienated audiences. The Shanghai market (which began to contract as refugees began to return home after 1939), thus remained under Hollywood dominance, and the Southeast Asian market became less profitable and predictable as Singapore and the Philippines began to develop their own cinema. Low-budget Cantonese films from Hong Kong also continued to vie for influence on the continent.[42] To survive, the industry had to expand its distribution network. But where was the new market?

A politically sensitive market did come up in the occupied regions around the lower Yangzi river delta. It was offered by Kawakita Nagamasa, a cosmopolitan movie entrepreneur who came from an old China hand family and was a graduate of Beijing University. When the Japanese military failed to infiltrate the Shanghai cinema, its headquarters in Tokyo approached Kawakita for help. Back in 1938, Kawakita had been one of the first Japanese to attempt penetrating the China market by making a movie in Manzhouguo. The feature, *Dongyang heping zhi dao* in Chinese (The way of East Asian Peace), starring Bai Guang, which openly promoted the "imperial way" in China, was a box-office disaster. When it was premiered in Tianjin only a few

Chinese viewers showed up; in Beijing not one bought a ticket.[43] This failure, along with his Chinese education, framed Kawakita's liberal belief that "the Chinese would see only films made by the Chinese." "Chinese films" here meant those without Japanese intervention and overt propagandistic values. According to his associates Huang Tianshi and Shimizu Akira, Kawakita agreed to work for the army after he was promised autonomy in shaping cinematic policy in the occupied regions across central China.[44]

Thus, in June 1939, Kawakita founded the *kokusaku* (national policy) company Zhonghua dianying gongsi (China Movie Company, or Zhongdian) in Nanjing, with a Shanghai office on Sichuan Road, near Fuzhou Road. It had sixteen employees, including Liu Naou, Huang Tianshi, and Huang Tianzuo. After the establishment of the Wang Jingwei regime, in December 1940 the company was reorganized into a Sino-Japanese venture, nominally controlled by Nanjing, which had the major holding (51 percent). Zhongdian's work consisted of making propaganda documentaries (*bunka eiga*), sending out "travelling movie units" to entertain the army in war zones, and distributing Japanese movies to Japanese-owned cinemas in occupied areas in central China (including Shanghai's Hongkou and Huxi). The most important purpose was to try to establish connections with the Shanghai film industry by distributing its products to the occupied regions.[45]

In mid-1939, through the office of Liu Naou and Huang Tianzuo, Kawakita met Zhang Shankun secretly. At the meeting, speaking in fluent Mandarin, Kawakita told Zhang that marketing Mandarin movies to the Chinese in occupied regions was not only a good business move but also an expression of patriotism. The occupied subjects in central China would then be able to reconnect with their homeland by way of consuming familiar images of the nation. Indeed, it was Chinese filmmakers' responsibility to provide the "Chinese in occupied areas with entertainment and comforts." Kawakita proposed several conditions for the marketing arrangement that included: (1) all Chinese films had first to go through the Japanese Office of Shanghai Film Censorship, which was made up of representatives of the army's press bureau, the military police (Kempeitai), and the Japanese consulate; (2) once approved, the Japanese would make advance payment for the films plus providing Fuji negative stock for making copies to be distributed in the occupied areas. At the end of the meeting, Kawakita intimated that, if he were recalled for failing in his mission, his successor would likely not be as generous and sympathetic as he. Then the survival of *gudao* Shanghai cinema would be in jeopardy.[46]

Zhang later accepted Kawakita's offer. He was worried that the movie business would soon be bankrupt if no new market and no new chemicals were made available. In fact, Kawakita's offers (pre-payment and film stock) were too good to pass up. He also probably believed that showing Chinese-made films to the Chinese in occupied regions should not be confused or identified with political compromise because occupied areas were, in the final analysis, an integral part of China. The captive audiences there had as much desire for entertainment and emotional outlets as their fellow countrymen in the unoccupied zones.[47] However, he seemed to overlook the very troubling questions of having to work through a Japanese distribution network and to subject himself to Japanese censorship, which amounted to no less than symbolic acceptance of the enemy's legitimacy. As he should have been aware, this was exactly what the *gudao* news industry had refused to do when it was asked to submit to Japanese censorship if it wanted access to markets beyond the city. It published instead under foreign registration. Filmmaking was of course a more capital-intensive and market-sensitive business than publishing; it required a constant effort to expand its audiences in order to survive in a highly competitive and volatile environment. Zhang's acceptance of Kawakita's offer was thus fundamentally a surrender to commercial imperatives. Furthermore, without knowing the consequences at the time, the agreement brought him into a close relationship with Kawakita, who, with him, was to shape and control the popular cinema of Shanghai after total occupation in 1941.

In any case, probably as a show of the underlying patriotic motive for his business decision, Zhang sold *Hua Mulan Joins the Army* to Zhongdian, which premiered it in Nanjing in July 1939 to box-office success. The film generated heated debate among the Japanese censors. While the Kempeitai agents disproved it on the ground that it projected Chinese nationalism, the Army Press Bureau representative Tsuji Hisakazu argued that it was just an entertaining period drama. Only on the insistence of Kawakita and Tokyo's intervention was *Hua Mulan Joins the Army* approved.[48] In late 1939, many *gudao* studios followed Zhang's lead.

This distribution practice provoked controversy within the film community. The controversy became ever more intense after the incident of the burning of *Hua Mulan Joins the Army* as a "traitorous movie" in Chongqing when it opened there in January 1940 (after being cleared by the Guomindang Central Film Censorship Committee in December 1939). The burning was instigated mainly by the young dramatist Ma Yanxiang (with the support of other prominent intellectuals like Hong shen), who published an open letter in *Dagong bao* denouncing *Hua Mulan Joins the Army* as a *hanjian yingpian* (traitors' film), because, among other accusations (1) Bu Wancang was a traitor; (2) Xinhua Studio was backed by the Japanese; (3) the film stock was Japanese-made; (4) the film made a mockery of the resistance army in the draftees scene; and (5) it tried to split up the racial solidarity between the Han and the Mongols by representing the latter as evil. Underlying these denunciations were the binary conceptions that Shanghai under partial occupation could produce only traitorous art.[49]

On January 27, 1940, in the middle of an afternoon show at Chongqing's Weiyi Theater, a man mounted the stage and spoke to the audience: "Do you all know who this movie's director is? It is the traitor Bu Wancang ... It is an utter disgrace that a traitorous film should be shown here, the capital of our National Resistance!" He then led the agitated crowd to break into the projection room and took the film out to burn it in front of the theater. Mob violence ensued and was calmed down only when the police intervened. The incident brought forth a spirited debate among intellectuals across the unoccupied zones: was *Hua Mulan Joins the Army* a traitorous film? Xia Yan, a venerable leader of the literary resistance, used his authority to frame the debate by speaking out in defence of Ouyang Yuqian. His acrid essay brought into focus the intellectuals' partisan spirit, prejudice against commercial filmmaking, and marginalization of Shanghai. Xia bifurcated the film to an opposition between Good script and Evil production. Acknowledging that he had not seen it, he none the less supported Ouyang, who was then living in Guilin, on the basis that he was "a genuine patriot." But Bu Wancang, on the other hand, he denounced in a strikingly patriarchal metaphor for "his loss of chastity" (*shijie*) because he had had contacts with the enemy. Continuing his moralistic diatribe, Xia criticized Zhang Shankun for "remaining in Shanghai to make movies . . . rather than engaging in National Resistance in the interior. This was surely unpatriotic behavior [*bu aiguo de xingwei*] . . . and we heard that he had compromised to some extent, so that his productions could be exhibited in occupied areas." Yet, he counseled, since Zhang was just a movie businessman, "we don't want to condemn him too harshly" as long as he did not openly collaborate with Japan. He thus concluded on a conciliatory note that *Hua Mulan Joins the Army* was in the final analysis not a "traitorous film."[50] But Xia Yan's bifurcation leaves one to wonder: if the story was not written by the liberal nationalist Ouyang Yuqian, in a tolerant mood of United Front policy, would Xia have defended the film?

In Shanghai, Zhang Shankun and Bu Wancang ran front-page advertisements in all major Chinese newspapers to express their innocence, and their outrage and disappointment at the burning of *Hua Mulan Joins the Army*. Zhang implored Chongqing and the Shanghai party branch to consider the fact that the film stock he had used was Kodak, not Fuji, that Bu Wancang was not a *hanjian*, and that Xinhua Studio had no Japanese capital. At around the same time, Zhang also registered Xinhua as an American corporation, and renamed it United China Motion Picture Company, probably as a way of showing his determination to resist Japanese infiltration. The film was re-released a few months later.

Having its most popular, best crafted, and most patriotic movie attacked because it was produced in Shanghai was surely a humiliation for the Shanghai people. It reminded them painfully of their marginality. Were they guilty just because they did not move to the interior? As the journalist Dong Guo complained: "*Hua Mulan Joins the Army* was immensely popular here, and all Shanghai audiences were proud of and enchanted by it. But the film was burnt in Chongqing. How can we not be sad and angry?"[51] Chen Yunshang explained her frustrations even more forcefully to some Hong Kong reporters:

> Bu Wancang is not a traitor. If they burnt the film because of rumors or because Bu remained in Shanghai, it will leave many idealistic film

workers who stay behind in *gudao* disappointed and at a total loss. In fact, living in a tiger's lair, the tenacious struggle and patriotic dedication of the many upright and courageous people [in semi-occupied Shanghai] are in no way inferior [in moral commitment] to those who can cheer and yell in the freedom of the interior.[52]

It was in the agonized context of frustration, outrage, and self-reflection that the 1940–1 controversy arose regarding the distribution of movies to occupied areas. To some commentators, business transactions of any form with the Japanese in a semi-occupied situation would inescapably involve various degrees of political compromise.[53] Thus, as a journalist aptly pointed out, the fundamental problem of the distribution system was that the moment the Chinese studio owners sold their film rights to the Japanese Zhongdian, which then made its own copies on Fuji film, they lost control over their products. What if, for example, the Japanese changed the content or imposed their message on it by way of subtitles, voice-over, or theme songs? Could the filmmakers still justify themselves as providing only movies of "familiar images" to the captive audience, who would otherwise be compelled to watch only propaganda put out by the enemy? Did they in effect compromise their political conscience for the sake of business interest?[54]

Yet some critics came out in defence of the film industry. They emphasized the painfully ambiguous situation in which the Shanghai cinema was struggling, all alone, to survive. Their endeavor to maintain a viable Chinese cinema in the semi-occupied city was unaided and spurned by the "resistance heroes" who saw the semi-occupied city as a suspicious other. As Dong Guo complained:

> Most people in the film community do not want to betray their country, but there are so many pressures out there to force them to compromise. Why can we not give them help ... [Despite all the criticisms from the unoccupied zone], no one has had the courage to come to Shanghai to provide guidance to the film industry. Nor has any one come forward to help the industry to expand its market to the interior ... Shanghai cinema is now facing the dilemma of whether to destroy itself heroically or to give itself up to the enemy. The destruction of Shanghai cinema would only enable the Japanese to take over the cinematic apparatus here. And if we return to the homeland [i.e. Chongqing], I am doubtful whether the cinema industry there, which is plagued by limited capacity and overemployment, can take in any of us. Thus [people in] Chongqing, it seems, are totally in the dark of the dilemma facing Shanghai filmmakers.

Dong Guo ended his bitter challenge against the marginalization of *gudao* Shanghai in the nationalist discourse by meekly pleading for the Nationalist party-state to recognize and actively guide the Chinese cinema in semi-occupied Shanghai.

All these agonizing debates and passionate pleas receded into history when the Japanese took over the whole of Shanghai on December 8, 1941. Under captivity, the ambivalence of Shanghai cinema and its marginalization in the nationalist discourse took on new significance.[55]

V

In semi-occupied Shanghai, where the semi-colonial system of extraterritoriality and fragmented imperialist domination created a space free from Japanese captivity, Chinese filmmakers sought to rebuild their ravaged cinema. These filmmakers, except for a few speculators, were interested in making money as well as making films to entertain and inspire the Shanghai public. They were not heroes, involving themselves in clandestine operations, fearlessly shooting or throwing bombs at the enemy. Rather they sought to discreetly negotiate with the enemy and adapt as best as they could to the brutality of everyday life in *gudao*.

The Chinese filmmakers found themselves in an ambivalent situation of conflicting demands and constantly shifting lines between possible defiance, necessary accommodation, and downright compromise. Unlike those who had exiled themselves to the interior, studio heads and artists remaining in Shanghai after the defeat were for the most part apolitical and distant from organized politics. Entertainment film was their forte. Thus when Zhang Shankun, Zhang Shichuan, and Yan Chuntang tried to rebuild the industry, they naturally turned to popular genres which they knew best and which they thought would avoid falling foul of the *gudao* authorities and Japanese army. They also expected that, as before the war, audiences went to the cinema primarily to be entertained, not to seek "truth." Box-office receipts confirmed their expectations, as the Shanghai public were eager to restore laughter and a sense of normality to their life.

While the filmmakers justified their production trend as a strategic adaptation to the poltical pressures of a semi-occupied city, *gudao* resisters associated entertainment as "contaminating" the body politic of National Resistance, selling "fantasies" for their self-interest, and chastised them for serving the interests of the marauders. These criticisms fed into and overlapped rumors and allegations of political treason that put the film community at risk from pro-Chongqing terrorism. At the same time, Japanese agents tried to position themselves in show business through harassing as well as offering capital to studio owners. The *Chahuanu* incident terrorized and scandalized the industry.

Thus the success of *Hua Mulan Joins the Army*, which was as entertaining as it was inspiringly defiant, called forth a cycle of patriotic drama in Shanghai cinema. But the quality varied greatly, and audiences soon grew weary of it. Some critics also clamored for films confronting contemporary issues instead of mystifying heroes of the past. Then the twin pressures of inflation and a contracting market forced Zhang Shankun and other industry leaders to agree to market Chinese films to the occupied areas. While they claimed they were making a necessary accommodation to survive the increasingly hostile business conditions of semi-occupied Shanghai, critics claimed the moral high ground by condemning their political compromise as selling out to the enemy.

Resistance intellectuals in Chongqing dramatized the debate when they led the campaign to burn *Hua Mulan Joins the Army* and castigated the entire Shanghai public as traitors for not joining real-life heroes in the unoccupied zones to fend off Japanese invasion. Thus, by valorizing the Chinese interior, the semi-occupied city, particularly its film community, became in effect an immoral other in the discourse of National Resistance. This marginalization of Shanghai and its cinema raised the question of who controlled the meaning of patriotism and, thus, the boundary between loyalty and compromise. If accommodation was necessary to survive in a semi-occupied city, who was to distinguish it from treason, and how? In a nation that was divided during the war into the occupied and the unoccupied, power relations were necessarily unequal and a singular, homogeneous national culture was illusionary. To be "chaste," to borrow Xia Yan's metaphor, meant to exile oneself to Free China. The semi-occupied Shanghai cinema, in retrospect, had limited space to survive and to be loyal at the same time.

NOTES

1 Benedict Anderson, *Imagined Communities: Reflections on the Origins and Spread of Nationalism*, London: Verso, 1993; Partha Chatterjee, *The Nation and its Fragments: Colonial and Postcolonial Histories*, Princeton: Princeton University Press, 1993; Susan Hayward, *French National Cinema*, London: Routledge, 1993.

2 Recently a surge of revisionist scholarship is beginning to challenge the binary paradigm. By bringing into focus the notions of historical complexity and wartime ambiguity, it opens up a new horizon of issues and perspectives. They include the analysis of Occupation literary trends (Edward Gunn, *Unwelcome Muse: Chinese Literature in Peking and Shanghai*, New York: Columbia University Press, 1980); the reevaluation of wartime state-building efforts (James Hsiung and Steven Levine, eds, *China's Bitter Victory: The War with Japan*, New York: Sharpe, 1992), the historical ambiguity of intellectual situation under Occupation (Poshek Fu, *Passivity, Resistance, and Collaboration: Intellectual Choices in Occupied Shanghai, 1937–1945*, Stanford: Stanford University Press, 1993); elite appropriation of "popular" cultural forms for patriotic propaganda (Chang-tai Hung, *War and Popular Culture: Resistance in Modern China*, Berkeley: University of California Press, 1994); and the ambiguous world of political terrorism in occupied Shanghai (Wen-hsin Yeh, "Dai Li and the Liu Geqing Affair: Heroism in the Chinese Secret Service during the War of Resistance," *Journal of Asian Studies*, 48, (1989), pp. 545–62, and Frederic Wakeman Jr., *The Shanghai Badlands: Wartime Terrorism and Urban Crimes, 1937–1941*, Cambridge: Cambridge University Press, 1996.

3 Cheng Jihua *et al.*, *Zhongguo dianying fazhan shi*, Beijing: Zhongguo dianying chubanshe, 1980, originally 1964, II, pp. 94–112.

4 For a fine book-length study, see Evelyn Ehrlich, *Cinema of Paradox: French*

Filmmaking under the German Occupation, New York: Columbia University Press, 1985.

5   See Huang Tianshi, "Yiduan bei yiwang de Zhongguo dianying shi" [A forgotten phase of Chinese film history], unpublished manuscript, pp. 2–3.

6   See Wang Qi, "Yinian lai zhi Xinhua" [Xinhua in the last year], *Xinhua huabao* 4, 1 (January, 1939).

7   Su Yadao, *Lunjin yinhe* [On Chinese cinema], Hong Kong: Boyi chubanshe, 1982, pp. 89–92.

8   Chen Dieyi, ed., *Zhongguo yingtan juren* [The giant of Chinese cinema], Hong Kong: n.d., pp. 3–33.

9   See Gongsun Lu, *Zhongguo dianying shihua* [History of Chinese cinema], Hong Kong: Chunqiu chubanshe, 1960, I, pp. 122–6; and Su Yadao, *Lunjin yinhe*, pp. 89–100.

10 Wang Qi, "Yinian lai zhi Zhonghua"; Gongsun Lu, *Zhongguo dianying shihua* I, pp. 125–6; Toshida Masatoshi, "Henbo shuru Shanhai Shina eiga kaku-sha" [Chinese production companies in Shanghai], *Eiga hyoron* 16 (March 1941), p. 67; Chen Chunren, *Kangzhan shidai shenghuo shi* [A history of life in wartime Shanghai], Hong Kong: Changxing shuqu, n.d.

11 See *Wenxian* 1, 4 (January 1939), pp. 16–18; *Xinhua huabao* 3, 3 (December 1938); Toshida Mastoshi, "Henbo shuru Shanhai Shina eiga kaku-sha"; and Yang Cun, *Zhongguo dianying sanshi nian* [Thirty years of Chinese cinema], Hong Kong: Shijie chubanshe, 1954, pp. 175–6.

12 "Shanghai dianying yuan xunli" [A tour of Shanghai movie theaters], *Dianying shijie* 2, 1 (January 1940); Tan Chunfa, "Yige teshu de dianying wenhua xianxiang" [A unique film cultural phenomenon], *Dianying shuanzhoukan* 257 (January 1989), p. 46.

13 "Shanghai dainying yuan xunli", *Xinhua huabao* 5, 5 (May 1940); *Dianying shenghuo* 14 (July 1940), 17 (October 1940).

14 See *Xinhua huabao* 5, 8 (August 1940); *Dianying shijie* 2, 1 (January 1940); Wang Qi, "Yinian lai zhi Xinhua" *Shen bao*, June 30, 1940.

15 See Poshek Fu, "Patriotism or Profit: Hong Kong Cinema during the Second World War," in Law Kar, ed., *Early Images of Hong Kong and China* (Hong Kong: Urban Council, 1995), pp. 69–73. The role of Southeast Asian film production and market in the artistic and institutional history of Chinese cinema is an important area of research that has barely begun.

16 Poshek Fu, *Passivity, Resistance, and Collaboration*, pp. 30–56; Wen-hsin Yeh, "Dai Li and the Liu Geqing Affair"; Frederic Wakeman, *The Shanghai Badlands*, pp. 27–127.

17 *Wenxian* 4 (January 1939) I, pp. 11–13; *Yilin* 48 (February 1939); *Xinhua huabao* 4, 1 (January 1939).

18 See Huang Tianshi, *Yiduan bei yiwang*, pp. 13–18; *Wenxian* 1, 4 (January 1939), pp. 6–8; Matsuzaki Keiji, *Shanhai jinbun ki* (Shanghai men of letters), Tokyo, Takayama Shoin, 1941. For Liu Naou's literary career, see Shu-mei Shih, "Gender, Race, and Semicolonialism: Liu Na'ou's Urban Shanghai Landscape," *Journal of Asian Studies* 35, 4 (November 1996), pp. 934–56.

19 For synopses and advertisements of these thirteen movies, see *Xinhua huabao* 3, 1 (December 1938).

20 "Shanghai ge bao fukan bianzhe zuozhe jinggao Shanghai dianyingjie," *Wenxian* 3 (February 1939), pp. H14–15.

21 Tan Zongxia, *Yiye huanghou* [An overnight queen], Hong Kong: Dianying xuanzhoukan, 1996, pp. 107–36.

22 For a detailed analysis of the publicity campaign, see Poshek Fu, "Selling Fantasies at War: Production and Promotion Practices of the Shanghai Film Industry, 1937–1941," paper presented at "Commercial Culture of Republican

Shanghai," Cornell University, July 21–2, 1995.

23 Long considered lost, *Mulan congjun* was found and restored in early 1990. I am grateful to the Hong Kong International Film Festival for making it available to me.

24 For publicity, see Nina, "Huanying Chen Yunshang lai Hu" [Welcome Chen Yunshang to Shanghai], *Xinhua huabao* 3, 3 (December 1938), and "Chen Yunshang yizhou jian" [Chen Yunxiang in a week], *Xinhua huabao* 4,1 (January 1939); Yang Cun, *Zhongguo dianying yanyuan cangsang lu* [Vicissitudes of Chinese movie actors], Shanghai: Shijie shuju, n.d., pp. 67–72. For Zhang's publicity strategy, see Tan Zongxia, *Yiye huanghou*, pp. 103–68. For a study of the popular mood of *gudao* Shanghai, see Poshek Fu, *Passivity, Resistance, and Collaboration*, chapter 1.

25 For an in-depth study of Hollywood narrative style, see David Bordwell, *Narration in the Fiction Film*, Madison: University of Wisconsin Press, 1985.

26 Ying Sun (A Ying), "Guanyu *Mulan congjun*" [On *Mulan joins the army*], *Wenxian* 6 (1939), p. F32.

27 As the unorthodox late Ming philosopher Lu K'un wrote of virtuous women like Hua Mulan in his celebrated *Guei fan:* "There are many virtuous . . . men, so why have I written about women? To manifest the teaching of woman. These are all women who are [examples of] benevolent people, filial sons, upright scholars, and loyal officials." In fact, Hua Mulan seized the imagination of many late Ming literati, as she was featured in several major plays and poems at the time, a time of social crisis. See Joanna Handlin, "Lu K'un's New Audience: The Influence of Women's Literacy on Sixteenth Century Thought," in Margery Wolf and Roxane Witke (eds), *Women in Chinese History*, Stanford: Stanford University Press, 1975, pp. 23–5. On traditional configurations of women, see Patricia Ebrey, *The Inner Quarters: Marriage and the Lives of Chinese Women in the Sung Period*, Berkeley: University of California Press, 1993; Mary Rankin, "The Emergence of Women at the End of the Ch'ing: The Case of Ch'iu Chin," in Wolf and Witke, *Women in Chinese Society*, pp. 52–6; Carolyn Brown, "Woman as Trope: Gender and Power in Lu Xun's 'Soap'," in Tani Barlow (ed.), *Gender Politics in Modern China*, Durham, N.C.: Duke University Press, 1993, pp. 74–89.

28 *Xinhua huabao* 4, 3 (1936).

29 A Ying made the point well when he summarized the three Hua Mulan plays published in the last decade of Qing rule: "In times of national crisis, when the nation is in its death throes, all people should dedicate themselves to the cause of the nation, and there should be no difference between man and woman." See his "Guanyu *Mulan congjun*," p. F33. For some fine studies of the issue of the nationalist construction of women in twentieth-century China, see Lydia Liu, "The Female Body and Nationalist Discourse: The Field of Life and Death Revisited," in C. Kaplan (ed.), *Scattered Hegemonies: Postmodernity and Transnational Feminist Practices*, Minneapolis: University of Minnesota Press, 1994, pp. 37–62; Prasenjit Duara, "The Order of Authenticity: National History and Gender in Modern China," paper presented at "Narratives, Arts, and Ritual: Imagining and Constructing Nationhood in Modern East Asia," University of Illinois, Urbana–Champaign, November 14–17, 1996; and Gail Hershatter, *Dangerous Pleasures: Prostitution and Modernity in Twentieth Century Shanghai*, Berkeley: University of California Press, 1997. For analyses of the female motifs in resistance literature in wartime, see Poshek Fu, *Passivity, Resistance, and Collaboration*, chapter 2; and Chang-tai Hung, *War and Popular Culture*, pp. 64–74. For nationalist patriarchy, see Chatterjee, *The Nation and its Fragments*, pp. 116–34.

30 See, for example, *Xinhua huabao* 4, 3 (1939).

31 See *Yilin* 50 (1939), p. 12. Dong Guo, "Xuduo de ganxiang" [Numerous reflections], *Dianying shijie* 11 (1940); and concerning rumors on Zhang's using Japanese film stock, see *Dianying shijie* 10 (1940).

32 See, for example, Liao Liao, "Jianli xin wenhua zhongxin" [Establish a new cultural center], *Li bao*, April 2, 1942.

33 Hua Mulan meets Liu Yuandu on the way to the front. His romantic attachment to her from the beginning functions in the narrative as a reminder to the viewer and Chen Yunshang alike that she is a girl, only in temporary disguise for a patriotic cause. Thus no question of gender confusion or reversal such as is common in such late twentieth-century movies as John Lone's *M Butterfly* or Lin Qingxia's *Peking Opera Blues* is ever raised.

34 See *Xinhua huabao* 4, 3 (1939) Tan Zongxia, *Yiye huanghou*, pp. 143–6.

35 Review in *Shenbao*, quoted in *Xinhua huabao*, 4, 3 (1943).

36 Quotes from reviews in *Da wanbao* and *Damei wanbao* in Tan Zongxia, *Yiye huanghou*, pp. 123–30.

37 Wu Yonggang, "Guanyu Yue Fei Jinzhong paoguo" [On Yue Fei], *Dianying shijie*, 2, 12 (1940) see also "Yijiu sanjiu nian Zhongguo yintan gaikuang" [Chinese cinema in 1939], *Dianying shijie* 2, 2 (1940) *Dianying shenghuo* 1 (1940).

38 Wakeman, *The Shanghai Badlands*, pp. 65–79.

39 *Dianying shijie* 2, 3 (1940) and Zhang Shankun, "Daoyan zhi yan" [From the director], originally written in September 1940, quoted from Tan Zongxia, *Yiye huanghou*, pp. 173–5.

40 *Xinhua huabao* 8 (1940).

41 See Su Yadao, *Lunjin yinghe*, pp. 103–7; *Dianying shijie* 2, 17 (1940); Tan Zongxia, *Yiye huanghou*, pp. 183–6.

42 *Xinhua huabao* 5, 11 (1940) *Yilin* 65 (1940) and 70 (1940).

43 See Dan Ding, trans., "Riben dianying de Dalu zhengce ji qi dongxiang zuotan" [A symposium on the mainland policy of Japanese filmmaking and its future development], *Wenxian* 4 (1939), pp. I13–25.

44 See Huang Tianshi, *Yiduan bei yiwang*, pp. 19–23; Shimizu Akira, *Shanhai sokai eiga watakushi shi* [Personal history of Shanghai's foreign concession cinema], Tokyo: Shinchosha, 1995, pp. 59–64.

45 Huang Tianshi, *Yiduan bei yiwang*, pp. 27–33; Tsuji Hisakazu, *Chunka denei shiwa* [A narrative history of Chinese cinema], Tokyo, Gaifusha, 1987, pp. 46–55; Huang Tianshi, "Zhongguo dianying gongsi tuozhan shilue" [A History of Zhongdian's Development], *Xin yingtan*, 1, 1 (1942).

46 Huang Tianshi, *Yiduan bei yiwang*, pp. 22–4; quotation from Tsuji Hisakazu, *Chunka denei*, pp. 64–86; Shimizu Akira, *Shanhai sokai eiga*, pp. 66–72.

47 Huang Tianshi, *Yiduan bei yiwang*, p. 23; *Dianyin shijie* 2, 3 (1940), pp. 12–19.

48 Tsuji Hisakazu, *Chunka denei*, pp. 86–8; Huang Tianshi, *Yiduan bei yiwang*, pp. 24–5. The film attracted widespread attention in the Japanese critical community in China; for two examples, see *Eiga hyron* 16 (1941), pp. 97–9.

49 A summary of Ma Yanxiang's open letter and the ensuing debate and editorial comments are collected in the special issue of *Dianying shijie* 8 (1940) and in *Yilin* 68 (1940), pp. 2–6. This is a critical event in wartime cultural history that demands further research, for it showed the widely held contempt and prejudice as well as ignorance on the part of the "Resistance hero" in Free China regarding Shanghai filmmaking.

50 Xia Yan, "Wenti yao feng qingchu" [We have to separate the questions], in *Dianying shijie* 8 (1940).

51 Dong Guo, "Xuduo de ganxiang."

52 "Chen Yunxiang zai Shanghai bannian" [Chen Yunxiang in Shanghai for half a year], *Yilin*, 69 (1940), p. 12.

53 For a rich study of business behavior and strategies in other industries in semi-occupied Shanghi, see Chapter 5 in this volume.

54 Pu Ti, "Zaitan *Mulan congjun*" [Reconsider *Hua Mulan Joins the Army*], *Dawan bao*, March 25, 1940.

55 For two studies of Shanghai cinema under occupation, see Poshek Fu, "Struggle to Entertain: The Political Ambivalence of the Shanghai Film Industry under the Japanese Occupation, 1941–1945," in Law Kar (ed.), *Cinema of Two Cities: Hong Kong–Shanghai*, Hong Kong: Urban Council, 1994, pp. 39–62; "The Ambiguity of Entertainment: Chinese Cinema in Japanese-occupied Shanghai, 1941–1945," *Cinema Journal*, 37, 1 (Fall 1997), pp. 66–84.

ACKNOWLEDGMENTS

I am grateful to Jin Qiang and Lau Yiu-Kuen for their help with research materials, and to David Desser, Patricia Ebrey, Daniel Littlefield, Lydia Liu, and participants of the Berkeley conference for their comments on an earlier version of this chapter.

Plate 1 Chinese refugees swarm into the foreign areas, August 1937

Plate 2 Suzhou Creek, flowing into the Huangpu River, separated the Japanese-occupied area from the Anglo-American International Settlement

Plate 3 Police quell a rice riot in the International Settlement, 1940

Plate 4 Chinese exchange shops in the International Settlement

Plate 5 Shanghai, 1940

Plate 6 Wang Jingwei on the third anniversary of the puppet regime in Nanjing, 1942

Plate 7 Wang Jingwei and German envoys to the Nanjing puppet government

Plate 8 Wang Jingwei and his entourage on a pilgrimage to a Meiji shrine in Japan, 1941

Plate 9 Zhu Minyi, Minister of Foreign Affairs in Wang Jingwei's puppet government, signing the agreement with the French consul by which the French Concession reverted to the Chinese, July 22, 1943

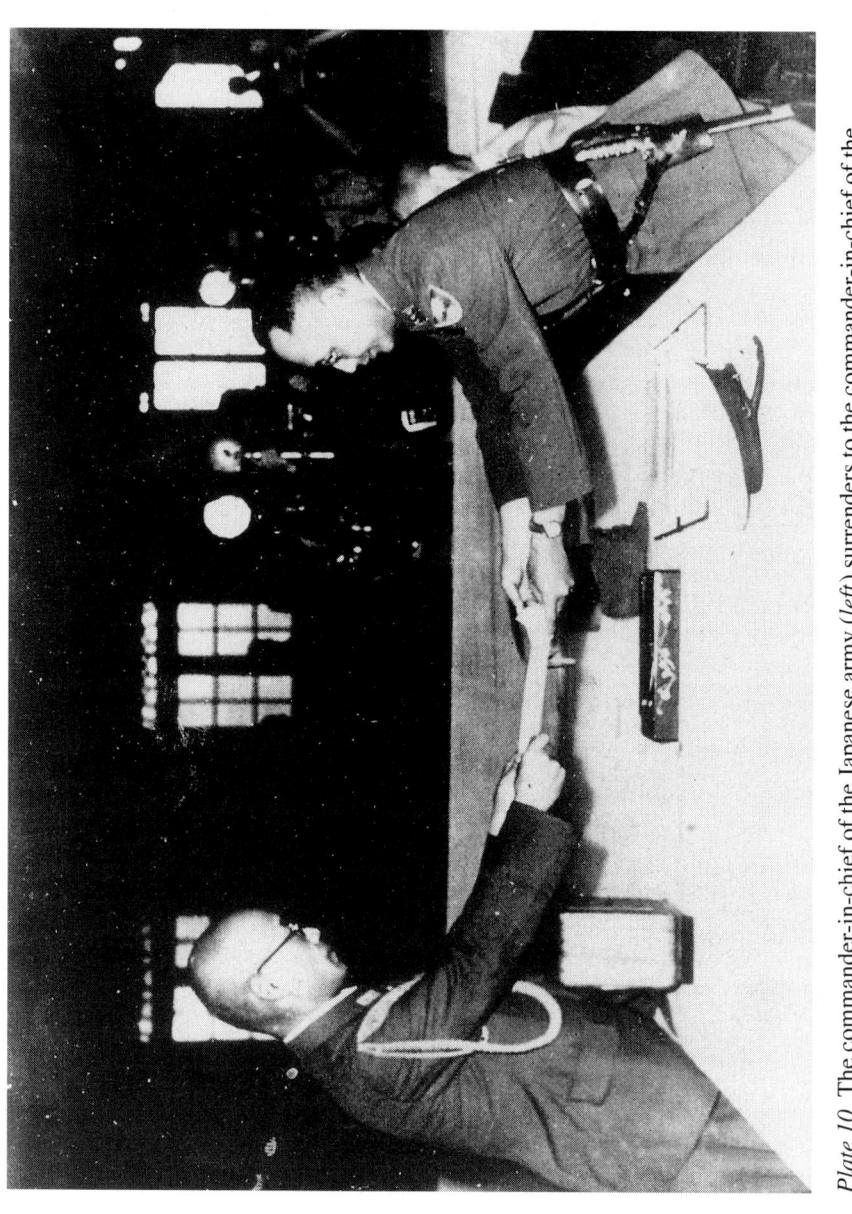

Plate 10 The commander-in-chief of the Japanese army (*left*) surrenders to the commander-in-chief of the Guomindang army, He Yingqin

Plate 11 Wang Jingwei, 1940

Plate 12 Wang Jingwei reviewing puppet army troops

Plate 13 Nanjing massacre, December 1937

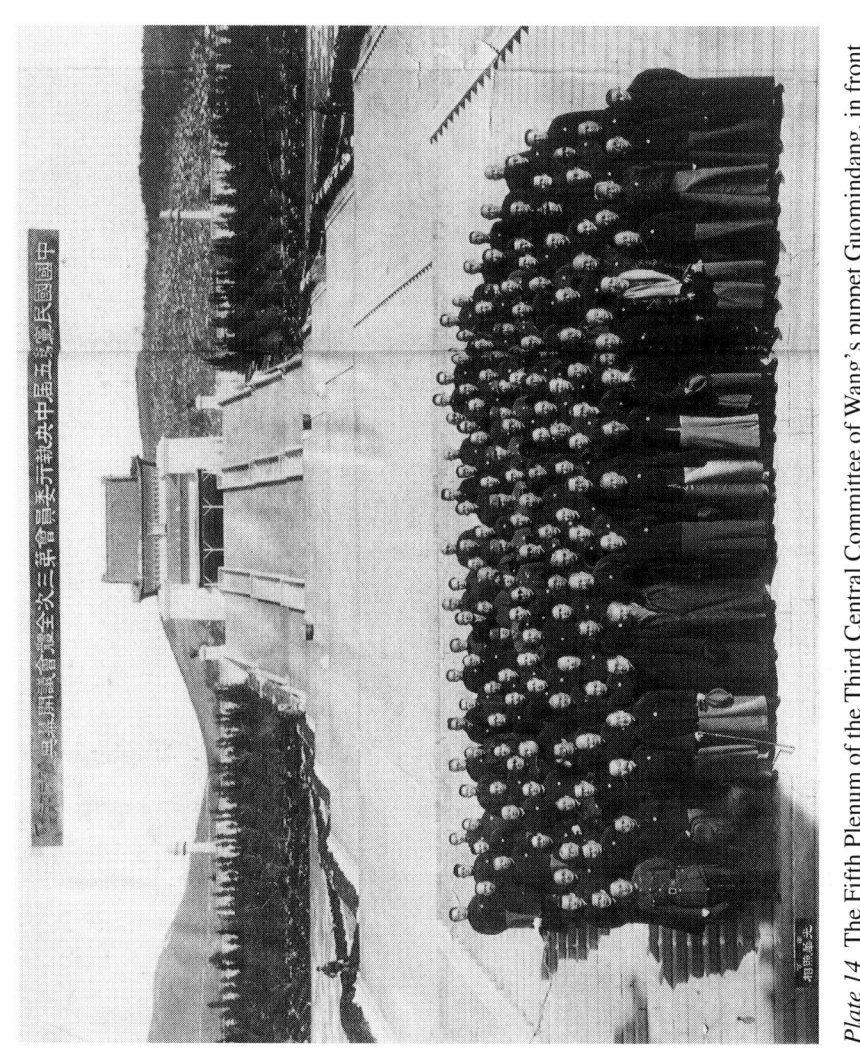

Plate 14 The Fifth Plenum of the Third Central Committee of Wang's puppet Guomindang, in front of Sun Yat-sen's tomb

Plate 15 The British Club in Shanghai, rebuilt in 1909, reputedly with the longest bar in the world

Plate 16 The major buildings along the Shanghai Bund: the Hong Kong and Shanghai Banking Corporation building, the Maritime Customs House, the Broadway Mansion, the Bank of China, and Sassoon Building

Plate 17 A Japanese soldier and a Chinese woman in the occupied zone

Plate 18 Japanese soldiers marching into the International Settlement,
December 9, 1941

7 Urban warfare and underground resistance

Heroism in the Chinese secret service during the War of Resistance

Wen-hsin Yeh

In the late 1930s and early 1940s, despite ardent hopes that the International Settlement would remain a safe haven for all who fled the brutalities of Japanese military occupation, the *gudao* became a scene of much violence. The predominantly British and American civilian authorities of the Shanghai Municipal Council were in no position to buck the demands of the Japanese military, who were poised to move in and take over the concessions. The Chinese population in the city, stirred by patriotic sentiment, were unable, meanwhile, to refrain from using the *gudao* as a base to launch anti-Japanese resistance. Nationalist and Communist activists alike used the foreign concessions to air anti-Japanese feelings, to gather intelligence, to procure war materials, to plot assassinations, and to stage a war of nerves against the Japanese. The Japanese, with the help of Chinese puppet police forces, retaliated in kind. The International Settlement and the French Concession, despite the declared neutrality, became a veritable battlefield between the warring parties.

Foremost among the combatants in this urban warfare were members of the Nationalist military intelligence service—the Military Bureau of Statistics and Investigation (Junshi Weiyuanhui Tongji Diaocha Ju, or Juntong), that was under the command of General Dai Li in Chongqing. Referred to some-times as the "Himmler of China" in the Western press, Dai, who swore unswerv-ing loyalty to the person of Chiang Kai-shek, was the master mind behind a series of assassinations carried out in Shanghai between 1939 and 1940, intended to intimidate individuals who were inclined to give in to the enemy.

In retrospect, Dai Li and his organization were the products of two sets of circumstances in republican Chinese history: the struggles between the Nationalists and the Communists in national politics, and the war between China and Japan. A much feared and highly secretive operation that had served as a powerful weapon against Chiang Kai-shek's political enemies, the bureau had long been a subject of sensational exposé and a target in left-wing propaganda against the Nationalists.

Information about the wartime activities of Dai Li and the Military Bureau of Statistics and Investigation did not come to light, however, until the 1960s, when personal memoirs and collections of documentary sources began to appear in quantity on both sides of the Taiwan (Formosa) Straits. In the Cold War atmosphere of the time, former members of Juntong who survived the 1949 takeover in China were invited by their Communist captors to denounce their own past. Their one-time colleagues in Taipei, meanwhile, proceeded to publish memoirs in which they eulogized the bureau's history. These materials contain profiles of key individuals, descriptions of organizational layouts, accounts of major events in the bureau's history, and discussions of the bureau's role in Nationalist politics. The two sets of accounts published on opposite sides of the Straits diverged predictably, condemning and praising in black and white. But these otherwise divergent accounts share a strikingly similar idiom that points to the presence of a shared imaginary world about the War of Resistance, articulated in a language derived from popular premodern historical novels such as the *Romance of the Three Kingdoms* and *The Water Margin*.

What was the significance of this language and imagination in the history of Juntong? What does this use of the past tell us about the men and the organization that played such a prominent role in the urban warfare of Shanghai during the War of Resistance? In what way does this help us grasp the nature of the Nationalist Chinese resistance on the streets of wartime Shanghai? This chapter tries to answer these questions by examining a critical moment in the history of Juntong in 1939, when rival spymasters competed with Dai Li in Shanghai for the loyalty of his field agents, and when the rhetoric of benevolence and righteousness was used in the best heroic tradition of the popular historical romance in order to motivate life-and-death struggles among armies of anonymous spies.

DAI LI AND THE CREATION OF JUNTONG

Juntong was the creation of Dai Li, who built it from scratch and turned it into a powerful base of personal power. The general regarded himself, meanwhile, as a personal instrument of Chiang Kai-shek, and used the bureau to serve the wishes of his master and leader. A central paradox thus lies at the heart of the organization that Dai Li had built. It was an organ of enormous power and influence in republican politics in its own right. This power, at the same time, derived from Dai Li's very dependence and total submission to the personal authority of Chiang Kai-shek.

Dai Li's lifelong relationship with Chiang Kai-shek began in 1924–5, when Dai, a native of Jiangshan, Zhejiang, arrived in Canton and matriculated in the sixth class of the Whampoa Military Academy, where he received instructions from Chiang Kai-shek, the headmaster of the school by the appointment of Sun Yat-sen, the founder of the Nationalist Party. Dai Li saw himself in subsequent years both as a traditional disciple of Chiang the mentor and teacher, and as a political follower of Chiang the supreme leader of a modern revolutionary party. In creating the Juntong, Dai Li drew upon Sun

Yat-sen's revolutionary ideology as well as the popular Confucian vocabulary of personal loyalty. He left a defining imprint on the bureau's training programs, organizational rules and personnel practices, and fostered an in-house political culture that combined the imperatives of a military bureaucratic operation with a cult of personal leadership.

Dai Li's intelligence work commenced in the mid-1920s when he was a Whampoa cadet, in the months and years after the death of Sun Yat-sen (1925). Sun's death set off a leadership struggle that ultimately doomed the fragile united front between the Chinese Nationalists and the Communists (1923–7). It also turned Whampoa and Canton into scenes of hot political contestations in which reliable political intelligence, of the sort that Dai Li worked assiduously to acquire, commanded premium value.

Dai Li's transformation from a one-man intelligence freelancer to the head of a special team of trained operators took place in the early 1930s, in the aftermath of Japan's military takeover of Manchuria. Early in 1932, a group of Whampoa graduates, stirred by patriotic fervor, founded the Lixing she (Vigorous Practice Society) to spearhead the reform of the Nationalist Party and to enhance the might of the Chinese state. They swore themselves to party discipline and unqualified allegiance to Chiang Kai-shek. They created a secret service unit (Tewu chu, or Special Affairs Department) under the society and asked Dai Li to serve as the head of it.

Dai Li received this assignment personally from Chiang Kai-shek, symbolically conferred in the Sun Yat-sen mausoleum in the suburbs of Nanjing in 1932. Chiang, speaking on that occasion as the former headmaster (*xiaozhang*) of the Whampoa Military Academy, instructed Dai Li to look into traditional popular historical novels such as the *Romance of the Three Kingdoms* and *The Water Margin* for inspirations in the creation of the Tewu chu.

Dai Li instantly saw the special assignment he had just received as calling for a sense of duty that would go beyond life and death.[1] He responded to Chiang by way of an oath: "From this day on my life is no longer in my hands. I will risk my life fighting the enemy for the success of our mission. If I fail I will submit myself to the punishment of death by my leader." Dai's resolve on this occasion was often compared by his followers to the determination of the assassin Jing Ke of Yan of the Warring States period (ca. 400–221 BC), who sang to his desperate prince before embarking upon a fateful mission in 227 BC: "The wind rustles through the dry leaves; the water of the river Yi chills the bones. The brave man sets forth with the determination never to return."[2]

Thereafter, even though the Tewu chu was to borrow freely from the KGB and the Gestapo for operational methods and organizational techniques, members of the service were to regard themselves neither as socialists nor as fascists. The Chinese secret service, Dai Li insisted, must adopt a system of values that was in harmony with traditional beliefs in benevolence and righteousness, loyalty and filial piety. These ideals, furthermore, must be expressed in a language of China's own. "Our comrades are all brothers; our collectivity [*tuanti*] is a family," Dai told his men. "Our comrades come together on the principles of benevolence and righteousness. We forge our communal bond on the basis of mutual loyalty and reciprocal obligations."[3]

The core group of the early Tewu chu, known as the Blue Shirts (Lanyi she), consisted of a "League of Ten" whose members were drawn almost without exception from the first six classes of the Whampoa Academy. From 1932 to 1937 these former classmates, under the leadership of Dai Li, operated on a small budget and shared an *ad hoc* office in Nanjing that also served as their living quarters. They saw themselves as members of a sworn brotherhood as well as of an extended family. The group maintained a rather egalitarian style of operation, and although Dai Li was its leader, he was only first among equals.

A dramatic moment of test of Dai Li's loyalty to Chiang came in December 1936, during the Xi'an Incident. On December 12, 1936, officers of the Northeastern Army under the command of General Zhang Xueliang, son of the assassinated Manchurian warlord Zhang Zuolin, launched a military *coup* and took Chiang Kai-shek hostage in their military headquarters in the old Tang capital. The insurgents demanded that the Nationalist government suspend military campaigns against its domestic foe, the Communists, who had retreated to northern Shaanxi, and declare war instead on the foreign aggressor, the Japanese. The officers threatened to put Chiang Kai-shek to death if their demands were not granted.

The Xi'an Incident threw the Nationalist government in Nanjing into a state of chaos and turmoil. As others scrambled to position themselves in the eventuality of Chiang Kai-shek's death, Dai Li set personal considerations aside and flew to Xi'an from Nanjing with Madame Chiang Kai-shek. He had already carried out enough secret executions to fear for his own life should he ever fall into Communist hands. He went forward accompanying Madame Chiang into enemy territory none the less, conscious of acting out a historical parallel.

Earlier, in 1922, Chiang Kai-shek had boarded the beleaguered cruiser *Yongfeng* in the waters of the Pearl river outside Canton to be at the side of his leader, Sun Yat-sen, who had been deserted by his comrades and attacked by the troops of the Cantonese warlord Chen Jiongming. Sun eventually escaped unscathed from that incident. Chiang Kai-shek, as the only committed follower who had stood firm by his leader under trying circumstances, emerged from the incident as the legitimate heir to the revolutionary legacy of Sun Yat-sen.[4]

Dai Li's act in 1936, known as *funan* (joining together in a time of difficulty), was meant to be an emulation of the courage displayed by his leader and teacher in 1922. The trip to Xi'an was deemed by many a deed of unflinching personal loyalty. The episode earned him not only Madame Chiang's friendship but also Chiang Kai-shek's full confidence—at a time when so many others of Chiang's aides and former students had chosen to stay behind in the safety of Nanjing.[5]

The Xi'an Incident was a major turning point that marked a decided change in official Chinese policy towards Japanese military aggression in China. It thereby set the stage for war. War broke out between China and Japan over the Marco Polo Bridge Incident in the suburb of Beiping on July 7 the following summer. The Tewu chu, in response to a significant increase in demands for its service, expanded dramatically until, after several rounds of reorganization, it became, in 1938, the Juntong. Headquartered in the Nationalists' wartime capital in Chongqing, with positions filled by the graduates of its own training classes, Juntong emerged to become a powerful arm under Chiang's Military Affairs Council. The bureau employed a growing number of uniformed code operators and information analysts along with a secret army of paramilitary units equipped with American hardware. The idiom of sworn brotherhood and the pathos of medieval chivalry, to be sure, continued to inspire personal heroism in the bureau's underground stations behind enemy lines. The bureaucratization and the profession-alization of Juntong analysts and technicians in its Chongqing headquarters, meanwhile, rendered the rhetoric of righteousness anachronistic.

The bureaucratization of the bureau formalized work relationships, but it did not displace the old bonds of brotherhood, nor did it change Dai Li's ideas about its political culture. Dai Li titled the bureau's in-house newsletter *Jiafeng* (Family tradition), and he ran his secret service as a *paterfamilias*. His organization, which placed strong emphasis on absolute obedience and total dedication, was characterized by authoritarian intervention into individual personal affairs. Invoking a phrase from the *Dynastic History of the Han* (*Han shu*), "Is personal happiness attainable before the extermination of Xiongnu?", Dai Li forbade those who worked for him to get married during the war. He also laid down strict rules against misbehavior such as smoking, gambling, and games of *majiang*. Violators of these in-house rules were routinely placed in solitary confinement. Scores of agents, furthermore, were executed each year for violating the bureau's disciplinary rules. These deaths were known as the *xunfa*, or a form of "martyrdom" that helped to assure the integrity of the bureau's draconian code of conduct.[6]

Dai Li demanded from his Juntong comrades such virtues as hard work, perseverance, dedication, and endurance. He reminded them repeatedly that they had joined the secret service for the purpose of making a special contribution to the country and to the people. Members of the secret service must therefore prepare themselves for total sacrifice in order to maintain the purity of Juntong's "family tradition"[7]—just as the "revolutionary soldiers" of the Vigorous Practice Society would under the personal leadership of Chiang Kai-shek.

Dai Li had professed, of course, a complete personal loyalty to Chiang Kai-shek that surpassed all his other allegiances and commitments. He dramatized the utmost importance of his vertical loyalty to "the Leader" (*lingxiu*) Chiang Kai-shek.[8] This insistence permitted him to demand, paradoxically, just as much loyalty from his own subordinates. The task of the Juntong, according to Dai Li, was to be Chiang's "eyes, ears, arms and legs." Members of the bureau must deny themselves a mind of their own. They were to serve the Leader "like dogs and horses" in response to the needs of their masters.[9]

This insistence upon a vertical line of allegiance between superiors and subordinates meant that, even within the brotherhood of Tewu chu, the formation of horizontal loyalty between comrades[10] was to be discouraged. Although familial filiality and fraternal righteousness do not necessarily lead to contradictory courses of action in a given context, the precise placement of the axis between vertical loyalty and horizontal ties and obligations carries significant implications with regard to the nature of an organization such as the Chinese secret service. Filial devotion, when pushed to the extreme, places absolute demands that lead to the total effacement of the self *vis-à-vis* the leadership and collectivity. Fraternal loyalty, on the other hand, permits the exercise of a certain discretion—and hence of autonomy. Although a sense of integrity does not always depend upon a prior element of self-determination, the nature of individual commitment to a course of action varies significantly whether one acts out of a sense of discretion and conviction or out of a sense of duty and obligation. The relationship between the self and the collectivity is quite different, furthermore, when individuals are permitted or forbidden to pursue matters upon their own judgment beyond the boundaries prescribed by the leadership. The potential paradoxes and ambiguities in the ideas held by Dai Li and his men, then, seemed endless.

Dai Li's pronouncements were intended as declarations of general principles as well as expedient responses to circumstances. Although many were straightforward injunctions (e.g. "Our comrades must work hard and endure hardship"), others were invocations of historical parallels. There was a certain coherence in the various slogans, speeches, rituals, and gestures employed by Dai Li, which was highly suggestive of the bureau's operating mentality.[11] But the habit of thinking and talking in terms of historical parallels introduced yet another dimension of complexity. Historical episodes, embedded as they were in specific narrative contexts, were often the vectors of a multiplicity of meaning. The meaning of these episodes, when invoked in response to a present-day condition, was far from fixed and stable. More often than not, Dai Li's resort to historical parallels thus left his men uncertain about his ultimate intent.

It was only with nearly complete self-effacement (at times even self-debasement) that Dai Li succeeded in earning the total trust of Chiang Kai-shek. Chiang had insisted that his followers must be content with their lot as "anonymous heroes"[12] of the revolutionary cause. This self-effacement, to the point of a total loss of the self, paradoxically opened up for Dai an avenue to self-aggrandizement through the sharing of secret power. The costs—and compensations—of this problematical sublimation were considerable. But the ambiguities intrinsic to the conflict between the principles of a sworn brotherhood and those of a patriarchal lineage, between horizontal righteousness and vertical loyalty, produced a problem of a different order.

In sum, Dai Li's ability to exploit areas of ambiguity was remarkable. He was the bureau's principal arbitrator of meaning; his interpretation had literal life-and-death significance to followers of his household rules. But within the realm of the brotherhood itself there were definite limits to the scope of his symbolic manipulation. For the symbols to retain their compelling force, it must never appear that Dai Li had perverted their substance in reality, or that he had betrayed righteousness for expediency. That is why the mysterious Liu Geqing affair, with its dramatization of epic heroism on the one hand and of double and triple treachery on the other, posed such a crucial challenge to Dai Li's ability to negotiate the meaning of his men's action.

THE LIU GEQING AFFAIR, SHANGHAI, 1939

Liu Geqing, one of the most accomplished assassins of Juntong, gained wide recognition as a hero in the killing of Chen Lu, a collaborator, in Shanghai in the winter of 1939. Although the death of Chen Lu was no trivial matter, the significance of the Liu Geqing affair lies not so much in the assassin's lauded deeds as in his unwavering loyalty to Dai Li.

The Liu Geqing affair took place at a time when Juntong's Shanghai station was nearly destroyed by its rivals and enemies, and the agents found their loyalty to their organization put to severe tests. Liu's immediate superior in Shanghai, station chief Wang Tianmu, had betrayed the organization and gone over to the enemy. In contrast to Wang, Liu proved with his deeds that his loyalty would never waver. In Juntong's official history, written at a later time, Liu Geqing thus emerges from the murky world of spies and counterspies as a true hero who recognized in Dai Li the legendary qualities of benevolence and righteousness. Liu's loyalty to Dai was that of a sworn brother and a subordinate in the time-honored manner of the knights errant. His style of conduct complemented that of his leader. In the bloody urban warfare that terrorized Shanghai in the late 1930s, the agents enacted the romantic tradition of chivalry and acted out the parts of leader, follower, rival, hero, and traitor through the medium of the historical romance.

Liu's recruitment

Liu Geqing was the son of an affluent overseas Chinese from Fujian and held a bachelor's degree from Jinan University in Shanghai. He met Dai Li by chance in the summer of 1935, and joined the bureau at the age of twenty-eight.[13] Liu's background was considered exceptional, because there were few college graduates in the secret service until the War of Resistance began.[14]

The majority of Juntong's secret service officers were products of a traditional education in the provinces—places that had been insulated from the urban-based intellectual ferment of the May Fourth Movement. Dai Li himself attended the Zhejiang Provincial First Normal School, which before

1919 offered a traditional literary curriculum. Other key figures of the secret service, from operations chiefs to middle-ranking officers, grew up with an education in the classics and dynastic histories. These men were immersed since childhood in a popular culture that glorified the assassins of the Warring States and the heroes of the Three Kingdoms.[15] Dai Jingyuan, a staff officer who went on an ill-fated mission to assassinate Wang Jingwei in Nanjing in 1940, was often seen drinking with friends and lamenting over China's chaotic state. He would cry out aloud: "Where are the Jing Kes and Nie Zhengs of our age, who will right wrongs and punish the shameless?"[16] After his capture by the Japanese military police in Shanghai in 1939, Yuan Liangchu, the liaison man from the bureau's Hong Kong station, penned these words in his detention cell: "The water of the empty River Yi flows on with lingering regrets."[17] Both phrases refer to heroic episodes of the Warring States period as recorded in the *Grand Historian's Record (Shiji)*.

In the context of dramatic changes in China's system of higher education in the twentieth century, these men of "middle peasant" provincial society were unable to compete successfully for admission to colleges and universities in Shanghai and Beijing, which stressed competence in English and mathematics. They were also profoundly suspicious of the westernized new elite of the May Fourth generation, who had given themselves to the rhetoric of cultural iconoclasm and social revolution. Like Dai Li, the officers of the military secret service inhabited a cultural universe of traditional heroic lore and historical allegories. They fashioned their own conduct, in turn, by the norms and rhetoric of this universe.

In his search for field agents, Dai Li looked for men schooled in traditional martial arts while possessing the kind of irreverent wit and personal valor as described in the chapters on knights errant in the *Grand Historian's Record* and other popular tales.[18] He invited to the bureau a kung fu master who was believed to be the real-life model for the hero of the *Jianghu qixia zhuan* (Legendary Roving Knights of the Rivers and Lakes), a Republican *wuxia* (martial valor and knight-errant) novel popular among the petty urbanites of the time[19]). The search for *jiang hu hao han* (true men of the rivers and lakes) led the Tewu chu to penetrate deep into the rough terrain of hill countries such as Shengxian in the central mountains of Zhejiang and Xiangfan along the upper reaches of the Han river for new recruits. These areas were noted for banditry and an uprooted peasantry in years of poor harvest. The popular lore of these regions was especially rich in tales of martial valor and the justice of the green woods.[20]

Dai Li recruited a core group of agents with this sort of provincial background and then methodically exploited their networks of relatives, classmates and native place associations for additional recruits. This recruitment strategy was practised especially in the prewar years before the establishment of Juntong's regular Training Class.[21] Because he relied heavily on these kinship and village ties, Dai Li built an organization strongly represented by men and women of three provinces: Zhejiang, Guangdong, and Hunan. These networks, however, eventually brought division into the secret service. When Dai Li died in an airplane crash in 1946, Juntong broke up along provincial cleavages into three contending factions over the question of Dai's successor.[22]

The bonds of personal loyalty and particularistic ties came under serious test once the War of Resistance broke out, and Dai Li's men found themselves fighting not only the Japanese but also their erstwhile Nationalist brethren under the command of the collaborator Wang Jingwei (1883–1944). Liu Geqing, whose background set him apart from a majority of his Juntong colleagues, was in many ways an outsider to the Juntong's inner core of networks and culture. A man of independent means, Liu was neither a former Whampoa cadet nor a fellow co-provincial. Precisely because his loyalty to Juntong was never the product of partisanship, his resolve to serve appeared all the more a result of genuine admiration for the sort of valor that Dai Li's leadership exemplified.

Liu Geqing in action

On February 18, 1939, Liu Geqing and a band of three men assassinated the Foreign Minister of the "reformed" puppet government of occupied China, Chen Lu. The day happened to be Chinese New Year's Eve. At the time of his death, Chen was at home in his mansion in the French Concession offering respects to the spirit of his ancestors. As the assassins opened fire, Chen Lu fell to the carpeted floor, killed by a spray of bullets. As a message of warning to other prospective collaborators, Liu Geqing left behind on the scene his "signature." It was a white scroll with characters written in black ink, declaring "Death to the collaborators! Long live Generalissimo Chiang Kai-shek!" Liu and his team fled the scene before the concession police responded to the summons of Chen Lu's family. The following day's pro-resistance newspapers in Shanghai headlined the assassination as yet another case in which the Nationalist government in Chongqing had punished Chinese collaborators. "A valiant man descended from the heavens last night," announced one paper in a pair of couplets reminiscent of chapter titles in old-fashioned popular novels. "The collaborator instantly entered his name in the roster of ghosts."[23]

Liu Geqing had acted on orders from Wang Tianmu, Juntong's station chief in Shanghai, who in turn reported to Dai Li in Chongqing.[24] To thwart Japanese attempts to reach partial peace settlements in China, Juntong had resorted to a method of systematic intimidation by the threat of assassination against prospective Chinese traitors. The assassination of Chen Lu, which came six months after the killing of another high-ranking collaborator in the sanctuary of his foreign concession home, was the second major case carried out under this policy. Six months earlier, in October 1938, Tang Shaoyi, a former ambassador and Cabinet Minister, was cut down in his own living room by an axe-wielding Juntong agent who had disguised himself as an antique dealer. The bureau, on that occasion, had received intelligence that Tang was the choice of Doihara Kenji, the Japanese army intelligence director, to head a puppet "central government" in occupied China. To nip the negotiations in the bud, the bureau eliminated Doihara's prospective candidate.[25]

Much of Juntong's visibility during this period came from its involvement with these assassinations. By one estimation, Dai Li's men, operating from the relative safety of the foreign concessions in Shanghai, carried out no fewer than 150 assassinations between August 1937 and October 1941, when the puppet secret service blew up the Shanghai station for the second time in two years. During the same time Juntong agents also attacked forty or more Japanese military officers and recorded more than fifty incidents of sabotage of enemy military installations, including airports and ammunition depots.[26] These deeds gave heart to Chongqing supporters in important ways. Pro-Chongqing newspapers reported every one of the incidents in lurid detail. Editorial comment hailed the assassins as modern day knights errant who had carried out justice with such daring ingenuity that they might have been aided by heaven.

The adversaries

The Japanese, in retaliation against Juntong attacks, resorted to the random execution of Shanghai civilians. Each Juntong attack would be followed promptly by Japanese killing of scores of innocent Chinese. These executions spread terror, but they were ineffective as a direct response to the Juntong challenge.

The assassination of Chen Lu drove home to the Japanese the necessity of creating a counter-operation of their own in order to assure the safety of prominent Chinese collaborators, to eliminate Chongqing agents in Shanghai, and to stifle anti-Japanese sentiment in the Chinese newspapers sheltered in the foreign concessions. The result was the creation of a Chinese-staffed puppet secret service known by its street number on the Jessfield Road as "No. 76," which was brought into being by the enterpreneurial Li Shiqun (1907–43).

The groundwork for this collaborative organ was laid in early February 1939, when Ding Mocun and Li Shiqun, both former agents of Zhongtong (Zhongguo Guomindang zhongyang weiyuan hui tongji diaocha ju) or the Bureau of Statistics and Investigation under the Central Committee of the Nationalist Party, presented themselves to Doihara Kenji in his "Little Tokyo" headquarters in Shanghai's Hongkou district.[27] Ding and Li offered their services to help "assemble a group of Nationalist comrades and to facilitate peace." The Japanese, for their part, were pleased to have acquired an instrument that would permit them to penetrate the seemingly impenetrable web of Chinese social networks—"the complicated Chinese social scene of personal relationships" that Chongqing agents had so masterfully manipulated in the past.[28]

Doihara's plan to support a puppet secret service was approved on February 10, 1939, by the army general staff in Tokyo. Li and Ding formally launched their operations, therefore, on March 1. Colonel Haruki Yoshitane was appointed as the liaison officer to represent the Plum Blossom Agency (Ume kikan), Colonel Kagesa Sadaaki's military intelligence unit that was responsible for the handling of Wang Jingwei's puppet government in Nanjing.[29] Ding and Li agreed that they would clear their operation details with the Japanese military police in advance. They also agreed to submit intelligence reports on a daily basis. In return, they were promised a regular supply of weapons, ammunition, and money. In early July the service set itself up in the mansion of the former Anhui warlord General Chen Diaoyuan in western Shanghai. Ding and Li built the mansion into an armed fortress with electrically charged iron gates and barricades of cement blocks. They also began to build up the capability of No. 76 for "action"—or kidnapping and assassination.

Ding Mocun and Li Shiqun were uniquely qualified for these tasks. Ding and Li were both Communist renegades in the late 1920s and Zhongtong agents in the 1930s. A major figure in the intelligence circles of the "CC clique"—the powerful political faction led by the brothers Chen Guofu and Chen Lifu who built their influence by controlling the Central Committee of the Nationalist Party—Ding was chief of the Third Section under the Military Affairs Council headed by Chiang Kai-shek in Wuhan in 1938, hence a colleague of Xu Enzeng, chief of the First Section, or Zhongtong, and of Dai Li, chief of the Second Section, or Juntong. In a reorganization of the intelligence apparatus of the Military Affairs Council in late 1938, Ding's Third Section was abolished, its function absorbed by Dai Li's Juntong. The reorganization most likely reflected the relative gain and loss of the Whampoa group in the power structure of Chongqing at the expense of the CC clique, which, in turn, may well have had something to do with Chiang Kai-shek's war policies against the Japanese. As a result of this reorganization, Ding Mocun was conveniently out of a job and disgruntled, hence available in the spring of 1939 to join Li Shiqun to collaborate with the Japanese in Shanghai.[30]

The actual "backstage boss" (*houtai laoban*) of No. 76 was Li Shiqun (1907–43), who had been active in the Shanghai–Nanjing area since the early 1930s and had gained entry to the Green Gang—Shanghai's opium and crime organization, led by Du Yuesheng—by becoming a disciple of one of the gang leaders, Ji Yunqing.[31] An enterprising man, Li Shiqun endeavored to build up an intelligence network for hire after his arrival in Shanghai in 1938. Initially a one-man spy operation, he bought information from his former colleagues in Zhongtong. Later he expanded his sources of information to include middle-ranking members of the Shanghai branch of the Nationalist Party plus followers of the local gangs. By the time Ding Mocun arrived, Li Shiqun had already assembled a core group of seven, most of them former Zhongtong and CC agents.[32] On May 8, 1939, Wang Jingwei arrived in Shanghai with his entourage. Li Shiqun enlisted the service of a gang of local thugs and bullies led by Wu Shibao, a Green Gang member, and asked these men to assure the personal safety of the Wang followers in Shanghai.[33] The group that Li Shiqun had assembled was thus drawn from social backgrounds remarkably similar to those of Dai Li's Juntong cadres. To announce the presence of No. 76 in the foreign concessions, Li Shiqun pursued a dual strategy. He would destroy Juntong organizations in the area and recruit some of the bureau's most seasoned operatives into his service. He would use a combination of inducement and coercion and exploit his knowledge of the Chongqing network to facilitate his goals.

In the summer and fall of 1939, Li Shiqun set to work. By September that year, he succeeded in bringing a critical number of Juntong agents under his command.[34] Li was so pleased with the results that in a visit to Tokyo later that year, he told his Japanese handlers that he had destroyed Juntong's functioning capability in the entire region of Jiangsu, Zhejiang, Anhui, Shanghai and Nanjing, and that he had either killed off or won over almost all of Dai Li's men in the field. Leading Juntong figures such as Lin Zhijiang (who assassinated Tang Shaoyi) and Wang Tianmu (the station chief of Shanghai) were now at Li Shiqun's beck and call. Li announced, with some exaggeration, that his No. 76 had triumphed not only over the Blue Shirts of Dai Li's Juntong but also the Zhongtong agents of the CC clique ("Zuo shou xiaomie Lanyi she, you shou dadao CC tuan").[35]

The defection of Wang Tianmu

Li Shiqun decisively attacked the Juntong field force in Shanghai in the late summer of 1939. Among his first targets was the bureau's station chief in Shanghai, Wang Tianmu. In broad daylight, Li Shiqun's men abducted Wang Tianmu on Nanjing Road, the busiest street of the international concessions. Wang Tianmu was taken to 76 Jessfield Road, confined but treated with courtesy for about three weeks, and then released.[36]

Shortly thereafter, however, Wang Tianmu found himself the target of an assassin's bullet fired by one of his own Juntong colleagues. Wang fortunately escaped with his life. He was embittered by the suspicion that the colleague had acted on the order of the "boss," Dai Li. His suspicion was encouraged by Chen Mingchu (Chen Dirong), another Juntong man, who showed him a telegram allegedly sent from Chongqing that ordered Wang's death.[37] Shaken and enraged, Wang Tianmu denounced Dai Li for breaching the bonds of benevolence and righteousness and declared himself a free agent from that point on.

Dai Li had been sedulously reminding his field agents of the obligation of benevolence and righteousness since March 1938, almost as soon as he sensed the rise of a rival spy master in the person of Li Shiqun.[38] Meanwhile he turned to a careful scrutiny of the conduct of his men, reviewing the slightest signs of wavering in the field and weighing the odds of slipping loyalty and imminent betrayal. Wang Tianmu's safe return from No. 76, a place referred to as "the gates of hell" by Chongqing agents, fatally compromised his credibility within Juntong and engendered strong suspicions about his loyalty.[39]

This was precisely what Li Shiqun had been hoping for. He had carefully engineered a situation that called to mind an episode in the *Romance of the Three Kingdoms*, creating conditions in which Dai Li was forced to choose between two courses of action.[40] In a famous chapter familiar to both men, General Guan Yu (d. AD 219), a sworn brother of Liu Bei (d. AD 223) and a hero famed for his valor and courage, fell into the hands of Liu Bei's enemy, Cao Cao (d. AD 220), the ambitious Prime Minister to the last emperor of the Han Dynasty. Cao Cao accorded Guan Yu great respect and much generosity. Guan Yu, however, was willing to serve Cao Cao only on a temporary basis. "His person was in the Cao camp; his heart was with the Han cause." When Guan Yu finally got word of the whereabouts of Liu Bei, he fought his way out of the Cao territories to rejoin his former lord and sworn brother, leaving behind all the gifts that Cao had showered upon him. Guan Yu was thus exemplary in his loyalty and righteousness and in his disregard for personal comfort and advancement.[41] Yet he was none the less tainted by the time he had spent in Cao Cao's company. There were residual doubts in the minds of his other sworn brothers about his ultimate loyalty. Guan Yu managed to prove himself again only after shedding, in the presence of the latter, the blood of Cao Cao's men who had come in pursuit of him.[42]

In the eyes of Dai Li's agents, Wang Tianmu's interlude in No. 76 was comparable to Guan Yu's service in Cao Cao's camp. To prove himself, Wang Tianmu would have to take the life of Wang Jingwei, the arch-collaborator with the enemy. But Wang Jingwei lived amid such tight security that the would-be assassin faced a daunting task. As Wang Tianmu's lack of success was only to be expected, it could not be viewed as a definitive proof of his infidelity.

In the world of romantic heroism, meanwhile, the lord must not even betray suspicion of his men's wavering, since the mere intimation of this lack of trust represents an insult to the integrity of the fraternal bond that alone makes the lord a deserving leader. In the *Romance of the Three Kingdoms* it was General Zhang Fei, a colleague and an equal, and not Liu Bei, the lord and leader, who demanded, indeed, Guan Yu's proof of loyalty. For Dai Li to call the integrity of the returned Wang into question, therefore, would be to cast the leader as a "mean person"—an undeserving recipient of the loyalty and gallantry of valiant and righteous followers. Yet to continue treating the presumably righteous with unattenuated trust, like a noble lord of the Warring States or Three Kingdoms period, posed a considerable risk for a twentieth-century secret service chief who knew only too well the permeability of personal networks of loyalty in an age far removed from antiquity.

Significantly, the official biography of Dai Li that was later prepared by the Bureau of Intelligence in Taiwan makes no mention of this episode.[43]

Had Dai Li ordered the death of Wang Tianmu, it would have diminished his stature as a righteous and benevolent leader of his men. Wang's colleagues at the time, however, suspected that Dai had given such an order. Wang, in this sense, was first betrayed by his chief. His fellow Juntong agents were consequently willing to accept Wang's open defection to the other side,[44] and Wang Tianmu certainly excused his own defection in just such terms.

Dai Li acted as if he had been keeping a meticulously balanced account of the loyalty and betrayal that he owed his men. The tallies on this balance sheet were reflected in his differential treatment of two traitors, Wang Tianmu and Chen Mingchu, who defected to the Japanese-sponsored secret service at about the same time. Unlike Wang Tianmu, Chen Mingchu had simply made up his mind to join the collaborators. It was probably Chen who later double-crossed Liu Geqing and delivered him into the hands of the puppet secret service.[45]

Dai Li unequivocally ordered Chen Mingchu's death. On Christmas Eve 1939 three Juntong agents accosted Chen in the Huierdeng night club near Zhaofeng Park in western Shanghai. They opened fire into a large crowd of Wang Jingwei's major supporters, who had gathered to spend Christmas Eve in the bars, casinos and dance halls of the club under the protection of some twenty guards of their own. Chen Mingchu was killed on the spot. The assailants escaped in the chaos that ensued, speeding away in a waiting car.

Whether Wang Tianmu was also intended as a victim was not clear; he happened to be away from the dance floor when the agents opened fire. But the collaborators obviously viewed him as not altogether above suspicion. He was immediately taken into No. 76 a second time and interrogated at length, but was soon released to assume his duties under Li Shiqun.[46] Meanwhile, as retaliation for the death of Chen Mingchu, three Juntong agents who had been captured by No. 76 earlier were taken out of their cells of confinement and executed in the puppet agency's courtyard on Christmas Day 1939.[47]

The killing of Chen Mingchu in the night club was not uncharacteristic of Dai Li's treatment of his former agents in 1939 and 1940. As Li Shiqun plotted to induce the defection of important Juntong figures, Dai Li stepped up his "punishment" of collaborators. Such killings provoked retaliation, and the gang war between the two secret services soon escalated into a full-scale urban warfare in the city.

In fall 1939, Li Shiqun claimed victory by blowing open Juntong's Shanghai station. Juntong, for its part, claimed the lives of no less than a dozen key figures in the puppet secret service.[48] Li Shiqun's men subsequently targeted notable civilian figures who were loyal to Chiang Kai-shek and active in anti-Japanese resistance. Pro-Chongqing newspaper editors and reporters in Shanghai became prime targets of attack. These men were soon forced to protect themselves by working behind closed gates and barred windows to avoid drive-by terrorist attacks. Chongqing-affiliated banking institutions received mail bombs and hand grenades.[49]

Rumors were rife that the puppet secret service kept a hit list with the names of more than 100 Shanghai educators, writers, publishers, journalists, financiers, industrialists, and jurists on it. Many prominent civilian leaders, including Dr Liu Zhan'en, president of the Baptist Shanghai College, were ambushed and gunned down on Shanghai streets during this time.[50]

Although the vendetta being waged in the streets of Shanghai gave the appearance of Juntong heroism against Japanese collaborators, in city after city behind enemy lines the bureau suffered the most serious setbacks that it had experienced since the outbreak of the war in 1937.[51] The defectors from the Shanghai station gave the Japanese military police the personnel rosters, addresses, and organization charts of all Juntong units in the area. Japanese military police, along with detectives from the International Settlement and the French Concession, raided thirteen bureau offices and safe houses. Moreover, because Chen Mingchu, the defected Shanghai agent, had formerly served as a personnel officer in the bureau's Nanjing station, Chen was able to brief the Japanese extensively on that operation. On August 12, 1939, the chief of the Anqing station, Cai Shenchu, was captured and tortured in Nanjing. On August 19 the bureau's Nanjing offices and safe houses were raided. Nanjing's deputy station chief, Tan Wenzhi, agreed to cooperate with the enemy. On September 11 the bureau's secret radio station in Nanjing fell into enemy hands.

Wang Tianmu's former contacts in the Beiping and Tianjin area, meanwhile, provided information to the Japanese that led to raids and arrests by the Japanese military police in north China. On September 27 the twenty-seven-year-old chief of the bureau's Tianjin region, Zeng Che, was identified and captured on the streets of Tianjin. The next morning the Japanese military police, assisted by the police forces of the English and French concessions, raided the bureau's offices and safe houses and captured, among others, the forty-one-year-old chief of the Tianjin station, Chen Ziyi. Zeng and Chen were both subsequently executed.

Wang Tianmu's defection in Shanghai encouraged the head of the bureau's action unit in Qingdao, Zhao Gangyi, to follow suit. Zhao and Wang had previously coordinated their moves, in fact, in Shanghai, when Zhao travelled there on bureau business. On November 15 Zhao Gangyi led the Japanese military police on raids and arrests in Qingdao. The acting station chief of the bureau in Qingdao handed over to the Japanese personnel rosters, addresses, and radio stations. On November 24, 1939, the bureau's regional office and ratio stations in Beiping fell. On September 8, 1940, deputy regional chief, Zhou Guangshi, was captured and executed.[52]

With information extracted from captured Juntong agents in the Beiping regional office, the Japanese military police methodically carried out raids and arrests in Zhangjiakou (Kalgan), Chahar, Suiyuan, Datong, Inner Mongolia and Taiyuan, imprisoning Nationalist informants, activists and guerrilla leaders, and blowing up radio stations.[53] By the outbreak of the Pacific war, the snowball effect of the Wang Tianmu defection that had begun with mutual distrust between Wang and Dai Li had cost Juntong almost its entire operation behind enemy lines.

The language and drama of righteousness

During this period, Liu Geqing found himself in the hands of Li Shiqun at his fortress headquarters at 76 Jessfield Road. Li Shiqun treated Liu Geqing with respect and hospitality, as he had Wang Tianmu. On the evening that Liu was captured he was permitted to contact his comrades. Li Shiqun also allowed Liu Geqing's woman friend, Lu Ti, who had served as his courier and cared for his needs in the past, to accompany Liu in confinement. Li Shiqun "put on the disguise" of a *junzi*, "a gentleman" of honor and principle, and "acted as if he knew how to treat a hero and a true man with generosity," according to Dai Li's official biographer.[54] He promised, furthermore, that Liu could receive visitors, who would be able to come and go of their free will. Two of Liu's friends—Bao Tianqing, a personal acquaintance, and Zhu Shanyuan, a bureau colleague—visited Liu Geqing in 76 Jessfield Road as soon as they were summoned. "Such unflinching loyalty to a comrade who had fallen into difficulty couldn't help but win the admiration even of someone like Li Shiqun," wrote Dai Li.[55] Liu Geqing asked Zhu Shanyuan to carry a note to Dai Li, in which he pledged not to trade his fealty to his chief for personal safety under any conditions.[56] On January 10, 1940, Dai Li ordered that this note be used as an exemplary text in Juntong's various training units. He called Liu's steady refusal to collaborate and Zhu Shanyuan's ready response to a comrade's summons to meet in a place of utmost danger "the valiant deeds of our collectivity, of which we are all proud." Such a fearless display of righteousness as loyalty both to the bureau and to a colleague, Dai Li commented, moved even the heart of the treacherous Li Shiqun.[57]

Dai Li especially appreciated Liu Geqing's gestures of loyalty at this juncture because they came in the wake of the defection of Wang Tianmu. Wang Tianmu was, after all, one of the original members of the "League of Ten." Wang's two daughters were once intimate with Dai Li's only son, and there were even expectations that the two families might be united by marriage.[58] In addition to the nearly complete destruction of Juntong's underground operations behind enemy lines, therefore, Wang's defection, according to his successor to the Shanghai station, shattered the mutual trust that bureau colleagues placed in one another.[59] Because the bureau was shaken by the desertion of Wang, an insider, it welcomed the timely pledges of unwavering loyalty from Liu Geqing, a man who had so recently joined the service out of personal admiration for the chief.

Some Juntong observers, however, refused to attribute the bureau's disastrous setback in underground warfare to the defection of one single disgruntled veteran. To a seasoned agent such as Chen Gongshu, the new station chief of Shanghai and Juntong's Jiangsu regional military liaison officer, there seemed sufficient clues pointing to the existence of a deeper mystery lying beneath what met the eye. "Although only two or three individuals had defected," Chen later recalled, "this betrayal was absolutely unprecedented. We faced a most intricate and puzzling situation. . . . Could this possibly be a planned scheme of 'major circuity' of counter-intelligence aiming at the distant future, with Tianmu being asked to play a big part in this tragedy?"[60] Was Dai Li, then, knowingly involved in an operation in which he shed the blood of his own men? Did he shield his true intentions from even his high-ranking officers? Was he capable of such heartless calculation and deception despite his rhetoric of benevolence and righteousness?

In so far as Li Shiqun treated Wang Tianmu and Liu Geqing as honorable "guests" and demonstrated his capacity to appreciate true men of courage, Li had cast himself as a righteous and benevolent leader worthy of the loyalty and devotion of true heroes. That role, first played by Cao Cao in his treatment of Guan Yu in *Romance of the Three Kingdoms*, not only dictated that Li Shiqun treat Liu Geqing with initial generosity; it ultimately mandated Liu Geqing's successful "escape" or perhaps release from a Nanjing prison after nearly six months of detention in 76 Jessfield Road.[61]

Early in 1940, Liu Geqing made his way back to Chongqing. Dai Li gave him a hero's welcome. There were formal banquets at the headquarters in his honor.[62] There were in-house poems that compared Liu's deeds to those of the ill-fated Jing Ke. Liu's safe return with his female friend called to mind yet another Warring States historical episode: the retirement of Fan Li, the great Minister of Wu, accompanied by Xi Shi, the most famous beauty of her time. A poem that paired Liu's return with Fan's retirement went like this: "With a dagger he stabbed the collaborator; the song of the Yi River is once more heard. The hero has returned, bringing with him his beautiful Xi Shi, who will follow him to the leisure and tranquillity of life on the five lakes.[63]

While Dai Li acted as if he had no doubts at all of Liu Geqing's true loyalty, Liu Gequing acted as if there were no bounds to the chief's capacity to trust. Liu requested that he be permitted to send a letter to his chief's enemy, Li Shiqun, and Dai Li generously consented. In his letter Liu Geqing referred to Li Shiqun as "a friend who has shown me true appreciation," and expressed the hope that the two men might meet again as true brothers were destined to do. Dai Li smiled on the missive, and since all correspondence between Chongqing and the Japanese-occupied territories was banned by his office, the chief of Juntong even arranged for Liu's letter to the puppet spymaster to be taken to Hong Kong to be posted.[64]

CONCLUSION

The patriarchal leader took a considerable chance when he tolerated obligations stemming from horizontal ties that posed a threat to the demands of vertical loyalty. In the *Romance of the Three Kingdoms* General Guan Yu ultimately failed to carry out his important assignment to capture the defeated Cao Cao because of residual regard for the arch-enemy of his lord.[65] Dai Li could not none the less lightly dismiss the weight of the language of righteousness and benevolence. He had built an organization with men drawn from social strata immersed in the cultural milieu of the heroic drama. The norms that prevailed in the fictional universe were also those governing real-life choices. Thus Dai Li, who had tapped the symbolic resource of the language of righteousness and benevolence in the first place, was compelled to see the reenactment of the historical drama through to the end.

Dai Li prominently advertised the Liu Geqing affair in order to demonstrate how fully he was able to play the historical role of the righteous and benevolent leader worthy of the loyalty of true men. Only a genuinely deserving leader could possibly be generous enough to accommodate his follower's flamboyant and uncompromising duty to a friend who happened to be his own arch-enemy. In the time-honored tradition of the elect brethren of the "rivers and lakes," Dai Li refused to allow his jealousy for Liu Geqing's undivided loyalty to himself and to his organization to interfere with Liu Geqing's obligations as a righteous man to his own friends. Such a gesture was also needed as an expression of confidence, for only by making it was Dai Li able to convey the impression that the vertical bond of filiality within the bureau had survived the defection of Wang Tianmu.

The human cost sustained by members of Juntong in underground activity in occupied China was great, with many lives lost through blunders, failures, betrayals and miscalculations. Whether by choice, many were martyred; others faced torture and imprisonment. Qiao Jiacai, who had served successively as the bureau's station chief in Beijing, as inspector of northern Chinese stations, and as inspector of internal discipline in Chongqing, returned home to Hebei in late fall 1939 to find his wife with a deep scar on her throat as a result of an attempt to hang herself. She was losing her mental faculties and failed to recognize him. This was the result of days of torture and interrogation by Japanese military police, who had suspected Qiao's identity.[66] Chen Gongshu, Wang Tianmu's successor as the chief of Juntong's Shanghai station, was captured by the puppet secret service in October 1941. Forty years later he wondered how he had survived the war. "To this day my heart beat quickens whenever there is a knock on the door; my muscles convulse whenever the phone rings."[67]

Dai Li told his men that their collective history was written with the blood, sweat, and tears of their comrades. When death seemed near, it was important for his men to believe in, and understand in their own language, the cause for which they were asked to give their life. He meant the pseudo-familial qualities and expectations of the bureau, expressed in the language of righteousness and benevolence, to meet certain important ethical obligations of his agents. Dai Li paid for the funeral expenses of Juntong agents' parents, cared for their widowed and orphaned, and sent their young ones to school. The benevolent bureau that he had created was intended as an organ that recognized the blood, sweat, and tears shed by the individual comrades and responded with a humane heart.

But the heroic image that Dai Li paired with this paternalistic collectivity was not so much the romantic ideal of the knight errant as that of the anonymous hero, a theme that enhanced the vertical rather than the horizontal chains of obligations between individuals. The anonymous hero upheld "the purity and integrity of our family tradition," and was committed to "the ideal of the Nationalist revolution," rather than the "pursuit of [individual] fame and gain." In Dai Li's view Juntong could lay claim to a special ancestry: "We will carry on the unfinished tasks of Dr Sun Yat-sen and the revolutionary martyrs." To fulfill that legacy he solemnly resolved with his men "to banish all thoughts of the self from our mind . . . [and] to be the anonymous hero."[68]

"It is an ancient saying that for every commanding officer who returns in triumph, there must be tens of thousands of soldiers reduced to ashes," Dai Li told his men.

The few moments of glory in history are attained by the sacrifices of tens of thousands of anonymous heroes. . . . Historical memories highlight glory and achievement. These deeds are written in black ink on white paper. . . . The place for you and me in history is the invisible background to those prominent deeds. We prepare the ground for the achievements of others. We are the anonymous heroes.[69]

Anonymous heroes, Dai Li continued, were always ready to make sacrifices. They were models of patience, perseverance, persistence and absolute silence.[70] They were the instrument and tool of the Leader, the one individual who accomplished great deeds and achieved historical immortality.[71] The stone tablet that Dai Li erected on the slope behind the bureau's headquarters in Chongqing, dedicated to the "anonymous hero," was smooth on both sides, without a single inscription. The monument thereby summed up one of the central paradoxes in the ethos of Dai Li's organization: a certain claim to the individual's sense of historical ancestry, continuity and immortality through the particularistic ties of the family, yet it was altogether abstract and depersonalized; it demanded heroic stature and personal sacrifices, yet was totally devoid of the autonomy and valor associated with heroes of a free-roaming age of the past.

In so far as Dai Li demanded that individuals surrender their discretion and hence their moral autonomy, the notion of the anonymous hero suited the organizational requirements of a secret service meant only to serve as an instrument of the Leader's ends. However, it clashed with the ideal of the classical knight errant of the historical romance that Dai Li's own field agents preferred. Because the core of the brotherhood persisted within the secret service even after Juntong became a formalized intelligence organization, Dai Li tried to use that appeal to his followers as well. In celebrating both the romantic and the anonymous hero, however, Dai Li subverted the purpose of each and both. Because he was trying to make the best of both sets of symbols, he enjoyed a certain freedom of manipulation. Even though he had to yield at times to the powerful imperatives of these cultural symbols, it was in his own interest to exploit their ambiguities and paradoxes whenever possible. His followers recognized his duplicity. Despite their ardent avowals of belief in the chief's principled humaneness, they also speculated endlessly about his true capacity for the contrary.

Dai Li was no Himmler of China; his symbolic repertoire was molded in a different cultural milieu. But neither was he the benevolent and righteous Confucian leader that his admirers later sought to portray. Dai Li stayed in control by exploiting the tension at the center of the paradox he professed to respect. The heart of his particular darkness was a world of ultimate ambivalence, a world in which terrifying possibilities existed, including torture and betrayal. Dai Li's men later glorified that world by depicting a domain of romantic heroes; they projected themselves into it as the knights errant of the modern age, fighting to protect China from the Japanese. And to demonstrate their filial bond to the idealized memory of their chief, they depicted Dai Li as a *paterfamilias*. Both attempts landed the hagiographers in the realm of fiction, their efforts subverted by the moral ambiguity that was the key to Dai Li's manipulation and control.

This chapter is a revised version of an earlier piece published as "Dai Li and the Liu Geqing Affair: Heroism in the Chinese Secret Service during the War of Resistance," *Journal of Asian Studies* 48, 3 (August 1989), pp. 545–62.

NOTES

1   Guofang Bu Qingbao Ju, ed., *Dai Yunong xiansheng quanji* [The complete works of Mr Dai Yunong], 2 vols, Taibei: Guofang Bu Qingbao Ju, 1979, I, p. 316. (Hereafter, *DYNQJ*.)
2   Ibid. XXI, pp. 316, 349.
3   Wei Daming, "Pingshu Dai Yunong xiansheng de shigong" [Dai Li's career and accomplishment: comments and accounts], *Zhuanji wenxue* 38, 1 and 2 (1981), pp. 40–5, at No. 2, p. 41; Liu P., *Fusheng lueying ji* [Fleeting images from a floating life], Taibei: Zhengzhong shuju, 1968, pp. 58–9; *DYNQJ* I, pp. 314–23.
4   Zhongguo Guomindang Zhongyang Weiyuan Hui Dangshi Weiyuan Hui, ed., *Xian zongtong Jianggong sixiang yanlun zongji* [Complete collection of the ideas, speeches, and writings of the late President Chiang Kai-shek], Taibei: Zhongguo Guomindang Zhongyang Weiyuan Hui Dangshi Weiyuanhui, 1984, I, p. 10. (Hereafter *JGZJ*.)
5   *DYNQJ* I, pp. 46–8; Wen Qiang, "Dai Li qiren" [Dai Li the man], in Shen Zui and Wen Qiang (eds), *Dai Li qiren* [Dai Li the man], Beijing: Wenshi ziliao chubanshe, 1980, pp. 196–7.
6   *DYNQJ* I, pp. 265–6, 311–12, 319–20; Zhang Jungu, 'Dai Li de gushi' [The story of Dai Li], *Zhuanji wenxue* 14, I, pp. 8–19.
7   *DYNQJ* I, pp. 397–405; *JGZI* XI, p. 336.
8   Wei, "Pingshu Dai Yunong," pp. 43–4.
9   *DYNQJ* I, pp. 262, 367–8, 382–3, 398–9; Shen and Wen, *Dai Li qiren*, pp. 58–9, 149.
10 Liu, *Fusheng lueying ji*, pp. 53–4.
11 J. J. Linz, "An Authoritarian Regime: Spain," in Eric Allard and Stein Rokkan,

eds, *Mass Politics: Studies in Political Sociology*, New York: Free Press, 1987, pp. 281–3.

12 Deng Wenyi, *Sanmin zhuyi lixing she shi* [History of the Vigorous Practice Society of the Three Principles of the People], Taibei: Shijian chubanshe, 1984, p. 117.

13 Qiao Jiacai, *Dai Li jiangjun he ta de tongzhi* [General Dai Li and his comrades], 2 vols, Taibei: Zhongwai tushu chubanshe, 1981, I, pp. 2–5.

14 *DYNQJ* I, p. 22.

15 Deng, *Sanmin zhuyi lixing she shi*, pp. 61–71.

16 *DYNQJ* I, p. 117.

17 Ibid. I, p. 107.

18 Wei, "Pingshu Dai Yunong," p. 42; Shen Zui, "Wo suo zhidao de Dai Li" [The Dai Li that I know] in Shen Zui and Wen Qiang, eds, *Dai Li qiren*, Beijing: Wenshi ziliao chubanshe, 1980, p. 78; Guofang bu qingbao ju, ed., *Zhongmei hezuo suo zhi* [History of Sino-American cooperative organization], Taibei: Guofang bu qingbao ju, 1970, pp. 15, 46, 56–60.

19 Shen, "Wo suo zhidao de Dai Li," pp. 132–3; Pingjiang buxiao sheng, *Jianghu qixia zhuan* [Legendary roving knights of the rivers and lakes], Shanghai: Shanghai shuju, 1923; P. Link, *Mandarin Ducks and Butterflies: Popular Fiction in Early Twentieth Century Chinese Cities*, Berkeley and Los Angeles: University of California Press, 1981, p. 22.

20 Wei, "Pingshu Dai Yunong," pp. 41–2.

21 Shen, "Wo suo zhidao de Dai Li," p. 87.

22 Wei, "Pingshu Dai Yunong" 2, pp. 48–9; *DYNQJ* I, p. 8; Shen and Wen, *Dai Li qiren*, p. 6; Wen, "Dai Li qiren," pp. 173–4.

23 Qiao, *Dai Li jiangjun he ta de tongzhi* I, pp. 11–12.

24 Ibid, pp. 14–17.

25 Masui Y., *Kankan saiban shi* [History of the trial of Chinese collaborators], Tokyo: Misuzu Shobo, 1977, p. 198; Jin Xiongbai, *Wang zhengquan shimo ji* [Wang Jingwei regime from start to finish], 2 vols., Hong Kong: Chunqiu zazhi she, 1965, I, p. 62; Huang M. and Zhang Y., eds, *Wang Jingwei guomin zhengfu chengli* [The founding of Wang Jingwei's Nationalist government], 2 vols, Shanghai: Renmin chubanshe, 1984, I, p. 297.

26 Chen G, *Beiguo chujian: Yingxiong wuming diyibu* [Weeding the evil in the north: Anonymous hero, part 1], Taibei: Zhuanji wenxue chubanshe, 1981, p. 10; Huang and Zhang, *Wang Jingwei guomin* I, p. 297.

27 Huang and Zhang, *Wang Jingwei* I, pp. 259–62, 267, 293.

28 Masui, *Kankan saiban shi*, p. 198; Huang and Zhang, *Wang Jingwei guomin* I, p. 298; Haruke Yoshitane, "Wo suo zhidao de qishiliu hao," [No. 76 as I knew it], *Shulin* 4, pp. 45–8.

29 J. H. Boyle, *China and Japan at War, 1937–1945: The Politics of Collaboration*, Stanford: Stanford University Press, 1972, pp. 238–9.

30 Huang and Zhang *Wang Jingwei guomin* I, pp. 266–7.

31 On the Green Gang and the career of Du Yusheng, see Brian G. Martin, *The Shanghai Green Gang: Politics and Organized Crime, 1919–1937*, Berkeley: University of California Press, 1996.

32 Huang and Zhang, *Wang Jingwei guomin* I, pp. 262–8, 281.

33 Ibid., pp. 272, 276a.

34 Ibid., p. 299.

35 Ibid., pp. 286, 279–80, 294.

36 Haruke, "Wo suo zhidao de qishiliu hao," pp. 47–8.

37 Qiao, *Dai Li jiangjun he ta de tongzhi* I, pp. 11–12.

38 *DYNQJ* I, pp. 551–2; Qiao, *Dai Li jiangjun he ta de tongzhe* I, pp. 17–18.

39 *DYNQJ* I, p. 114.

40   Haruke, "Wo suo zhidao de qishiliu hao," p. 48.
41   Luo Guanzhong, *Sanguo yanyi* [A romance of the Three Kingdoms], Hong Kong: Zhonghua shuju, 1970, pp. 200–3, 210–13.
42   Ibid., pp. 225–7.
43   *DYNQJ* I, p. 112.
44   Qiao, *Dai Li jiangjun he ta de tongzhi* I, pp. 17–19.
45   Ibid., pp. 25–6; *DYNQJ*, p. 114.
46   *DYNQJ* I, pp. 113, 116; Jin, *Wang zhengquan shimo ji*, I, p. 66; Chen, *Beiguo chujian*, pp. 134–6; Qiao, *Dai Li jiangjun he ta de tongzhe* I, pp. 28–9; Zheng J., ed., *Wangni tegong zongbu neimu* [Inside the headquarters of the secret service of Wang Jingwei], Guilin: Guofang shudian, n.d., pp. 12–13; Huang and Zhang, *Wang Jingwei guomin* I, p. 287.
47   Chen, *Beiguo chujian*, pp. 262–3.
48   Jin, *Wang zhengquan shimo ji* I, p. 64.
49   See Chapter 1 in this volume for a discussion of the incidents in the residential quarters of the Bank of China and the Jiangsu Provincial Bank in March 1941.
50   Jin, *Wang zhengquan shimo ji* I, pp. 66–80; Huang and Zhang, *Wang Jingwei guomin* I, p. 294.
51   *DYNQJ* I, pp. 105–6.
52   *DYNQJ* I, pp. 106–9; Chen Gongshu, *Shanghai kangri dihou xingdong* [Fighting the Japanese behind enemy lines in Shanghai], Taibei: Zhengzhong shuju (1984), p. 127; Qiao, *Dai Li jiangjun he ta de tongzhi* I, p. 103.
53   Qiao, *Dai Li jiangjun he ta de tongzhi* I, pp. 95–7, 103–4, 107–8.
54   *DYNQJ* I, p. 114.
55   Ibid., I, p. 502.
56   Qiao, *Dai Li jiangjun he ta de tongzhi* I, pp. 23–4.
57   *DYNQJ* I, p. 502.
58   Chen, *Shanghai kangri*, p. 6.
59   Ibid., p. 8.
60   Ibid., pp. 9–10.
61   Qiao, *Dai Li jiangjun he ta de tongzhi* I, pp. 31–4.
62   Ibid., p. 1.
63   Ibid., p. 35.
64   Ibid., p. 34.
65   Luo, *Sanguo yanyi*, pp. 400–1.
66   Qiao Jiacai, *Haoran ji* [The brave and the imperishable], Taibei: Zhongwai tushu chubanshe (1981), III, pp. 129–30, 135–7.
67   Chen, *Beiguo chujian* I, p. 22.
68   *DYNQJ* I, pp. 409–10.
69   Ibid., I, pp. 409–10.
70   Ibid., I, p. 401.
71   Ibid., I, p. 399.

8   Urban controls in wartime Shanghai

Frederic Wakeman, Jr.

During early Nationalist rule, the Shanghai Public Security Bureau became a test case for the new regime's ability to rule effectively while modernizing the municipal administration and seeking to regain sovereign rights over the foreign concessions.[1] Although the Nationalists succeeded in suppressing the Communist movement in Shanghai, they had failed in both latter respects by the time they were driven out of the city by the Japanese in August 1937.[2] The puppet regime of Wang Jingwei ostensibly recovered national sovereignty over the entire city, but the price was rampant corruption and degrading collaboration under the *de facto* occupation of the Japanese.[3] Paradoxically, however, the period of puppet administration after Japanese military forces seized the International Settlement on December 8, 1941, saw a tightening of Chinese police control over the urban population while the Communist Party was simultaneously discovering fresh opportunities to expand its underground activities within the city.[4] In this chapter I would like to show how new urban control mechanisms were crafted in Shanghai under the various puppet regimes and Japanese occupation forces between 1937 and 1945. These mechanisms were bequeathed, so to speak, to the Nationalists, who assumed rule over a city now entirely theirs in 1945, and to the Communists, who won Shanghai in 1949 after the Nationalists fled.[5]

BOOM AND BUST

Shanghai was the first of the world's metropolises to suffer the destruction of World War II. During the battle of Shanghai (August–November 1937), 900 mills, workshops, and factories were consumed, destroying 70 percent of the city's industrial potential and throwing 600,000 people out of work.[6] Refugees poured into the ten square miles of the French Concession and the International Settlement, swelling the population from 1.5 million to 4 million and increasing the size of the average household to thirty-one people. Many sought shelter in the makeshift 175 refugee camps thrown up by the city's various political authorities and charities, but tens of thousands of homeless still clogged the streets, sleeping in office corridors, temples, and guild halls. With winter came starvation and exposure; by the end of the year more than 100,000 corpses had been picked up in the streets or among the ruins.[7]

Yet, incredibly enough, the "solitary island" (*gudao*) of Shanghai began to enjoy an economic boom.[8] Textile mills inside the International Settlement resumed operation under British and American names and seven new plants were constructed.[9] Four hundred small enterprises sprang up in the International Settlement, manufacturing industrial chemicals, medicines, lamp bulbs, thermos bottles, electric fans, and cigarettes. The American-controlled Shanghai Power Company spent US$2 million on new equipment. Shipping and insurance increased as well.[10]

Part of this boom was stimulated by the increased demand of the immigrant population, including European refugees fleeing fascism. Another source of growing demand was an annual trade of US$120 million through Japanese lines with "Free China" in the hinterland.[11] The export trade also improved, owing to the fifty German firms that shipped Shanghai goods to feed, clothe, and shoe the wartime populace of the Third Reich.[12]

As the economy boomed, the contrast between wealthy war profiteers and homeless refugees was glaring. The two classes kept their distance:

> Neither interfered with the other, since the poor begged only in the major thoroughfares and bustling marketplaces and stayed away from the quiet residential areas of the rich. They asked for money only from those on foot, unable to catch up with the rich in their sleek cars. [But social disorder flourished and]: Slums gradually spread like ringworm over the face of the city. Political terrorist incidents occurred nearly every day.[13]

In other words, the initial prosperity of 1938 that generated this profound social stratification in Shanghai also fostered general urban disorder that required heightened measures of control. This was all the more the case as the wind went out of the city's economic sails when the initial boom sagged.[14]

The prosperity of the refugee-driven economy of 1937–8 began to slump by the fall of 1939, when the Japanese commenced closing the Yangzi river to commercial traffic, cutting Shanghai off from its hinterland. Commodity prices soared. Public workers went on strike. Copper and nickel coins were confiscated and postage stamps were used for currency. After the 1940 New Year celebrations the Shanghai stock market went out of control. Speculators quoted "war baby" shares at outlandishly high values, and the exchange "dashed up and down with every rumor."[15]

By May 1940 Shanghai speculators were hoarding huge stocks of cotton at $1,000 per bale, planning to ship them to Europe via French Indochina. By June they had run the price up to $2,000. On June 25, France signed her armistice with Italy and Germany, and Japan prompted the new Vichy authorities in Indochina to close Haiphong to vessels from China. The artificially inflated cotton market collapsed. As requests for margin could not be met, over fifty import–export companies went bankrupt, further depressing the stock exchange.[16]

None the less, profiteers abounded and foreign businessmen, paid in American dollars or British pounds, lived quite well as the value of the Chinese dollar fell. By early 1941 it was next to impossible to get a room reservation or advance booking for a weekend movie, and the night clubs were packed in the foreign concessions where the wealthy engaged in feverish consumption. This fever was the symptom of inflation, which struck Chinese white-collar and blue-collar labor alike.[17]

If the cost of living of Shanghai workers in 1936 is indexed at 100, then in March 1941 the price of foodstuffs was 774; of rent, 385; of clothing, 503; of fuel, 636; and of miscellaneous goods, 599. South City (Nandao) stagnated, its central market deserted. While the gap continued to grow between rich and poor, on the eve of Pearl Harbor both staggered under the weight of growing wartime inflation. For Chinese workers prices had risen tenfold since just before the War of Resistance began in 1937, and for foreigners the cost of living was climbing at a rate of nearly 9 percent a month.[18] As the War of Resistance took its economic toll, street crime increased, and the need for stricter police controls grew accordingly.[19]

EXPANSION OF THE PUPPET POLICE

But as long as the foreign concessions continued to survive, police administration and sovereignty were hopelessly entangled among four different authorities: the Japanese military and consular police in charge of the occupied zone, the Chinese puppet police under the former's jurisdiction, the International Settlement police officered primarily by the British, and the French Concession police. These forces vied with each other for control of disputed areas of Shanghai. Especially acute was the long-standing dispute between the International Settlement's Shanghai Municipal Police (SMP) and the Chinese police over the extra-boundary roads outside the International Settlement and French Concession. For over fifteen years, the SMP and the Chinese police had struggled over these roads and the properties built along them. The contest intensified throughout 1938 and 1939 as crime thrived in the disputed "badlands" of western Shanghai (Huxi).[20]

On January 22, 1939, copies of a notice from the Western Branch of the Shanghai Police Bureau—that is, the puppet government's police—were posted outside police stations throughout Huxi. The notice, signed by Western Branch chief Wang Delin in his headquarters at No. 92 Jessfield Road, ordered the population to immediately cease dealing with the SMP and thereafter report all cases to the Western Branch police bureau.[21]

At that time—January 1939—the puppet police did not have the manpower to bring law and order to Huxi. But Shanghai police chief Lu Ying was steadily increasing the size of his force in the Western District: from sixty-four constables in January to 230 in early February. And the puppet constables were also backed up by the Kaneya Military Police detachment at 94 Jessfield Road.[22] As its ranks expanded in Huxi, the Chinese police grew more assertive towards the SMP, "stiffen[ing] its attitude towards the Settlement authorities regarding matters concerning jurisdiction over the extra-Settlement [area] in the Western District."[23]

By April 1939, the puppet government's regular police roster had grown to 5,155 members, an increase of nearly 60 percent since February.[24] At that time the Japanese Special Services Section also established a Military Armed Police (Wuzhuang jingcha) force consisting of 400 Chinese guerrillas who had surrendered, along with their weapons, in return for a one-time payment of $10 and the promise of $20 a month thereafter. The Military Armed Police were headquartered at Huangjiahua yuan in the Western District under the command of Han Jun, a former brigadier-general in Wu Peifu's service. The Japanese Special Services Section advisor was one Colonel Nishimura, and the intelligence office was headed by Gu Zhuhua and Hu Anbang, a Green Gang drug lord.[25] The Japanese planned eventually to enlist 15,000 paramilitary policemen in the Military Armed Police.[26] In May 1939, a former magistrate and detective sub-inspector in the SMP was appointed chief of staff of the Military Armed Police, who were given jurisdiction in Pudong over criminal cases involving anti-Japanese elements.[27]

In plain clothes these hastily recruited rowdies were sometimes mistaken for armed robbers themselves.[28] Indeed, to the British inspectors of the Shanghai Municipal Police these new puppet police were no better than bandits. Ballistic reports showed that 90 percent of the pistols seized or bullets recovered from armed crimes were "hot" weapons stolen from SMP constables on duty in Huxi.[29] Blatant felonies were routinely ignored by the Military Armed Police. On January 4, 1939, for example, armed gangsters held up twelve Britons and Americans right in front of the Columbia and Great Western Roads sub-station. The puppet police made no attempt to intervene.[30]

TERRITORIAL DISPUTES

International Settlement police and Chinese puppet police relations were ever more strained owing to the expansive growth of the Chinese police outside of Shanghai proper.[31] The expansion occurred after regular Japanese forces defeated or coopted Chinese loyalist guerrillas operating in the suburbs. Before March 1939 Fengxian district in Pudong, for example, was completely under the control of guerrillas. But after army units under General Nakajima launched a one-month mopping-up operation, the district was cleared of resistance.[32] Mayor Fu Zongyao then ordered Shanghai police chief Lu Ying to establish a new branch bureau there under the command of Yin Zhongli, advised by Special Services Section agent Yamashita.[33]

By June 1939 the Shanghai puppet police comprised eleven branch bureaus, five police stations, and eight other police units (detective corps, garrison, police reserve unit, river police corps, police training depot, police van, detention house, and police hospital) with a total strength of 5,662 men and women, an increase of 507 persons since April.[34] In July, the police enjoyed another increase in strength after Interior Minister Chen Qun ordered Chief Lu Ying to assume jurisdiction over Jiading prefecture and Chongming Island.[35] Lu Ying promptly appointed his secretary, Jin Dianyang, chief of the Jiading police force, and named Fengxian bureau chief Yin Zhongli head of Chongming Island's police.[36] The Shanghai puppet police now had a total roster of 6,125.[37]

By September 1939 the puppet detective corps under Guo Shaoyi numbered 300.[38] On October 7, the Japanese instructed Lu Ying to transform this corps into a Special Intelligence Branch (Tegaoke) to handle foreign affairs, investigate political dissidents, censor cultural works, and conduct special operations.[39] Simultaneously, 700 former Nationalist guerrillas in Pudong who had surrendered to form a Nanhuai Anti-Communist Self-defense Corps began to function as a regular police unit under Lu Jie and Jiang Miaogen.[40]

As the puppet police extended their sway over the suburbs, backed up by the Japanese army, confrontations with the SMP in Huxi increased.[41] On August 19, 1939, Settlement police officers shot and killed a puppet police sub-inspector and sergeant on Jessfield Road. Mayor Fu's government subsequently exhorted the Western District police to "adopt a strong and undaunted attitude towards the Settlement police," and authorized their constables to use force against anyone, regardless of nationality, who dared to interfere with their duties in Huxi.[42] This fresh determination to assert Chinese police sovereignty over the extra-boundary roads was supported by the Japanese once the British declared war against Germany on September 3, 1939.[43] Japanese gendarmes took over several large residences along Jessfield Road and set up sandbagged machine-gun emplacements outside their gates.[44] They also turned a former gambling casino at 448 Avenue Haig into a billet for Japanese military police. On September 14 a notice over Wang Delin's signature was posted at the entrance to 92 Jessfield Road announcing that the Western District was now under the jurisdiction of the Reform government and inviting members of the SMP to join the city police at an equivalent rate of pay.[45]

The Settlement authorities initially refused to recognize the puppet regime's claims, and retaliated instantly when Chinese and Sikh constables were shot on traffic duty on the outside roads.[46] On October 22, in the early hours of the morning, a thirty-minute gun battle broke out between SMP sergeants and elements of the puppet secret police from 76 Jessfield Road.[47]

By then, the Japanese consular and military authorities were vehemently arguing that anti-Japanese terrorism and the continuing crime wave in the International Settlement proved that the SMP were incapable of ensuring law and order, making it necessary for the Chinese to police Huxi themselves and even to recover the foreign concessions.[48] Reviving arguments that the foreign concessions provided criminals with a secure haven of operations, the puppet press chimed in with the claim that the Shanghai city police had successfully overcome crime and disorder in the areas under their jurisdiction.

MOMENTARY COMPROMISE

The collaborators' claim of law and order in Huxi was made in the context of negotiations between the Japanese and Wang Jingwei to form a new Nationalist government. One of the key points of those negotiations, intended to shore up Wang's patriotic mandate, was the restoration of Chinese sovereignty over the concessions. A major assertion, in this regard, was the linkage between extraterritoriality and crime.[49]

> The Settlements constitute the number one shelter for crime in China, and in order to purge the city of lawless elements, the retrocession of all foreign settlements should be given immediate attention. So long as the foreign settlements remain unrecovered, Shanghai will never have peace or security.[50]

The British government was acutely aware that, once established, a collaborationist regime under Wang Jingwei would have much more leverage over the disposition of the foreign concessions than the current Reform government with its culturally conservative and politically reactionary gang of unsavory puppets, slavishly answering to every whim of the Japanese special services. The British authorities in the International Settlement were therefore increasingly disposed to negotiate an agreement with lame-duck Mayor Fu Zongyao over police jurisdiction in Huxi.[51]

Discussions opened just after New Year, 1940, between Mayor Fu's representatives and Godfrey Phillips, secretary and commissioner-general of the Shanghai Municipal Council. Although Japanese and puppet secret agents from 76 Jessfield Road tried to delay a compromise settlement by murdering Phillips, the assassination attempt failed and an agreement "in principle" was worked out with Mayor Fu to form a special Western District police force with "certain principal officers" to be appointed from among candidates recommended by the Shanghai Municipal Council of the International Settlement.[52] The agreement, which was signed by the Chinese mayor and the Shanghai Municipal Council on February 16, 1940, was hailed by the *Xin Shenbao* as

> a satisfactory solution of the outstanding extra-settlement roads question.... The goal of new China is to work for her independence, to remove all aggressive influence, and to abolish all the unequal treaties. The settlement of the outside roads question in the Western District marks the beginning of this.[53]

On March 30, 1940, Wang Jingwei formally inaugurated the new national puppet government in Nanjing.[54] Its executive Vice-president, Minister of Finance, General Director of the Central Reserve Bank, Vice-Chairman of the Military Affairs Commission, Minister of Police, and chief of the secret police were one and the same person: Zhou Fohai.[55] Zhou had graduated from Kyoto Imperial University in 1924 before returning to China to systematize Sun Yat-sen's writings in his own *Sanminzhuyi zhi lilun de tixi* (Theoretical system of the three people's principles, 1928) and serve as editor of the Guomindang's *New Life Monthly*.[56]

Responding to the Wang regime's establishment, *Xin Shenbao* took on a new tone as early as April 1, criticizing the foreign concession authorities' failure to check the "terroristic elements in the employ of ... Chungking" (Chongqing) who were trying to block "the progressive development of the peace movement."[57]

> Our new central government is now in existence. Not only does our government desire to recover the foreign settlements in China, but our friendly nation Japan has given indication of a desire to render assistance to China in the retrocession of these settlements.[58]

WANG JINGWEI'S SECRET POLICE

Puppet claims for the peaceful police administration of Huxi were belied by the activities of the Special Services Section at 76 Jessfield Road, the palace of horrors run by Li Shiqun and Ding Mocun, the two former Communist renegades who had joined Nationalist Intelligence only to betray their new secret service masters by defecting to the Japanese.[59]

Li Shiqun was originally head of the Nationalist Special Services Brigade for the Shanghai region. In 1938 he defected to the Japanese along with a number of other leading Nationalist intelligence officers. Li, who was a member of Shanghai's Green Gang, used the informers and agents that he had run as a Nationalist case officer to work as mercenaries for the Japanese. He also quickly secured the allegiance of Wu Shibao, another Green Gang member, who enlisted local gangsters to serve as bodyguards for Wang Jingwei and other prominent collaborators.[60]

Ding Mocun, who had supervised Li Shiqun's work as an editor of the "CC clique's" *Shehui xinwen* (Social news) in Shanghai during 1933, had been chief of the Third Department of Zhongtong (Central Statistics—a euphemism for the Nationalist Party's secret police) until that section was reorganized in August 1938 and handed over to Dai Li, head of Juntong (Military Statistics—the army's secret police).[61] Ostensibly retiring from intelligence work, "Little Devil Ding" (who was only 5 ft 1 in.) went to Hong Kong without Chiang Kai-shek's permission and was hired by Li Shiqun in 1939 to come to Shanghai and work for the Japanese.[62]

In early 1939 Li Shiqun invited Ding Mocun to Shanghai. After he arrived, the two men together went to see General Doihara Kenji in the Special Service's Section's headquarters in Hongkou. Ding and Li offered to help General Doihara "assemble a group of Nationalist comrades and to facilitate peace." General Doihara was pleased to acquire a means to infiltrate "the complicated Chinese social scene of personal relationships" that Chongqing agents had exploited in the past. Doihara's plan for a puppet secret service was consequently approved by Tokyo on February 10, 1939, and Li and Ding's operations were formally inaugurated on March 1 under the aegis of Colonel Haruke Yoshitane from the Plum Blossom Agency (Ume Kikan), Colonel Kagesa Sadaaki's military intelligence unit that dominated the Nanjing puppet government. All of Ding and Li's operational plans were supposedly cleared with the Japanese military police in advance and the two Chinese defectors were required in turn to submit daily intelligence reports to their Japanese masters in exchange for a steady supply of money and weapons. In July 1939 the Li-Ding operation moved into 76 Jessfield Road and began encouraging the defection of Nationalist secret agents on the one hand, while crushing the organizational units behind them on the other.[63]

According to SMP reports, "No. 76" was also responsible for a series of brazen and brutal assassinations that multiplied during the following year.[64] By April 1940 Shanghai Municipal Council secretary Phillips felt obliged to write to Commander L. Neyrone, the Italian consul-general who was dean of the Shanghai diplomatic corps. In the letter he expressed anxiety about the activities of the Special Services Brigade of the China Guomindang Anti-Comintern and National Salvation Army headquarters at "76." This group, he said, "constitutes an appallingly grave menace to peace and order in Shanghai."[65] Phillips believed that unless the organization was curbed, it was doubtful that the newly envisaged Western District police force was going to be able to bring law and order to Huxi.[66]

SUBVERTING THE FOREIGN POLICE

Because of the fall of France, the wraps were almost completely off in the French Concession. In June 1940, the new Vichy authorities turned over the policing of Xujiahui to the puppets, who were also allowed to operate in the French Concession against pro-Chongqing terrorists.[67] This new arrangement with the local Wang Jingwei regime was one of the inspirations behind the effort in the late summer and early fall of 1940 to suborn the International Settlement's SMP.[68]

On September 16, 1940, two men tried but failed to kill Deputy Commissioner R. W. Yorke, chief of the SMP Special Branch. The attempt at assassination took place the day after the SMP had suspended over sixty policemen on suspicion of being suborned. Since Yorke was in charge of the investigation of this subversion, and since his counterpart in the French Concession police, Lieutenant Blanchet, had nearly been killed by assassins from 76 Jessfield Road three weeks earlier, the connection seemed obvious.[69] As Consul-General A. H. George explained to the British ambassador:

> It appears that the Shanghai office of the Ministry of Police of the Nanking "government" situated at No. 76 Jessfield Road is making determined

attempts to suborn members of the French and Shanghai municipal police forces, with the apparent object of inducing members of the two foreign-controlled police forces to render full facilities to the members of the Special Service Group attached to the Shanghai office of the Ministry of Police in the execution of their "duties" in the foreign-controlled areas prior to the actual "recovery" of these areas by the *de facto* authorities. As a *quid pro quo*, members of the foreign police forces are promised employment after the foreign areas have been "recovered," and necessary relief should they be dismissed in the event of their political activities being discovered by the foreign police authorities.[70]

The subversion effort was the responsibility of Pan Zhijie (also known as Pan Da and C.C. Pan), chief of the Fourth Department at 76 Jessfield Road. Inspector Pan was said to have suborned 460 SMP and French police officers with monthly retainers. Now, Pan Zhijie was designated by the city government as commissioner of the special police force for the Western District that the puppets expected to establish.[71]

THE WESTERN SHANGHAI AREA SPECIAL POLICE FORCE

Throughout the fall and early winter of 1940, Pan Zhijie's appointment and the hard line taken by the collaborationist mayor, Chen Gongbo, made it difficult to implement the police agreement signed "in principle" in February 1940 by the late Mayor Fu Zongyao and the then Shanghai Municipal Council chairman, Cornell S. Franklin.[72] But Major Kenneth Bourne of the SMP and Colonel Lu Ying of the Shanghai Municipal Government puppet police continued to negotiate, and—spurred on by the usual New Year's crime wave—managed in January 1941 to come to a tentative agreement on forming a special Huxi police force for the badlands, officered by a combination of Settlement, puppet, and Japanese inspectors.[73] When they submitted the tentative agreement to the Shanghai Municipal Council and to the Chinese authorities in Nanjing, it was approved.[74]

On February 1, Mayor Chen Gongbo and Shanghai Municipal Council chairman W. J. Keswick met at the Chinese city hall in Jiangwan to sign the police accord together.[75] The agreement announced the establishment of a Western Shanghai Area Special Police Force (WSP for short), or *Huxi tebie jingcha zongshu*, to control the area formerly under the jurisdiction of the West Shanghai police division, a section of the jurisdiction of the Xujiahui police division, and districts presently guarded by the Shanghai foreign defense forces.[76]

The new WSP was to be composed of the existing police main corps, the whole West Shanghai division, part of the Xujiahui division, and officers of the detective branch corps together with officers recommended by the municipal council. According to the regulations, it was to be the only organization to exercise police power in the above areas, and it would do so under the direction of the Shanghai city police bureau.[77] The maximum strength was to be 1,466, men with an additional reserve of twelve men, grouped into five police divisions and a number of stations and sub-stations.[78]

Officers in charge of divisions where most of the residents were foreign nationals would be appointed by the puppet city government from a list of candidates (including men of Chinese nationality) recommended by the Shanghai Municipal Council. Basically each division would have a mixture of nationalities, with a preponderance of Japanese and Europeans in command. If there were disagreement over cases concerning foreigners then the matter would be settled by the commissioners of the Shanghai Municipal Government police and of the SMP; if that failed, a final decision would be made by the mayor and the chairman of the Shanghai Municipal Council.

According to the agreement, the police forces of the city government and of the International Settlement would cooperate, via liaison officers, in intelligence matters, searches, and extradition cases. All three police forces in "close pursuit" of criminals or terrorists could cross city boundaries. If the WSP harbored "reasonable suspicion" that confederates of a criminal gang were hiding in the Settlement, then the suspects would be apprehended and handed over to the WSP, which had a week either to report evidence of guilt or return the accused to the SMP "in good condition."[79]

A special annex to the accord stipulated that "all illegitimate businesses (such as the running of gambling dens, trafficking in opium and narcotics, and providing addicts with such narcotics) shall be forbidden to exist within the area under its jurisdiction."[80] During the earlier negotiations, the collabora-tionist police authorities had dragged their feet over the annex precisely because the Wang Jingwei government was a "Monte Carlo regime," dependent for a good portion of its revenue on the sale of narcotics, the licensing of prostitution, and fees and kickbacks from gambling casinos.[81] Needless to say, after the WSP opened its station doors at 57A Great Western Road and Chief Pan Zhijie sent his constables out on patrol in their new police uniforms on March 17, 1941, gambling and drug trafficking continued to flourish.[82]

CHEN GONGBO'S CRACKDOWN ON VICE

Because of the struggle within the Wang Jingwei regime between Zhou Fohai and Li Shiqun, the latter relinquished his position as head of the Shanghai Special Services Section (Tegong zongbu) in January 1941 to his deputy, Wu Shibao, popularly called the "king of racketeers." In early March 1941 Mayor Chen Gongbo ordered all of the gambling dens in Huxi closed. At least four major casinos continued to keep their doors open because their owners had an "understanding" with Wu Shibao and the Japanese military police whereby a daily protection fee of $12,000 was paid over to the "East Asia Charity Association" (Lane 1032, 25 Yuyuan Road), headed by a senior Japanese police officer. Thanks to the "understanding," Wu Shibao warned Commissioner Lu Ying that if the city government attempted to close the casinos down there could be unpleasant consequences. Wu asked Colonel Lu to convey the intelligence to Mayor Chen that there was a stockpile of firearms at the China Club and that the gambling house owners were prepared to offer armed resistance, backed by the Japanese military police. Chen Gongbo still wanted the gambling dens shut, but the casino owners by then had increased their daily protection "contributions" to $15,000 to be sure of Japanese and secret police armed support in the event of a conflict with the Chinese city government.[83]

Meanwhile, Tokyo was becoming concerned about the extent of crime in the parts of Shanghai controlled by the Nanjing regime. In May 1941 *Asahi* published an editorial arguing that the most effective way to strengthen the Nanjing regime would be to do away with China's long-standing public vices by pressing Wang Jingwei to introduce reforms. As Japanese politicians talked about ways of bolstering Nanjing, Ambassador Honda Kumataro returned to Tokyo, where he publicly urged support for the puppet government. The result of this flurry was growing Japanese pressure on Wang Jingwei, during his June 1941 visit to Tokyo, to clean up some of Shanghai's more egregious vices.[84]

Wang Jingwei had already ordered Chief Pan Zhijie to close all of the casinos between May 31 and June 2. Mayor Chen Gongbo heartily supported this decision. None the less, Special Services chief Wu Shibao managed to thwart Wang's plans by introducing Nanjing's vice-minister of police, Deng Zuyou, to the lavish pleasures of night-time Shanghai. The day after Deng's debauchery, the gambling houses were reopened.[85] That same day, June 16, 1941, Commissioner Pan publicly vowed to punish those responsible for this malfeasance. He did personally lead a raid five days later on the Eventail and the Welcome Café, but nearby casinos operating full blast were not at all disturbed.[86] Moreover, only some of the gambling paraphernalia were seized, and the "joints" were not forced to close.[87]

The puppet newspaper *Shanghai* continued to make extravagant claims about the success of Mayor Chen's campaign against gambling. It declared that as of May 31 all the Chinese-operated gambling dens had been closed, "never to reopen again," and that Commissioner Pan had permanently shut down the foreign-owned clubs in Huxi.[88] But this was not enough to forestall the Nationalist government in Chongqing from making excellent propaganda use of the Wang Jingwei regime's toleration of vice in Shanghai. Chiang Kai-shek actually sent a note in July 1941 to the Shanghai press excoriating the puppets and calling for a campaign against narcotics and gambling.[89] Mayor Chen Gongbo subsequently insisted upon closing down foreign-run gambling houses in the concessions (by then there was only one fly-by-night casino managed by a Frenchman), and then supported an effort by the regular Chinese police to take over WSP operations in Huxi.[90]

In late July 1941 Colonel Lu Ying, director of the Shanghai Special

Municipality police, headquartered in Nandao, finally moved in on Commissioner Pan Zhijie's Huxi bailiwick. Colonel Lu sent his assistants to the headquarters of the Western District Special Police with instructions to serve as liaison between Commissioner Pan's office and the police establishment downtown. Their real mission was to wrest control of the WSP headquarters from Pan Zhijie, which they rapidly succeeding in doing. That *coup* was followed by another directed against the secret police. On August 16, Captain Wu Shibao was removed from his post at 76 Jessfield Road and ordered to report to Changzhou to do rural pacification work. Wu had no choice but to resign, but he refused to abandon his racketeering activities in Shanghai, where he remained under other guises thereafter.[91]

MUTUAL RESPONSIBILITY SYSTEMS

The Japanese colonial authorities in Taiwan had perfected their own version of the Chinese mutual responsibility system of *baojia*, which they called *hokô*, much earlier in the twentieth century. The key difference between their Taiwanese adaptation and the original Chinese version of this ancient local control system was the linkage of the household with a modern, professional police system.[92] Instead of functioning as a kind of self-governing unit, in which responsibility rested with a rotationally appointed headman, the *hokô* system required that the Taiwanese chief of the unit report regularly and directly to the local *kôban* or police box, manned by a resident Japanese colonial policeman.[93]

The Japanese military brought *hokô* to north China in 1937. Severe restrictions were imposed upon the population, which had to take part in a census and maintain a wooden tablet on every residential and commercial door, listing the names of all inhabitants. Anyone missing during spot checks by Japanese troops was presumed to be a guerrilla. When the system was transferred to south China, however, the occupation authorities did not have enough soldiers in rural areas to function as policemen, and consequently had to rely upon local *hokô* leaders (who were in effect collaborators) to participate in local administration and to establish self-defense corps.[94]

In November 1940 the deputy chief of staff of the imperial headquarters in Tokyo, Lieutenant-General Sawada Shigeru, was transferred to eastern China to command the Thirteenth Army. Wang Jingwei's puppet troops were still unable to control the countryside, even just outside the capital at Nanjing. General Sawada was eager to pacify the region, and so turned to Lieutenant-Colonel Haruke Yoshitane, a counter-insurgency specialist on Major-General Kagesa Sadaaki's staff, for a pacification plan. Colonel Haruke had closely studied Zeng Guofan and Chiang Kai-shek's suppression campaigns, and he proposed the establishment of "model peace zones" (*mohanteki wahei chiku*) with the help of Chinese collaborators who would build a primary or grassroots level political system based upon "self-government" (*jichi*), "self-defense" (*jiei*), and "economic self-improvement" (*jisei*). The model peace zone would be created, after Japanese mop-up operations, by walling off the subjugated area with bamboo palisades, electrified barbed wire, and watch towers.[95] Within the zone, there would be created *baojia* with Chinese collaborators, a police system, a secret service system, and a self-defense corps.[96]

The first model peace zone was to comprise the five counties of Changshu, Jiangyin, Kunshan, Wuxi, and Taicang, just west of Greater Shanghai. Although this plan received the support of General Hata Shunroku (China theater commander), the Wang Jingwei regime wavered. A rural pacification committee was not formed until May 22, 1941, by which time initiative for the venture had slipped into the hands of Police Minister Li Shiqun.[97]

Working under Colonel Haruke, who installed an office in Suzhou, Li Shiqun brought in some of his agents from Shanghai to form an intelligence network and trained 5,000 cadres and police, most of whom came down from north China to collaborate with Li Shiqun and puppet governor Gao Guanwu. With the help of Japanese soldiers, the police and cadres suppressed most of the Guomindang "Loyal and Patriotic Army" (Zhongyi jiuguo jun) and at least one-quarter of the Communist New Fourth Army units in the zone.[98] Households were registered under the *baojia* system, and all males between fourteen and forty-five were enrolled in a self-defense corps, which was not, however, allowed to carry guns on patrol.[99] In the end, as Japanese military fortunes tumbled elsewhere, the local collaborators who were crucial to the system ceased cooperating, but at least until late 1942 the model peace zone system constituted a rural model for parallel control mechanisms in urban centers such as Shanghai.[100]

RICE AND RESTRAINT

After occupying the Chinese-held sectors of Shanghai in 1937, the Japanese and puppet authorities had thoroughly enforced the household registration system developed by the Nationalist police in the Special Municipality during the Nanjing decade.[101] The *baojia* system, however, was not so much for census-taking as for social control. It was the special contribution of the puppet regime, therefore, to apply the Japanese colonial version of *baojia*— that is, the Taiwanese *hokô* system—to semi-colonial Shanghai by requiring the mutual responsibility head to report direct to the local police precinct station.[102]

In addition, under the special conditions of wartime food shortages, the Japanese and puppet authorities coupled this more highly evolved and state-linked mutual responsibility organization with the government's rice ration-ing system. When the journalist Vanya Oakes left Shanghai in 1940, just as Japanese puppets were being picked off right and left, she felt around her a do-or-die determination to resist the aggressor. When she returned in 1941, she could sense the collapse of Chinese spirit. Why, she asked her Chinese friends, had they become so passive and accepting of the Japanese occupation? Their answer was simply: "Rice."[103]

The Japanese used rice as a weapon to dominate Shanghai much as Hitler used the control of food supplies to subjugate Europe. That is, Chinese rice grown in the provinces was used to feed the Japanese army or the civilian population in Japan. Cities such as Tianjin and Shanghai, where under the ration system each individual was supposed to get 1.5 *sheng* (about 2.7 pounds) of stone-laden rice once a week, had been living on rice imported from Indochina, so that "when Japan secured control of Indochina's entire output of nearly six million tons, she naturally came into possession of a weapon with which to force 'cooperation' upon Occupied China."[104]

This weapon was used very concretely as a means of social control. For example, there were five cases of Japanese being shot between September 29 and October 18, 1940. In retaliation, the Japanese military police sealed off the lanes of suspected areas, and "subjected [them] to a vigorous blockade, which in some sections was sustained long enough, according to current reports, to cause several deaths through starvation."[105]

Rice shortages and inflated prices shortened tempers and inflamed public opinion. On March 15, 1941, the Shanghai Municipal Police and a Chinese team played a soccer match at the Canidrome in the French Concession. After a foul, a Chinese player was ordered off the field. His fellow team mates marched off with him, causing the 20,000 Chinese spectators to stream on to the field, tear up the goal posts, and throw stones and bricks at the policemen who tried to break up the riot. Police reinforcements and the fire brigade, which turned its hoses on the crowd, managed to force the rioters out into the street. More than thirty people were injured.[106]

The Canidrome riot was taken as a sign of worse to come should rice prices continue to rise, and both the Wang Jingwei puppet regime and the two foreign settlements' administrations bought what rice they could to distribute or sell at a considerable discount in order to keep the lid on at a time when political relations with the Japanese were increasingly strained and when Shanghai's urban economy continued to deteriorate.[107]

After Pearl Harbor, in fact, even the rice provisioning system began to break down. During the two years between 1943 and 1945, there were only seventy provisions provided, with many weeks missing in between, so that out of a supposed total of 730 days of rations, each person legally received only about 140–50 days of rice supplies. The result was a tremendous rise in the price of black-market rice, and a siphoning off of schoolteachers and clerks into smuggling and other forms of crime.[108]

Meanwhile the supply of electricity for municipal lighting and industry declined radically as the Japanese commandeered coal. By December 1943, less than 40 percent of the textile industry and only 27 percent of Shanghai's flour mills were still in operation; domestic electricity was approximately 70 percent of the amount consumed in 1941. Individuals were only permitted to use twenty-five units of light and eight units of power per month. Trams stopped running at 8.30 in the evening. Eggs cost $5.50 apiece, rice was $2,500 a picul, and firewood was selling for $500 per hundred catties.[109] In addition, the introduction of the Central Reserve Bank note (CRB) in May 1942 had led to an upward spiral of prices, which—given the scarcity of consumer goods—inevitably led to the virtual collapse of Shanghai's economy.[110]

EXTENDING *BAOJIA* TO THE CONCESSIONS

The *baojia* control system had never been applied to the foreign settlements in Shanghai. In fact, because the International Settlement and French Concession did not have a household registration system, the Japanese authorities who took over the police in February 1942 had to launch an initial census of their own, using figures on grain allocation and tax payments to get a rough fix on the population.[111] It was difficult to get accurate figures because males concealed the names and addresses of concubines or mistresses living in separate locations, and even completely respectable wives pretended to be "secret women" (*mimi nüren*) in "little households" (*xiao fangzi*) in order to stay hidden from the occupation authorities. Nevertheless, the government announced by February 19 that there were 1,586,021 Chinese and foreigners residing in the Settlement, and 854,380 people living in the French Concession. South City (Nanshi) had a population of 647,411.[112]

Shortly after the census figures were announced in mid-February, pro-Chongqing terrorists attacked the Louza (Laozha) Road police station in the International Settlement. Two Chinese collaborators, Jiang Tingyao and Xu Chang, promptly petitioned the Japanese, requesting that *baojia* be imposed upon the foreigners. The Chinese, they said, had experienced "indescribable" sufferings at the hands of the Western imperialists.

> Happily, on 8 December last year, following the outbreak of the War for the Emancipation of Great East Asia, the imperial [Japanese] forces entered and occupied the Settlement to drive out British and American influences in order to free the Chinese from the yoke of oppression.... The entire Chinese community in this city are [*sic*] rejoiced to find an opportunity for national regeneration, for the preservation of territorial integrity, and for the enjoyment of a bright future.[113]

For too long the concessions had been a sanctuary for criminals and "a paradise for the wealthy." The time had come to bring "peace and good order" to the Settlement by instituting *baojia*.[114]

After the Laozha Road bombings the police blockaded all alleyways with iron, wooden, and bamboo gates; closed major intersections with barbed wire; and installed siren alarm systems along Chengdu and Bubbling Well Roads. Now, at the behest of their Japanese overlords, the British-commanded SMP also announced plans to extend *baojia* to the International Settlement. On March 16, a preparatory committee was set up in the Ningbo tongxiang hui

(Ningbo Fellow Countrymen's Association); it was succeeded in turn by a regular *baojia* office, which opened its doors at 200 Fuzhou Road on April 24 to issue citizenship certificates. The area south of Suzhou Creek was divided into seven *baojia* districts, congruent with police precincts, e.g. Central district, with four sections, thirty-five *bao*, 600 *jia*, and 6,355 *hu* (households).[115] The heads of these various levels in the control system were recommended by constituent members, but the actual appointments were to be made by the police.[116]

The system was dominated by Japanese police advisors, whose salaries came out of the general *baojia* budget. In addition, more than 400 staff persons had to be hired, fed, and provided with supplies, office rent, utilities, and so on, for a total of $550,000. Members of the still existing Shanghai Municipal Council proposed that this "huge sum of money" be raised by imposing an Emergency Rate on Shanghai taxpayers. Given the strident opposition of Japanese ratepayers to increased municipal taxes, however, the only realistic way of financing *baojia* had to be levies on Chinese-owned firms and shops. These assessments, which were collected by the *bao* and *jia* chiefs themselves, were nominally loans, but as far as one can tell, the moneys were never refunded by the Shanghai Municipal Council.[117]

The Shanghai Municipal Council, still led by British and American elected officers, resisted both mandatory levies and compulsory service. But in July 1942 the Japanese required all British officers to resign from the Settlement police and the force was reorganized along Japanese lines. At the same time, the occupation authorities pressed ahead to implement the new *baojia* system by conducting a census, issuing identity cards, and creating a self-defense corps.[118]

Baojia officials, under the supervision of the SMP, began taking the census early in March 1942. Using specially prepared forms, they had each head of household (*huzhang*) in the same *jia* sign a mutual guarantee and joint responsibility bond. When the census was completed, a *baojia* certificate was issued to each household to be affixed in a conspicuous position outside the main entrance to the premises. Thereafter, each *huzhang* had to report to the *jia* head—in addition to births and deaths in the family—whenever a suspicious person entered the household, whenever a guest spent the night, and whenever a family member went away overnight.[119]

During the census, each *hu* member was issued a "citizen's card" (*liangminzheng*) stamped by the regular police and by the Japanese military police. That card had to be carried on the person all the time. "Checks are made daily in restaurants and other public places, and waiters and servants are questioned by the police and plain-clothes men regarding customers and establishment."[120]

After the census was completed, a People's Self-protection Corps was formed. *Bao* heads prepared a roster of all males between twenty and forty-five, and forwarded it to police headquarters. Members of the corps were expected to serve three-hour shifts equipped with a police whistle, baton, rope, raincoat, armlets and electric torch. They were, in effect, police auxiliaries, operating under their local *baojia* direction bureau (which normally had a Japanese advisor or two in tacit command along with an intelligence officer) to render assistance during blockades, help apprehend criminals, and man wooden kiosks at important road crossings and street corners.[121] Their skills were periodically tested by Japanese military police-men disguised as terrorists in plain clothes. Their expenses, which were borne by the local *baojia* committee, were not inconsiderable, since the total number of corpsmen in the seven police districts of the Settlement totaled 86,921, with approximately 13,000 on duty every day.[122]

TIGHTENING CONTROL

On October 13, 1943, the Wang Jingwei government's Ministry of the Interior promulgated a set of twenty-eight organizational regulations (*Neizheng bu zuzhi fa*) that brought internal affairs under the Ministry (article 1), and placed all police matters throughout occupied China under its Police Administration Office (Jingzheng si, articles 4 and 8).[123] This move toward greater national police integration—a policy that Chiang Kai-shek's police officials had been unable to implement during 1934–7—meant that all municipal police forces had to report direct to the central government. The sole exception to this nationalization policy of the Wang regime was the Shanghai police force, which remained under the control of the municipal government and which reported directly to the mayor of Shanghai (articles 1 and 3 of the "Shanghai tebie shi di yi jingcha ju zhanxing" [Temporary regulations of the No. 1 Police Bureau of Shanghai Special Municipality]).[124]

According to the legalistic governing philosophy of the Wang Jingwei regime, and appropriate to its highly coercive nature, all social activities concerned the police and were necessarily determined by laws. "A philoso-pher once said, 'We humans live by laws, act by laws, survive by laws.'" The rule of law itself was divided into the realm of *fa* (laws as such), set by legal (*lifa*) organizations; and the realm of *ling* (decrees), issued by administrative (*xingzheng*) organizations. The one cannot contradict the other, and while the police are concerned with the administration of all the internal affairs (*neiwu*) of a nation, they were instructed to observe this general legal domain as well.[125]

The Sino-Japanese colonialized version of *baojia* helped sustain this newly extended legalism at the expense of a subjugated population. It also brought the state closer than ever to its subjects by welding together, for the first time, the age-old mutual responsibility system and modern instruments of police control developed after the Xinzheng state-building reforms of the early twentieth century.[126] In Shanghai itself, the new *baojia* system continued to develop apace, growing more complex—and more bureaucratic—over the remaining years of the war. The thirty-nine-article *baojia* regulations issued in February 1944 by the municipal government stipulated proper functions, duties, procedures, and attitudes for members of this urban militia.[127] And though the auxiliary police corps was disbanded when the Nationalists liberated the city in 1945, the control system remained intact. Identity cards (*shenfenzheng*) were issued by the Guomindang authorities, and the household registration infrastructure survived, just as it would persist through 1949 and the period of Communist "liberation" as well.

NOTES

1 F. Wakeman, Jr., "Policing Modern Shanghai," *China Quarterly* 115 (1988), pp. 408–40.
2 F. Wakeman, Jr., *Policing Shanghai, 1927–1937*, Berkeley: University of California Press, 1995.
3 F. Wakeman, Jr., *Shanghai Badlands: Wartime Terrorism and Urban Crime, 1937–1941*, New York: Cambridge University Press, 1996.
4 F. Wakeman, Jr., "Liberation," manuscript in progress.
5 The dramatic extension of wartime mechanisms of urban control was part of a longer trajectory of political centralization and and administrative integration that resulted in growing state power over the course of the twentieth centuy. See F. Wakeman, Jr., "Models of Historical Change: The Chinese State and Society, 1938–1989," in K. Lieberthal, J. Kallgren, R. MacFarquhar, and F. Wakeman, Jr., eds, *Perspectives on Modern China: Four Anniversaries*, Armonk, N.Y., and London: Sharpe, 1991, pp. 68–102; and F. Wakeman, Jr., "The Civil Society and Public Sphere Debate: Western Reflections on Chinese Political Culture," *Modern China* 19, 2 (April 1993), pp. 108–38.
6 P. Finch, *Shanghai and Beyond*, New York: Scribner, 1953, p. 259. See also E. O. Hauser, *Shanghai: City for Sale*, New York: Harcourt Brace, 1940, p. 313; C. Henriot, "Le gouvernement municipal de Shanghai," thèse pour le doctorat de troisième cycle présenté à l'Université de la Sorbonne Nouvelle (Paris III), 1983, p. 324.
7 Finch, *Shanghai and Beyond*, pp. 261–2.
8 P. Fu, "Intellectual Resistance in Shanghai: Wang Tongzhao and a Concept of Resistance Enlightenment, 1937–9," paper delivered at the Association for Asian Studies meetings, San Francisco, March 24, 1988, pp. 3–4.
9 E. Honig, "Women Cotton Mill Workers in Shanghai, 1919–49," Ph.D. dissertation, Stanford, Cal., 1982, pp. 27–8.
10 V. Oakes, *White Man's Folly*, Boston: Houghton Mifflin, 1943, pp. 372–3.
11 Ibid., p. 374; L. Eastman, "Facets of an Ambivalent Relationship: Smuggling, Puppets, and Atrocities during the War, 1937–1945," in *The Chinese and the Japanese: Essays in Political and Cultural Interactions,* ed. Akira Iriye, Princeton: Princeton University Press, 1980, p. 278.
12 Oakes, *White Man's Folly*, pp. 348–9. After Germany and the Soviet Union signed their pact, and before Hitler invaded Russia, the Germans were shipping 100,000 tons a month of products over the Trans-Siberian railway. In 1940, German–Chinese trade amounted to US$9.7 million, with Shanghai accounting for about half of that amount. Shanghai's exports to the United States by February 1939 amounted to approximately US$1 million per month, which was roughly half the amount exported in February 1937, before hostilities began. Records of the Department of State relating to the Internal Affairs of China, 1930–1939, (hereafter: *RDS China*) 893.00 P.R. Shanghai/125 (February 1939), p. 17.

13 C. Ch'ien, *Fortress Besieged*, trans. by Jeanne Kelly and Nathan K. Mao, Bloomington and London: Indiana University Press, 1979, p. 325.

14 Oakes, *White Man's Folly*, 362; "Shanghai Mayor keeps his Promise to the Public," pp. 2–3.

15 Zhang Y., *Lunxian qianhou de Shanghai*, pp. 57–8; Ch'ien, *Fortress Besieged*, p. 325; Oakes, *White Man's Folly*, pp. 375, 381.

16 Zhang F., *Jinrong manji* [Random notes on finance], Shanghai: n.p., 1942, p. 31.

17 "What had cost $100 to buy now cost $365. By comparison, wages had increased only an infinitesimal amount," *White Man's Folly*, pp. 357–9.

18 "The High Cost of Living and the Labour Situation," *Shanghai* 1, 3 (July 1941), pp. 13–14; *China Weekly Review*, [hereafter *CWR*] October 11, 1941, p. 153.

19 China Intelligence Wing Report No. C-35-85, May 8, 1944, in FO371/41680, British Foreign Office Records [hereafter: BFOR].

20 In 1939 there were sixty-three true cases of murder, against forty-two true cases in 1938, and twenty-two in 1937, in the International Settlement. That same year, 1939, saw 42 percent of crime cases unsolved, as opposed to 37 percent in 1937 and percentages in the mid-30s in 1936 and 1935. Wakeman, *Policing Shanghai*, chapter 15; A. Silliman, "Sino-foreign Conflict and the extra-Settlement Roads of Shanghai," *passim*, *Annual Report of the Shanghai Municipal Council, 1939*, pp. 100–1.

21 Notice included in Shanghai Municipal Police (International Settlement) Files [hereafter SMP], microfilms from the US National Archives, D-8155, 24/1/39.

22 SMP, D-8155,2/2/39, 7/2/39, 9/2/39, 14/5/39; *CWR*, August 2, 1941, p. 269.

23 SMP, D-8155, 13/3/39, 14/5/39, 24/2/39, 22/3/39.

24 Ibid., 1/5/39.

25 Ibid., 1/6/39.

26 Two hundred of these puppet gendarmes, who were paid $30 a month to combat guerrillas, were stationed at police headquarters; the rest were distributed among branch bureaus (*fenju*) in Huxi and Pudong, where loyalist guerrillas had been ousted by regular Japanese forces.

27 The new chief of staff was Yao Zhiduan, alias Yao Asheng and Yao Zidu. He had worked for the CID. SMP, D-8155(2), 8/6/39; D-8155B, 1/6/39; D-8155G, 7/3/39, 11/4/39, 19/5/39.

28 Ibid., 22/5/39.

29 *CWR*, March 1, 1941, p. 462.

30 Ibid., January 14, 1939, p. 213.

31 *RDS*, 893.00 PR Shanghai/126 (March 1939), p. 14. See the article "SMC assumes Arrogant Attitude in Western District," from *Xin Shenbao*, July 11, 1939. *Xin Shenbao* was the leading puppet daily newspaper published in Shanghai. This excerpt was translated in SMP, D-8116, 12/7/39. (I am unable to give citations from the original newspaper because I have not gained access to copies of the periodical other than those articles clipped in the SMP files.) Under puppet Mayor Fu Zongyao's administration, twenty recent graduates of the Nanjing government's police academy were appointed sub-inspectors at the various Shanghai branch bureaus and the monthly budget of the Shanghai city government police was increased from $160,000 to $200,000 in May 1939. SMP, D-8155 (2), 8/6/39.

32 One group of guerrillas joined the Nanhui Anti-Communist Self-defense Corps mentioned below. See SMP, D-8155, 13/10/39.

33 Ibid. Yin was also known as Yin Zhongyu.

34 Ibid.

35 This was done to increase the supervision of the Japanese Special Services Section over these areas, using the puppet police it already controlled. Ibid.,

D-8155 (2), 10/8/39. See also the requests from the Chongming police chief to the Japanese concerning local pacification in *Ri wei Shanghai shi zhengfu*, pp. 221–4.

36 SMP, D-8155, 21/7/39. The Nanjing Ministry of the Interior also ordered that all branch bureaus (*fenju*) and stations (*suo*) be renamed bureaus (*shu*).

37 Ibid., 10/8/39.

38 Ibid., 11/9/39.

39 There existed also an independent Special Branch of the Shanghai government under one of Mayor Fu's aides, Gong Wenfang, whose assignment was to report on the movements of anti-Japanese elements. Ibid., 21/7/39, 10/10/39.

40 On October 12, 1939, Chief Lu Ying, accompanied by Chief Detective Guo Shaoyi, River Police Chief Bao Ziying, and their Special Services Section adviser Agent Takeguchi, inspected the corps by way of bringing these former guerrillas under formal police control. Ibid., 13/10/39, 1/11/39.

41 Ibid., 4/8/39.

42 Constables wounded in the event of an affray would be given $500 by way of compensation. The families of policemen killed in this line of duty would receive $2,000-$20,000, depending upon rank and seniority. Ibid., 24/8/39.

43 L. T. White III, "Non-governmentalism in the Historical Development of Modern Shanghai," in L. J. C. Ma and E. W. Hanten, eds, *Urban Development in Modern China*, Boulder, Colo.: Westview Press, 1981, pp. 48–9. On September 9, 100 members of the puppet police's reserve unit were transferred from the Toyoda cotton mill to 92 Jessfield Road, where they brought the number of Chinese city government police to 360 men. With these new forces, the puppet police began to patrol extra-Settlement streets in that area, including Rockhill Avenue and Avenue Haig. SMP, D-8155, 11/9/39.

44 Ibid., 13/9/39.

45 Ibid., 14/9/39, 15/9/39.

46 When the Shanghai city police established a traffic post at the corner of Robeson and Kiaochow [Qiaozhou] Roads, the SMP immediately protested to Count Bentivoglio, commander of the Italian marines. In less than three hours the post was removed. Ibid., 29/9/39.

47 Shanghai dispatch 1059, 7/11/39, W0208-246A, British War Office Records [hereafter BWOR].

48 Oakes, *White Man's Folly*, pp. 362–3.

49 Wakeman, *Policing Shanghai*, chapter 4.

50 "Banditry rampant in Foreign Settlements," *Xin Shenbao*, February 4, 1940, trans. in SMP, D-8116, 11/2/40.

51 The "Outline of Readjustment of Sino-Japanese Relations" (*Ri-Zhi xin guanxi tiaozheng yaogang*), which was based upon Wang Jingwei and Colonel Kagesa's negotiations in Shanghai in June 1939 and which was formally signed on October 30, contained many concessions to Japan, including jurisdiction over Inner Mongolia, the virtual independence of north China, the assignment of Japanese advisers to all levels of organizations, and the promise to compensate Japanese civilians for war damage. However, the meeting of the three main puppet leaders—Wang Jingwei, Liang Hongzhi, and Wang Kemin—at Qingdao on January 23–4, 1940, finally led to the formation of a unitary national government. Huang Meizhen and Zhang Yun, *Wang Jingwei guomin zhengfu chengli*, [The founding of Wang Jingwei's Nationalist government], Shanghai: Shanghai renmin chubanshe, 1984, pp. 92–4, 109–16, 421–7, 662–5; Wu, "Contending Political Forces during the War of Resistance," pp. 68–70.

52 BFOR, FO371-24682, F312, 13/1/40, and F1534, 4/3/40; SMP, D-8373/12, 28/11/40; J. V. Davidson-Houston, *Yellow Creek: The Story of Shanghai*, Philadelphia: Defour Editions, 1964, pp. 163–4.

53 Translated in SMP, D-8116, 22/2/40. See also BFOR, FO371-24682, F226, 10/1/40; F839, 6/2/40; F1209, 18/2/40.

54 Zhou Fohai had begun recruiting personnel in Shanghai in late 1939, before the Nanjing government was actually even organized, so the new puppet government was already a prominent presence by the time of its formal inauguration on March 30. S. H. Marsh, "Chou Fo-hai: The Making of a Collaborator," in Akira Iriye, ed., *The Chinese and the Japanese: Essays in Political and Cultural Interactions*, Princeton: Princeton University Press, 1980, pp. 318–19.

55 *CWR*, November 16, 1940, p. 351.

56 Marsh, "Chou Fo-hai," pp. 323–4; H. L. Boorman *et al.*, eds, *Biographical Dictionary of Republican China*, New York: Columbia University Press, 1967–71, 1979, p. 405.

57 *Xin Shenbao*, April 1, 1940, trans. in SMP, D-8116, 4/4/40.

58 *Xin shenbao*, April 10, 1940, trans. in SMP, D-8116, 15/4/40.

59 See chapter 7 in this volume. For the horror-chamber quality of the compound, see Tao Juyin, *Tianliang qian de gudao* [The isolated island before daybreak], Shanghai: Zhonghua, 1947, pp. 72–3.

60 Chen Gongshu, *Kangzhan hougi fanjian houdong* [Counter-espionage activity in the later phase of the War of Resistance], Taibei: Zhuanji wenxue chubanshe, 1986, p. 206; Nao Xiaotian and Wang Mengyun, "Wang wei 'tegong zongbu' qishiliu hao de jianli" [The creation of No. 76 "special mission headquarters" of Wang the usurper]. in Huang Meizhen and Zhang Yun (eds), *Wang Jingwei guomin zhengfu chengli* [The founding of Wang Jingwei's Nationalist government], Shanghai: Renmin chubanshe, 1984, pp. 268–78; *CWR*, November 16, 1940, p. 351; Zhang Weihan, "Dai Li yu 'Juntong ju'" [Dai Li and the Military Statistics Bureau], in Wenshi ziliao yanjui weiyuanhui (eds), *Zhejiang wenshi ziliao xuanji* [Collection of historical materials on Zhejiang] 23, Zhejiang: Renmin chubanshe, 1984, p. 145.

61 Section One, which became Zhongtong, was directed by Xu Enzeng. Section Two, which absorbed Section Three and became Juntong in August 1938, was directed by Dai Li.

62 Ch'en Li-fu Materials, "Ting Mo-ts'un File," pp. 1–3; Zhang Weihan, "Dai Li yu 'Juntong ju'," p. 145; Mao Xiaotian and Wang Mengyun, "Wang wei 'tegong zongbu' qishiliu hao de jianli," pp. 259–62. See also Pan Ling, *Old Shanghai*, p. 120; Tao Juyin, *Tianliang qian de gudao*, p. 70.

63 Wen-hsin Yeh, "Dai Li and the Liu Geqing affair," *Journal of Asian Studies* 48,3 (1989), p. 552. A few Western journalists, such as Jack Belden, had vague inklings of these developments, including attacks on underground Communists. Israel Epstein, *The Unfinished Revolution in China*, Boston, Mass.: Little Brown, 1947, p. 135.

64 BFOR, FO371-24663, 3/4/40.

65 The headquarters corps consisted of over 500 intelligence workers and armed guards, and there were an additional seven branches, each with ten to twenty members, throughout the city.

66 BFOR, FO37124663, enclosure No. 2 in dispatch No. 268, 2/5/40. Earlier, on April 16, the British and American diplomatic authorities brought to the attention of the Japanese consul a confidential police report indicating that there would be attempts instigated by the Japanese to assassinate newly elected members of the Shanghai Municipal Council. FRUS 1940, p. 735.

67 Davidson-Houston, *Yellow Creek*, 164.

68 BFOR, letter from Consul-general A. H. George to the ambassador, in FO371-24663 (16/9/40).

69 Ibid.

70 Ibid.

71 Ibid.; *CWR*, February 8, 1941, p. 330.
72 *CWR*, January 11, 1941, p. 198.
73 The strength of the Shanghai Municipal Government police bureau under the Wang Jingwei regime in January 1941 was 7,501. This was a slight decline from the previous roster of 7,801. Of the total, 6,381 were constables. SMP, D-8115(1), 24/1/41.
74 *CWR*, January 11, 1941, pp. 198–9.
75 Ibid., February 8, 1941, p. 330; *Municipal Gazette*, February 12, 1941, p. 32.
76 *Municipal Gazette*, February 12, 1941, p. 29.
77 The official language of the WSP was Chinese.
78 However, there were two additions planned: a reserve unit of seventy-eight riot police plus a second group of 131 seconded from the city police. Thereafter the strength of the WSP was not to be altered without the agreement of the Shanghai Municipal Government and the Shanghai Municipal Council. Ibid., pp. 29, 34. For the jurisdiction of each of the five divisions, see *CWR*, February 8, 1941, p. 331. The WSP would also have had seven branches: Police Affairs, Executive, Special, Foreign Affairs, Crime, Internal Affairs, and a secretariat. *Municipal Gazette*, February 12, 1941, p. 30; *CWR*, February 8, 1941, p. 331.
79 *Municipal Gazette*, February 12, 1941, pp. 31–4; *CWR*, February 8, 1941, pp. 330–3.
80 *Municipal Gazette*, February 12, 1941, p. 35. See also *CWR*, March 1, 1941, p. 462; Oakes, *White Man's Folly*, p. 357.
81 Wakeman, *Shanghai Badlands*.
82 *CWR*, February 8, 1941, p. 331, March 8, 1941, p. 22, March 22, 1941, p. 87, and March 29, 1941, p. 112; *Municipal Gazette*, February 12, 1941, p. 29; "Shanghai Mayor Keeps his Promise to the Public," p. 2.
83 SMP, D-8039A, 15/3/41.
84 *CWR*, June 28, 1941, p. 108.
85 Ibid., pp. 108–9. In July 1941 the manager of the Argentine at 625 Avenue Haig, where gambling had gone on for several weeks in the upstairs rooms, published a notice in the newspaper declaring that his establishment had no connection with the gambling den upstairs. Ibid., July 12, 1941, p. 173.
86 Ibid., p. 109.
87 Ibid., August 2, 1941, p. 269. It was even reported that a major new casino was opening on Columbia Road in one of Shanghai's best residential districts. Ibid., July 26, 1941, p. 234.
88 "Shanghai Mayor Keeps his Promise to the Public," p. 2.
89 *CWR*, July 12, 1941, p. 173.
90 Ibid.
91 *CWR*, August 2, 1941, p. 269; September 6, 1941, p. 11.
92 F. Wakeman, Jr., "The Evolution of Local Government in late Imperial China," in F. Wakeman and C. Grant (eds), *Conflict and Control in Late Imperial China*, Berkeley: University of California Press, 1975.
93 Ching-chih Chen, "The Japanese Adoption of the *Pao-chia* System in Taiwan, 1895–1945," *Journal of Asian Studies* 34 (1975), pp. 391–416.
94 F. M. Bunge and R. S. Shinn (eds), *China: A Country Study*, Washington, D. C.: US Government, Department of the Army, 1981.
95 See, for "mopping-up" operations and attendant atrocities in North China: J. W. Dower, *War without Mercy: Race and Power in the Pacific War*, New York: Pantheon, 1986, p. 43.
96 Chen Gongshu, *Kangzhan houqi fanjian huodong*, pp. 81–2.
97 Yeh, "Dai Li and the Liu Geqing Affair," p. 553; Shi Yuanhua, "Li Shiqun," in Huang Meizhen (ed.), *Wang wei shi hanjian* [Ten Wang puppet traitors], Shanghai: Shanghai renmin chubanshe, 1986, pp. 429–75.

98 Li Shiqun also extended their counter-insurgency *qing xiang* (cleaning up the villages) activities north to Baoshan and across the Yangzi into Jiangbei. *Baoshan xianzhi*, 1992, p. 721.

99 Chen Gongshu, *Kangzhan houqi fanjian huodong*, pp. 83–8. Li Shiqun was soon to be poisoned by the Japanese, either at the request of Zhou Fohai or because of certain connections that Li Shiqun had clandestinely developed with the Communist New Fourth Army outside of Yangzhou. Zhang Weihan, "Dai Li yu 'Juntong ju'", 145; Chen Gongshu, *Kangzhan houqi fanjian huodong*, pp. 370–1.

100 "In late 1942 and early 1943 the Japanese began to seek non-monetary means of encouraging Chinese collaboration. For the first time, they took concrete steps to convince the Chinese of Japanese respect for Chinese nationalism. They renounced extraterritoriality and returned the foreign concessions they had seized, and they reduced overt interference in 'Chinese internal affairs' (i.e. in the puppet government). These gestures, however, came too late." Chen Gongshu, *Kangzhan houqi fanjian huodong*, p. 97.

101 Wakeman, *Policing Shanghai*.

102 "Pao Chia System—Regulations," 1, pp. 11–13; Wakeman, *Policing Shanghai*.

103 Oakes, *White Man's Folly*, p. 360.

104 Japan barred the import of grain from the Yangzi delta into Shanghai. The rice, which was often discarded by the Japanese army, was mixed with gravel and hulls, and was often rotten. Poshek Fu, "Struggle to Entertain," unpublished paper, Champaign–Urbana: University of Illinois, 1995, p. 9; Oakes, *White Man's Folly*, p. 360.

105 FO371/24663, BFOR. "After the murder on November 30 [1940] of a Japanese gendarme by a Chinese gunman, the Japanese military blockaded until December 14 a large district in the western extra-Settlement roads area of Shanghai.... Very little food and other supplies were permitted to enter the area." CSDCF 1940–4, 893.00 P.R. (Political Reports)/Shanghai, 147, December 1940, p. 19.

106 BWOR, extract from Shanghai Naval and Military Intelligence Summary No. 7, 9/4/41, W0208-246A. For rice riots and the *baojia* system in Shanghai's Jewish ghetto, see E. G. Heppner, *Shanghai Refuge: A Memoir of the World War II Jewish Ghetto*, Lincoln: University of Nebraska Press, 1993, pp. 77 and 114.

107 "The High Cost of Living," pp. 14–15.

108 One picul (133 1/3 lb avoirdupois) of rice went from CRB $600 in May 1942 to $1,913 in July 1943, to $9,000 in June 1944, and to $1million in 1945. In 1943 a primary school teacher in Shanghai made about $200–$300 per month, which was not even enough for half a picul of black-market rice. Fu, "Struggle to Entertain," pp. 9–10.

109 China Intelligence Wing Report No. C-35-83, April 26, 1944, in FO371/41680, BFOR.

110 Fu, "Struggle to Entertain," pp. 8–10.

111 Tao Juyin, *Tianliang qian de gudao*, pp. 50–1. In February 1942, the commander of the Shanghai Municipal Police, Colonel Smyth, and the British commander of the Shanghai Volunteer Corps, Colonel Mann, were forced by the Japanese to resign. Davidson-Houston, *Yellow Creek*, p. 178.

112 Tao Juyin, *Tianliang qian de gudao*, pp. 50–1.

113 "'Pao Chia' System for Settlement Recommended," translation of petition to Secretary Teraska from Jiang Tingyas and Xu Chang, March 4, 1942, in SMP (International Settlement) Files, N-1437-1-4, Microfilms from the US National Archives, pp. 1–2.

114 "'Pao Chia' System for Settlement Recommended," p. 2.

115 Each residence, shop, temple, and so on, was known as a *hu*, with one chief. Ten *hu*, formed a *jia* with one chief. Large buildings such as hotels, apartments, and

factories could be considered as one or more *jia*, the size of which was adjustable. "Progress re Enforcement of Pao Chia System in the Settlement," 2.

116 "Progress re Enforcement of Pao Chia System in the Settlement," report, April 7, 1942, Shanghai Municipal Police (International Settlement) Files, N-1437-1(6), Microfilms from the US National Archives, pp. 1, 4–6; "Pao Chia System—Regulations," 1–5; White, "Non-governmentalism," p. 50. See, for the hapless role of the neighborhood surveillance chief: Nai-shan Ch'eng, *The Banker*. Transl. Brutlen Dean, San Francisco: China Books and Periodicals, 1992, p. 425.

117 SMP, N-1437, April 30, to June 30, 1942.

118 "Pao Chia System—Regulations," 1, 11–13; Davidson-Houston 1964, 178–9.

119 Progress re Enforcement of Pao Chia System in the Settlement," 2; "Pao Chia System—Regulations," 8–9.

120 "Interview with Mao Tsu-p'ei," 2; "Pao Chia System—Regulations," 2; L. T. White III, "Deviance, Modernization, Rations, and Household Registers in Urban China," in A. A. Wilson, S. L. Greenblatt, and R. W. Wilson, eds, *Deviance and Social Control in Chinese Society*, New York: Praeger, 1977, pp. 151–72, at p. 157).

121 In October 1943, after the Wang Jingwei government recovered national sovereignty over Shanghai, 399 street names (including 129 in the French Concession) were changed: e.g. Avenue Joffre became Huaihai lu, Route Cardinal Mercier became Maoming nanlu, Avenue Pétain became Hengshan lu, and so forth.

122 "Pao Chia System—Regulations," 2-4; "Progress re Enforcement of Pao Chia System in the Settlement," 3, 10; SMP, N-1437, April 30 to May 31, 1942. The French Concession also organized a civil policing corps on the basis of the *baojia* system. SMP, N-1437, December 8, 1942.

123 *Jingcha faling* [Police laws], Nanjing: Ministry of the Interior, 1944.

124 *Jingcha faling* 1944. This exceptionality probably reflected the wishes of the Japanese gendarmerie (military police) and the Special Organ (Tokumu jikan) of the Imperial Japanese Army. The various offices (*chu*)—general affairs, police defense (including air defense), economic peace preservation, peace preservation administration, judicial affairs, fire protection, and inspector-general—included one for *baojia* (Japanese *hokô*) and a special higher office (*tegao chu*) responsible for political police affairs, foreign affairs, propaganda, and special services (*tewu*). Article 7, "Shanghai tebie shi di yi jingcha ju zhanxing," *Jingcha faling*.

125 *Jingcha faling*, 1944, pp. 1–2.

126 Wakeman, *Policing Shanghai*.

127 *Jingcha faling*, pp. 107–19.

9   The purge in Shanghai, 1945–6

The Sarly affair and the end of the French Concession

Marie-Claire Bergère

During the night of December 14, 1945, soldiers from the Wusong–Shanghai garrison arrived at the home of Roland Sarly, the Assistant Director of Police in what had been the French Concession, and arrested him. In the course of the next few days, Sarly was handed over to the Chinese municipal police, who had him brought before the prosecutor of the High Court of Shanghai (Shanghai gaodeng fayuan).[1]

According to the investigation carried out by the garrison, Sarly was guilty of collaboration and treason. He was accused of having held the post of inspector with responsibility for external relations in the municipal police force of the puppet government of Wang Jingwei, from August 1943 to March 1945.[2] It was claimed that even before 1943 he had cooperated with this police force, handing over to it Guomindang undercover agents who were operating in the French Concession.[3] He was said even to have given some members of the puppet police force permission to carry arms within the concession territory. He was also accused of collaborating with the Japanese: in particular, by agreeing to hand over to them Chinese soldiers who, following the defeat of the Nationalist troops in the autumn of 1937, had sought refuge in the French Concession and had there been disarmed and interned. The investigators furthermore accused Sarly of having provided the Japanese authorities with an inventory of materials stocked in the concession and of having relinquished to them all the weapons seized from the Nationalist soldiers at the time of their internment.[4]

Over and above these charges of collaboration and treason, the investigation of the municipal police, for its part, accused Sarly of corruption. The charges were not exactly identical to those made by the military. According to the municipal police, Sarly had taken part in the hunt for "terrorists" carried out by the Japanese in the French Concession in December 1941; he had exploited his powers of control over the prices and rationing of goods to extort money from the wholesalers of cotton textiles, assisted the Japanese in their policy of confiscating "enemy property" (i.e. property belonging to nationals of the Allied countries) and in the application of measures discriminating against the latter.[5] Finally, following the Japanese capitulation in August 1945, he had encroached upon the prerogatives of the Chinese police and had violated the sovereignty of China by having French agents standing sentry in front of a building in the former French Concession that was being used by the American forces, and by instigating searches and arrests of French residents of Shanghai.

The wide variety and the gravity of the crimes with which Sarly was charged are an indication of the importance of the responsibilities of this police officer and of the role that he had played in the French Concession.

A FRENCH SHANGHAI POLICEMAN

Roland Sarly was still in his twenties when he first arrived in Shanghai, just after World War I. The young man, of Franco-African descent, had received no special training following his secondary schooling. He entered the concession's police force as a uniformed policeman. There were not many policemen of French origin in Shanghai and it was not long before Sarly made his mark, standing out "like a heron among chickens" (as the Chinese police file put it). Captain Fiori, then director of the French Concession's policing services, noticed him. The young Sarly, who was physically striking and intelligent, a hard worker and a skillful flatterer, made a good impression. Fiori, not as a rule a trusting man, came to place his confidence in him.[6]

In the spring of 1927, thanks to the relations he had cultivated with the Chinese inspectors of the French Concession, Sarly learned of the measures that Chiang Kai-shek was intending to take against the Communists, employing Shanghai gangsters as his agents. The French police turned a blind eye, thereby indirectly greatly facilitating the *coup* of 12 April.[7] Sarly was rewarded by being promoted to the rank of chief inspector and was put in charge of the newly created Political Service, which soon became "the real centre of power in the French Concession."[8]

Sarly now began to grow rich. As a well placed observer, Joseph Shieh (Xie Gengxin), himself a former Chinese chief inspector in the French Concession, remarked, "In truth, it was impossible to be totally honest if one was a Shanghai policeman in 1930."[9] The "protection money" paid by politicians of every kind seeking refuge in the French Concession, the "registration fees" required from companies, the "gifts" offered by gaming houses and opium dens, the "monthly subscriptions" from coolie garbage collectors, and the bribes paid by the Nationalist authorities in return for information about their opponents all helped to swell the income of any official who went along with the local customs. Sarly's professional scruples probably stretched only as far as keeping his cupidity and acceptance of hand-backs within limits judged to be reasonable by his colleagues and partners.

But Sarly managed to escape the upheavals of 1932. After three years of deepening corruption favoured by the weakness of the consul-general, the French Concession fell under the control of the powerful secret society of the

Green Gang and its leader Du Yusheng. The local administration, openly financed by the illicit profits from opium and gambling, was discredited. The reestablishment of order was instigated by Paris, which appointed a new consul-general, Jacques Meyrier, and a new chief of police, Commandant Fabre.[10] The restoration of authority and public probity was accompanied by a rigorous police purge. Whether by pure chance or through forewarned prudence, Sarly was at this time on vacation in France. Upon his return to Shanghai, he was able to ingratiate himself with his new superior, Commandant Fabre, a man of integrity, and, in the course of the 1930s the Political Service of the French Concession, headed by Sarly, became one of the best centres of intelligence in East Asia.

As war approached, Roland Sarly was recalled to France to serve as an army captain: he was twice cited in dispatches.[11] After the defeat he was demobilized, and in March 1941 he returned to Shanghai, where he resumed his duties at the head of the Political Service and at the same time became the Assistant Director of Police, working alongside Commandant Fabre. He also became one of the principal collaborators of Roland de Margerie, the new consul-general appointed by the Vichy government. In July 1943, when that government, under pressure from Japan, decided to renounce the rights and privileges granted to France by the nineteenth-century treaties and to restore the French Concession to the puppet regime of Wang Jingwei, Roland Sarly (along with several hundred other employees of the former French municipality) passed into the service of that regime.[12]

He retained the functions of inspector in the Chinese police until the Japanese strike against the French administrations and troops of both Indochina and Shanghai, in March 1945.[13] August 1945, a few months later, found Roland Sarly in the post of adviser to the consulate-general of France, recently resuscitated by the Allied victory.

The man whom the Chinese authorities accused of collaboration and treason was thus certainly one of the foremost figures in the French administration and community of Shanghai. At the age of forty-four, this energetic and ambitious man was still young, but in possession of a wealth of long experience of a wide range of Shanghai circles, with which his official duties enabled him to establish many links, most of them founded upon services both received and rendered. He had never lost the trust of his superiors: Commandant (now Colonel) Fabre had always praised the "courage and resolution" of his assistant; and Consul-general Roland de Margerie, who had written the most glowing references for him, had no hesitation in giving evidence in his favour in the Chinese courts, in February 1946, and then again in December 1948.[14] In the eyes of the former residents and "notables" of the French Concession, Sarly was (after Colonel Fabre) "the figure who best embodied French authority in Shanghai over the past ten to fifteen years."[15] That was no doubt precisely why his trial immediately turned into an "affair" with many diplomatic and political implications.

THE SARLY TRIAL

After his arrest, Sarly appeared before the prosecutor for the High Court of Shanghai, who subjected him to two interrogations, one on December 27, 1945, the other on February 14, 1946. Sarly was required to answer questions relating to his activities both as a policeman and as an individual. The matters under investigation were numerous and in general concerned problems already raised in the investigation files compiled by the garrison and the municipal police. But the prosecutor also raised a few new questions: he tried to identify a "Sarly network" within the staff of the French police force and to establish Sarly's responsibility in the activities of the Maron brigade.[16]

Sarly pleaded not guilty, declaring, "I am a friend of China. I hate the Japanese."[17] According to him the whole affair was nothing but a tissue of "false accusations."[18] He denied them all. In the December interrogation he nevertheless admitted that in 1942 he had granted a few permits to carry arms to the puppet police of 76 Jessfield Road.[19] However, in the interrogation of February 1946 he withdrew that statement. And in the *pro domo* statement in his defence that he produced for the Chinese prosecutor the following March, from his prison, he protested his innocence, denying some accusations, laying certain responsibilities either at the door of other colleagues (Joseph Shieh, for example, in the case of the 1943 racket involving the wholesalers of cotton textiles) or else at that of his hierarchical superiors, whose orders he claimed to have been simply carrying out.[20]

While these investigations were taking place, Sarly was held in preventive detention. The Chinese press described his living conditions in the Chinese prison as "comfortable": he had bread every day and soup twice daily, visits and parcels from his family, and one hour's exercise a day. Sarly nevertheless wrote a letter of protest to the League of Human Rights.[21]

The vice was closing in on him. One after another his subordinates and close colleagues were arrested and charged, in their turn, with collaboration and treason: in January, the Annamese non-commissioned officer Nguyen Van-hoong, formerly Fabre's secretary and also close to Sarly, against whose arrest he had mounted an active campaign;[22] in February, the ex-Inspector George Emelianoff, a former Russian officer with naturalized French nationality, who was a good linguist and analyst and the author of "a highly regarded report on the communist problem in the Far East."[23] In March, it was the turn of Lambalot and Oussakovsky. The former, an assistant director of the French police, was an old friend of Sarly's, who had the reputation of being involved in "every violent operation" and whom Joseph Shieh described as "brutal" and "prone to lay about with his truncheon."[24] The latter, a White Russian, who had arrived in Shanghai in 1927, was considered a good intelligence agent who, again according to Joseph Shieh, had during the war allowed "some of the information that should have been kept for the French to filter through" (to the Japanese).[25]

In mid-April, Sarly was served with a writ summoning him to appear before the court.[26] He was accused of collaboration on seven charges. The Chinese press, which was hostile to him, stressed his offhand attitude when he appeared in court: he chewed gum and lounged with his legs crossed, listening to the examination of witnesses as if to a play in a theater.[27] Passing judgment on June 17, 1946, the court dismissed all but two charges: the one of granting agents of 76 Jessfield Road permits to carry arms, the other of carrying out the duties of an inspector in Shanghai's puppet police force from July 1943 to March 1945. On these he was found guilty and was sentenced to three years in prison, with the confiscation of all his possessions.[28]

The defence immediately decided to appeal, claiming that the court had not had the opportunity of examining a number of official French documents, documents of a kind to prove the innocence of the accused.[29] The Chinese prosecutor also appealed, protesting that the High Court had not considered five of the seven charges on which Sarly was indicted.[30]

Pending the decision of the Court of Appeal, Sarly was released on bail.[31] Many witnesses came forward to testify in his favour. Roland de Margerie, the former consul-general of Shanghai, and M. Grosbois, the French Concession's former Inspector of Education, had already written letters in his defence, which were included in his file.[32] Now a letter from a "Shanghai well-known Resident" was added to these. It was dated June 18, 1946, and was addressed to Prime Minister Félix Gouin, asking him to intervene directly through his Chinese counterpart, the president of the Executive Yuan, T. V. Soong.[33] The hand-written notes added by Quai d'Orsay diplomats in the margin of this text describe the praises showered upon Sarly by the author of the letter as "ridiculously exaggerated", but at the same time acknowledge that they reflect the opinion of much of the French community of Shanghai.

Yielding to considerations of a general political nature more than to pressure from the residents of Shanghai, the Quai d'Orsay agreed to make available to Sarly's lawyer official documents of a kind to strengthen his defence. These constituted French "diplomatic and consular authoritative evidence in his defence, even though this ran counter to international practice."[34]

On April 11, 1947, following a further inquiry, the Supreme Court of Nanking quashed the judgment, condemning Sarly and returning the case to the High Court of Shanghai for reexamination.[35] Sarly's second trial began on May 17, 1947.[36] The court was instructed to concentrate upon the five charges left aside in the first trial. On November 11 it partially acquitted Sarly. The only charge remaining was that of having granted agents of the puppet police permits to carry arms.[37] On January 2, 1948, the prosecutor appealed against this decision. But the Supreme Court of Nanking upheld the partial acquittal.[38] A definitive acquittal was declared on December 15, following the testimony of the former consul-general, Roland de Margerie, who acknowledged his own responsibility in the granting of permits for the carrying of arms.[39]

THE PURGE OF FRENCH COLLABORATORS

Sarly's acquittal brought to an end the series of proceedings taken by the Chinese police and courts against French nationals accused of collaboration and treason. According to the French consul-general in Shanghai, the request for the inquiry addressed by the Waijiaobu (the Chinese Ministry of Foreign Affairs) to the municipal police concerned about fifty "war criminals", over forty of whom had already left Shanghai. But the Chinese Minister of Justice mentioned only thirty-five names, twenty-two of which were those of "accused who were absent."[40]

Some of the French nationals brought before Chinese courts were sentenced to a few years in prison, then acquitted on appeal, others had their cases dismissed, yet others found the proceedings against them quite simply dropped. By the end of 1947, the Chinese authorities had decided to call a halt to the trials for collaboration and were preparing amnesty measures for "minor war criminals."[41]

All these trials, Sarly's included, ended amid public indifference on both the French and the Chinese sides. The history of the Sino-Japanese war and, even more, that of the French Concession belonged to what seemed an already distant past. Many of the foreign residents had left Shanghai and the former French community, now dispersed, was no longer affected by the politico-judicial ups and downs or the human dramas unfolding in the local courtrooms. In France itself, rightwing and moderate forces had already launched a campaign that was to end with the amnesty laws of 1951 and 1953. As for the Chinese, their attention was increasingly focused on the vagaries of the civil war and the prospect of a Communist victory.

In China, as elsewhere, purge trials were political trials. Chinese courts, like French courts, endeavoured to reconcile the application of the law with the desire for revenge and punishment harbored by former opponents and victims: but they were even less successful than their French counterparts, on account of the fragility of modern judicial practices only recently imported from the West and also the violent pressure exerted by relatively uncontrolled political and military forces.

In this respect, the report of the Sarly inquiry produced by the Shanghai police makes significant reading. The nine proofs appended to the report in support of the charges are almost all constituted by official texts submitted by the French municipal or consular authorities or by the Japanese occupation authorities, none of which imputed any personal responsibility to Sarly. As for the crimes with which Sarly, as an individual, was charged—such as fatally assaulting a Chinese employed by the police, following a theft from the Assistant Director's office—no evidence at all was produced.[42] The report of the investigation carried out by the garrison explained, for its part, that no proofs actually existed, that many people who could have brought witness for the prosecution had died, that Sarly was a cunning man and had operated in secret.[43] When, on March 26, 1946, the former consulary judge, Horace

Kaufman, a sworn enemy of Sarly, was questioned by the Chinese magistrate in the course of preparations for the case, he likewise was unable to make any precise allegations and mostly produced replies such as "I do not know the details" (of Sarly's relations with the puppet regime), "It would be better to ask his subordinates," or "It was said" (that Sarly had arrested Chinese undercover agents) "but I myself did not see this," or "I do not really know" (whether Sarly supplied the Japanese with military intelligence) but "I do know that he is a bad man."[44]

Well known French residents, such as M. Cochin, the president of the French Chamber of Commerce in China, were not alone in complaining of the abuses or shortcomings of Chinese justice.[45] An editorial in the *China Weekly Review* complained of the Chinese courts' subordination to political and military factions: "China's courts are not free agents. The judiciary is not independent. It is too often the tool of military and political factions. The Shanghai-Wusong garrison ... arrests a man, announces to the press that he is guilty and follows him into the courtroom."[46]

The numerous acquittals in 1947 no doubt reflect not only the political desire for reconciliation but also the fact that judicial proceedings had been placed on a more regular footing, thanks to the fact that the Shanghai court could be overruled by the Supreme court of Nanking and the Minister of Justice, both anxious not to jeopardize the abolition of the privileges of extraterritoriality.[47]

The purge process was complicated not only by questionable legal process, but also by the many ambiguous aspects of resistance and collaboration in Shanghai. Sarly's trial, like the trials of the other accused, was affected by the whole history of China, Shanghai and its concessions, from the outbreak of the Sino-Japanese war in the summer of 1937 through to the end of the war in the Pacific, in August 1945. It was a complex history, with features reminiscent of those of the history of France itself over the same period: partial occupation of the territory by enemy forces; rivalry between the government of free China (that of Chiang Kai-shek, holed up in Chongqing) and a collaborating government (that of Wang Jingwei, installed in Nanking); rapidly developing Communist forces, carried along by the impetus of national resistance and regarded as a threat by both governments. In Shanghai, as in Paris, there was a black market and rationing, profiteers unashamedly paraded their affluence, and assassinations, denunciations, arrests, and torture were all rife.

But the Far Eastern context conferred a number of peculiarities upon Chinese collaboration and resistance. Japanese militarism was not founded upon the same ideological bases or the same ambitions as Nazism. The presence of Western imperialism complicated the political choices of Chinese patriots. And the growing strength of Communism encouraged the conclusion of secret alliances between Chongqing and Nanking or even with the Japanese.

In France, despite the relative strength of Pétainist tendencies in some early resistance movements and the ambiguities created by the establishment of the

French state in 1940, commitment choices were relatively clear.[48] In Shanghai, what predominated was the idea that it might prove possible to "save the nation by devious means"[49] and what was adopted more or less generally was a strategy of double or even triple games, governed by considerations more political than ideological, frequently prompted by personal friendships or personal interests: Shanghai, or the triumph of opportunism.

All these factors certainly did not make the purge process any easier. Sarly's judicial file bears the mark of these ambiguities. A systematic analysis of it would call for an in-depth study of the history of Shanghai and the French Concession from 1937 through 1945 and is clearly not possible within the framework of the present chapter. So I will limit myself to exploring some of what was at stake in the trial in its early stages, during the winter of 1945 and the spring of 1946, when certain issues could not be confined to the courtrooms but were mobilizing public opinion generally.

At the time, these were burning issues of a diplomatic and political nature, and it was they that turned the trial into an "affair." They were linked with both the disturbed context of the end of the imperialism of the Western powers and also the ups and downs of the never-ending Franco-French conflict.[50] Through Sarly, it was not only the attitude of the authorities of the French Concession during the occupation that was brought into question, but the very legitimacy and future of the French presence in Shanghai. The judicial procedure that was used to advance the Chinese Nationalist claims seems also to have served as an instrument for one section of the French community to get at another. For the charges brought against Sarly by the Shanghai court were largely based on denunciations by his own compatriots. Here, as in France, the occupation, followed by the purges, brought back into play the old rift between the left and the right, the socialists and the Church, minor employees and the administrative and economic elites. And political divisions combined with and poisoned the personal rivalries that were always ready to develop in this small community of expatriates.

This Franco-French aspect of the Sarly affair is not always easy to seize upon, because some archives remain inaccessible. Furthermore, such an aspect hardly affected the history of China and Franco-Chinese relations. That is why, in this chapter, I shall limit myself to exploring what was at stake diplomatically in Sarly's trial, which precipitated the return of the former French Concession to Chinese sovereignty and provided concrete evidence of the new situation.

FRENCH AFTERTHOUGHTS, FOLLOWING THE LIBERATION

For many Chinese, the collapse of Japan in 1945 raised hopes of a profound change, a new era in which China, delivered from the weight of unequal treaties, would recover its full sovereignty and, having been accepted as one of the Big Five, would accede to the rank of a world power. For Chinese public opinion and the Chinese authorities, the Sarly trial provided an opportunity to express a definitive rejection of the old colonial order. It was the whole management of the French Concession that was under attack in the person of the police officer. Since that management had, from 1940 on, been the responsibility of an administration appointed by the Vichy government, the charges of collaboration brought against Sarly were intended to discredit that entire administration and to speed up the liquidation of the concession and of the French presence in Shanghai.

By the end of the war in the Pacific, that presence was already very weak. Under Japanese pressure, and following the example of the British and the Americans, France had agreed to renounce its extraterritorial privileges and to restore Chinese sovereignty over its concessions. Following a "declaration of principle," made by the Vichy government on February 24, 1943, an agreement of intent was signed with Nanking on May 18. On the following July 30, the Shanghai French Concession was handed back to the government of Wang Jingwei. The consul-general, Roland de Margerie presided over the official ceremony. Although present in Shanghai, the French ambassador, Henri Cosme, did not attend. (It is true that he was accredited to the government of Chiang Kai-shek in Chongqing and had no official relations with Wang Jingwei's government in Nanking.) The return of the French Concession was thus concluded between two governments—that of Vichy and that of Nanking—neither of which recognized the other and neither of which any longer existed by the autumn of 1945. For some of the French, the ambiguity of this situation generated hopes of a return to the old *status quo.*

Those French afterthoughts were encouraged by the uncertainties of the process of transition from the collaborationist regime to the Nationalist one, which took place in Shanghai during the late summer and the autumn of 1945. The Japanese capitulation had taken the Chongqing government by surprise. It took Chiang Kai-shek, still holed up in his mountain fastness of Sichuan, in the west of the Chinese mainland, several weeks to organize transport to carry the Nationalist forces to the eastern coastal provinces. In the meantime, Shanghai was left to its own devices. Right up until the end of September, the armed Japanese military were still moving freely about the city, where they continued to ensure public law and order. Eventually they "interned themselves" in camps that they themselves set up and guarded.[51] German Nazis continued to occupy the fine residences that they had requisitioned;[52] meanwhile, with no money or lodgings, the 6,600 interned allies remained in their camps.[53] Following the flight of the chief leaders of the Nanking government to Japan, Chiang Kai-shek made the (collaborationist) mayor of Shanghai, Zhou Fuhai, responsible for maintaining order until the arrival of the Nationalist troops, in mid-September.[54] The appointment of new authorities at this point did nothing to improve the situation. The new mayor, General Jian Dajun, was a courageous fighter but had no administrative experience and was soon at loggerheads with General Tang Enpo, the commander of the military region of Shanghai.[55] As for the deputy mayor, Wu Shaoshu, he was a local Guomindang cadre, reckoned to be "a pleasant nonentity" by some and "notoriously xenophobic" by others.[56] Notwithstanding the confused situation, security was maintained. But the city suffered from serious shortages and a measure of social unrest.[57]

Confronted with this administrative void and these political uncertainties, many French residents could dream of nothing but a return to the prewar situation. "They do not yet understand why the French Concession has not returned to normal."[58] As soon as the Japanese capitulation was announced, certain members of the consulate staff—apparently inspired and supported by Sarly—took action with a view to reaffirming French authority within the territory of the former French Concession: they sent several groups, each a dozen men strong, equipped with tricolor armbands and revolvers, to patrol the main thoroughfares of the ex-French Concession. They tried to get the Japanese to hand over, directly to them, the French buildings that had been confiscated during the war; they endeavoured to ensure the protection of premises occupied by the American information services; and they proceeded to arrest and intern certain of their compatriots, just as if France still enjoyed its old extraterritorial privileges.[59]

In the consulate-general, there was apparently a clash of views on these initiatives. While the consul-general, Baron Guy Fain, tolerated or encouraged them, his assistant, Consul Salade, repeatedly offered his apologies to the Chinese authorities.[60] By late autumn, the situation had become rather more stable. However, the French diplomatic representative, clinging to a juridical point of view, still considered that the exterritorial status must continue until such time as it was abolished by a treaty in due and proper form with the Nationalist government. That, at any rate, was the argument put forward when, on December 3, 1945, the consul-general ordered the arrest of a notorious collaborator, Paul-François Carcopino;[61] when he pressed the Chinese authorities to hand over other French collaborators whom they had seized, such as René d'Alessy[62] and Alexandre Gerspach;[63] and when he refused to hand over to those authorities the brothers Arthur and Théodore Sofer, also accused of collaboration and held (or perhaps given refuge?) on the premises of the consulate-general.[64]

From a technical point of view, there was some justification for the position adopted by the French diplomat. However, it reflected a very insensitive appreciation of the political context and failed to take into consideration the force of triumphant Chinese nationalism, the desire to avenge imperialism, and the appetites aroused by the prospect of laying hands on the foreign businesses and services of Shanghai.

CHINESE INTRANSIGENCE AND APPETITES

The new authorities installed by the Chongqing government immediately revealed themselves to be difficult partners, "more nationalistic, more anti-foreign and less reasonable than the former puppets," in the opinion of one British journalist.[65] The general tone was set by General He Yingqin. On September 8, the Chinese commander-in-chief had set up his headquarters in Nanking. On the 9th, he received the official surrender of the Japanese troops in China. On the 17th, he gave a press conference in Shanghai:

> The national army has returned in triumph to Shanghai. Now we have won the war … With the unequal treaties abolished, Shanghai is now completely under Chinese sovereignty. From now on, no one in Shanghai, regardless of his nationality, is to observe any law other than that of this country.[66]

A few weeks later, the general headquarters of the Chinese forces in Shanghai announced that "foreigners guilty of collaboration with the Japanese and the puppet authorities will have charges brought against them by the Chinese courts," and it urged the public to denounce all those guilty.[67] Then, in mid-December, the Waijiaobu's special delegate in Shanghai offically turned down the French request for the Frenchman Alexandre Gerspach to be handed over to the consular authorities.[68]

Not only were the Chinese authorities determined not to relinquish a single inch of the territory reconquered since 1943, but they endeavoured to make the most of the new situation created by the Japanese defeat to complete that reconquest and erase the last traces of the French presence in Shanghai. They accordingly tried to repossess a number of buildings and properties of the former municipality, which, at the time of the handover in 1943, the consul-general Roland de Margerie had managed to exclude from the negotiations and retain for France, by transforming them *in extremis* into state property.[69]

The Chinese authorities produced a stream of arguments to justify their actions. The Director of Hygiene, who wanted to extend his authority to the Institut Pasteur and the Sainte-Marie Hospital, invoked the manner in which these establishments had compromised themselves with the puppet municipality.[70] The police, who were laying claim to the former municipal infirmary, hoping to use it as their own hospital, accused the former authorities of the French Concession of duplicity, asserting, "It is quite clear that … before the retrocession, they intended to dissimulate and to usurp the buildings and grounds of the infirmary."[71] The Waijiaobu's office in Shanghai supported these actions, but—as the consul-general noted—"without particular insistence or acrimony." No doubt this settling of old scores between Shanghaiese did not affect Chinese sovereignty as directly as the resurrection of extraterritoriality.

However, at a local level, tensions ran high as the Chinese tried to eliminate or confiscate the major French businesses that had continued to function throughout the war, in some cases by dint of entering into deals with the puppet authorities or the Japanese. The Société d'Oxygène et d'Acétylène d'Extrême-Orient, a subsidiary of Air Liquide, was forced to close down. It was feared that the Compagnie des Messageries Maritimes and its naval yard of Kiou Sin (Jiuxin) might be forced to do likewise.[72] The Compagnie Française des Tramways, de l'Eau et de l'Électricité de Shanghai was also under threat. The director and his assistant were summoned to justify the company's attitude under the occupation, first at the Shanghai town hall, then before the courts. In their defence, they claimed that they had never willingly supplied any materials at all to the Japanese.[73]

French possessions were not the only ones at risk[74] but, because of France's political and military weakness in East Asia, they were particularly vulnerable. In Europe, the battles fought by the Free French and the resistance, and the part played by the reconstituted French army in the invasion of Germany, conferred a degree of legitimacy upon the role claimed by De Gaulle and recognized by the Allies. In the Far East, however, in the eyes of Chinese and Allies alike, the French who had been defeated without fighting were no longer seen as a great power. At best they were "considered the weakest of the Big Powers."[75] So it was they who came under the most violent attack. Increasingly heavy pressure was applied through manipulated strikes and through interventions on the part of the municipality, the army and the police force. These were frequently made in the name of taking revenge on 'Vichy traitors'.[76] Arrests of collaborators—whether real or supposed— constituted part of this campaign, which, according to the observations of one British journalist, was resulting in reducing the French to the sad situation of Jewish refugees or White Russians, who had always been denied consular protection.[77]

FROM THE *EMILE BERTIN* CRISIS TO THE FRANCO-CHINESE TREATY OF FEBRUARY 1946

The *Emile Bertin* was a French warship that left Shanghai on January 3, 1946, bound for Saigon, carrying a passenger officially required to be on board, Paul-François Carcopino. This pro-German collaborator and propagandist had been summoned before the French consular tribunal on December 28, in accordance with the right of extraterritoriality that the French authorities continued to claim despite protests from the Chinese. The consular tribunal declared itself unqualified to deal with the matter and referred it to the Saigon tribunal. Hence the precipitate departure of Carcopino, which the mayor of Shanghai and the local representative of the Waijiaobu had opposed in vain.[78]

The official protests and popular demonstrations that followed the ship's departure soon assumed veritable crisis proportions that threatened the French presence and interests in Shanghai, and were sometimes tinged with a more general xenophobia. This was the context in which the Sarly affair materialized. Sarly's arrest by the Chinese on December 14 was a riposte to Carcopino's by the French ten days earlier. The case of these two French citizens, both charged with collaboration, one of them summoned to face Chinese justice while the other was more or less kidnapped and removed to be tried in Saigon, provides an illustration of the difficulties of a transition that the war made inevitable, at the same time ruling out any possibility of preparation for it.

At first, the crisis was diplomatic in nature. The arguments of Consul-general Filliol, based on the continuing existence of French extraterritorial rights, exasperated the Waijiaobu, which proceeded to demand the recall of the French official,[79] and set out its own reasons for doing so. Passing in silence over the retrocession of the French Concession to the government of Wang Jingwei that had taken place in July 1943, the Waijiaobu invoked the unilateral declaration of May 19, 1943 made by the Chongqing government. This had followed a declaration of intent on the part of the Vichy government on February 24, 1943,[80] and an agreement of principle between Vichy and Nanking, signed on the following May 18. It repudiated the extraterritorial privileges granted to France by the nineteenth-century treaties. Could a unilateral declaration stand up against an international treaty? It would be pointless to dwell on these juridical and diplomatic considerations, for very soon the press campaign and popular demonstrations conferred upon the crisis a political urgency that pushed the juridical arguments into the background.

On December 26, the *Xinwenbao* reported the arrest of ten (!) French Nazis by the consulate-general.[81] On January 4, this newspaper accused Filliol of having assisted the flight of the "war criminal" Carcopino.[82] On January 7, it censured him for having represented the problems raised by the treatment of war criminals as merely so many local incidents (*difang shijian*).[83]

Tension mounted. The Chinese authorities threatened to seize the Sofer collaborators, two brothers held inside the consulate-general, and to ban French warships from the port of Shanghai.[84] The unrest spread to student circles and tracts began to circulate.[85] On January 14, a demonstration attracted between 20,000 and 30,000 students, who gathered in front of the French consulate-general. They asked for "the French traitors to be handed over to the Chinese authorities," the recall of Filliol, apologies from Paris, and the secession of the Compagnie Française des Tramways and also of the Franco-Chinese School. The Shanghai Federation of Industrial and Trade Associations, (Shanghai tongye gonghui) sent a telegram of support to the protesters and the mayor of Shanghai agreed to parley with them.[86] Furthermore, 723 policemen of the former French Concession came out against the consul-general.[87] These were Annamese guards of the former municipality whom the vicissitudes of war had prevented from being repatriated to Indochina. Having rebelled against their officers in July 1945, declaring themselves in support of the Vietnamese independence movement, and having been protected by the Japanese military, who had in August 1945 been replaced by the Guomindang government, these lost soldiers quite naturally espoused the anti-French cause of the Chinese Nationalists.[88]

In accordance with the well tried tactics of the 1920s and the 1930s, the unrest spread from political and intellectual circles to the workers— encouraged by Du Yuesheng, the leader of the Green Gang, who was attempting to regain his former control over the local gangsters and trade unions.[89]

Any solution to the crisis precipitated by the arrests of Carcopino and Sarly would clearly have to involve a redefinition of Franco-Chinese relations. The need to provide new juridical and diplomatic bases for France's relations with China was clearly perceived in both Paris and Chongqing. When called in for consultation, the jurist and former adviser to the Chinese government, Jean Escarra, recommended a pragmatic solution.[90] At the height of the *Emile Bertin* crisis, the moderation of the notes emanating from the Quai d'Orsay and the telegrams from the ambassador, Jacques Meyrier, contrasted sharply with the intransigence of Consul-general Filliol. At one moment, in order to affirm the continuing existence of French extraterritorial rights, the latter, using everything to hand as grist to his mill, would be arguing that the agreements of July 1943 on the retrocession of the French Concession were null and void; the next, he would be referring to the terms of those very agreements, in order to support the French state's ownership of certain buildings in the former concession.[91] Paris tried to moderate the zeal of this official and advised him to cease referring to agreements "concluded between authorities whom neither the French government nor the Chinese government recognized." But the warning appeared to go unheeded and had to be repeated.[92] As for Ambassador Meyrier, he was of the opinion that France's renunciation of its extraterritorial rights ought to be considered as established *de facto*, even if in 1943 it had not been possible to ratify that renunciation by a treaty.[93]

Certainly, a few French attempts were made to negotiate the application of emergency procedures: it was claimed that, where political offenses were concerned, cases pending at the time of the closing down of consular tribunals should be transferred to French courts or else to a court of international justice. This request had been made several several times and was repeated in early January 1945.[94] But the *Emile Bertin* crisis and developments in the Sarly affair scuttled these efforts.

In general, however, French diplomacy adopted a conciliatory attitude. No official protest was made following the demonstrations of January 14, and the decision of January 21 to close down consular tribunals was made several weeks in advance of the signing of the Franco-Chinese treaty.[95] This low profile not only reflected acceptance of a situation regarded as irreversible, but also testified to the secondary importance attributed to Shanghai affairs by a French government anxious primarily to settle the Indochinese problem. For Paris, what was above all at stake in the diplomatic negotiations held in Chongqing during the winter of 1945–6 was not the fate of the former French concessions in China but the evacuation of the Chinese troops which, by virtue of the Potsdam agreement of August 1945, had occupied Tonking, Annam and Laos to the north of the sixteenth parallel, preventing the French forces from regaining a footing in these regions and from reaffirming French sovereignty there.

So not one but two Franco-Chinese treaties were signed in Chongqing on February 28, 1946. In the first, the French renounced all extraterritorial rights in China and retroceded their former concessions. In the second, China—in exchange for a number of compensations—agreed that its armies should be replaced by French forces in northern Indochina.[96]

The Sarly trial now lost its political importance. The Chinese authorities seem to have claimed the right to judge the French collaborators solely the better to affirm the end of the extraterritorial regime. In reality, the fate of the collaborators was of scant interest to them,[97] which no doubt explains the indulgence with which those charged were treated: although not all were innocent, all were in the end either acquitted or had their cases dismissed. As for the French authorities, what they had feared above all was that the Sarly trial would put the concession as a whole in the dock and would compromise a Franco-Chinese agreement that was indispensable to the settlement of affairs in Tonking. The signing of the treaties in February removed both those threats and brought the Sarly affair to an end.

THE TRIAL GOES ON

Although the Sarly affair was over, the trial went ahead. The arguments that took place from 1946 to 1948 in the courtrooms of Shanghai and Nanking raised a number of essential problems: those of state collaboration and individual responsibility, active and passive collaboration, vengeance and law. Why was the trial continued when the affair was over? For two main reasons, I think. The first was the presence in Shanghai of former French resistance members, victims of the Vichyist policies of the consular authorities, whose instrument Sarly had been. Among them, Horace Kaufman, the former consular judge, dismissed in 1940 "on account of his Israelite status," was to be called as a witness for the prosecution in the preparation of Sarly's case.[98] Also noteworthy is the return to Shanghai, in November 1945, of Roderick Egal,[99] General De Gaulle's unofficial representative in Shanghai, from 1940 on, the organizer of the France Quand Même group and a recruiter of volunteers for the Free French forces. In April 1941, Egal had been arrested and sent off to Saigon aboard the *Kindhia*, to stand trial before a naval tribunal for the crime of complicity in desertion in a time of war. These men were certainly anxious that justice should take its course.

The Chinese judges, for their part, seem to have shared that anxiety, but for different reasons. Because of the controversy that surrounded its early days, the Sarly trial attracted considerable attention. It was the first major trial of a foreigner in a China newly restored to its sovereignty. And it represented a test of China's ability to exercise that new-found sovereignty. The French consul-general commented as follows:

> One is tempted to believe that the sustained attention that my foreign colleagues and I myself have devoted to all the trials of our own nationals

before local courts, and the criticisms of the Chinese courts that the foreign press has persisted in making have little by little forced the authorities, concerned for the prestige of their courts following the abolition of extraterritoriality, to oversee their activities more closely.[100]

Whatever the reasons may have been, it is only fair to underline the care with which Chinese justice conducted Sarly's trial, the progressive improvement in its procedures and its recognition of the particular problems posed by the definition of and penalties for crimes of collaboration. Moving from the very wide concept expressed in the decree of 23 November 1945, which condemned as "Chinese traitors" (*Hanjian*), all those who had worked in Japanese or puppet organizations, who had run businesses in the occupied zone, or who had pursued cultural activities or liberal professions there,[101] a shift took place to very much more nuanced views. Among the reasons for its decision, declared along with the acquittal of Lambalot in June 1947, the Chinese court stated clearly that having worked for a puppet government service did not constitute sufficient grounds for being judged guilty of collaboration.[102]

The obstacles with which the purge process met in Shanghai were of the same kind as those encountered in France and in Europe. The legal process was neither precise in its definition nor regular in its application. Moreover the Shanghai purge was carried out at a time when Western imperialism was in its death throes, when the Chinese were clamouring for their sovereign rights back but still lacked experience in exercising them. What was really at stake in the legal proceedings taken against foreign collaborationists was the assertion of Chinese national identity. Sarly's trial was among the most important ones. It gave the Chinese an opportunity of condemning French local presence and political activities.

If sources allowed us to also investigate proceedings instituted against Chinese collaborationists, we might better realize how nationalism interfered with the specific aims of post-liberation purges. After the 1945 victory, the process of delegitimizing the Wang Jingwei regime was hardly started. Some years later, after their takeover, the Communists would again raise the issues of collaborationists' responsibility and guilt. But they did so with a view to getting rid of their political enemies, in a spirit of instant political efficacy. Japan is not the only East Asian country which failed to come to terms with the past, leaving the untold tragedies of recent history hanging over today's developments.

NOTES

1 Archives du Ministère des Affaires Étrangères, Série Asie-Océanie 1944–1955, sous-série Chine, vol. 318 (hereafter MAE, vol. 318), "Note de la direction Asie-Océanie," January 14, 1946; Shanghai Municipal Archives, 'Shanghaishi gong jian fa junshi guanzhi weiyuanhui zhengzhi dang'an (Political archives of the

Shanghai Military Control Commission, Public Security Office, Procuratorate and Law Courts), file 187-2-142 (hereafter SMA, 187-2-142), "Shanghai gaodeng fayuan xingshi juanzong. Hanjian gengshen. Sa'erli" (Files of criminal cases, Shanghai High Court, Judgements on appeal of "Chinese traitors." Sarly), (hereafter Sarly), 2d vol., 2d part, "Waihuan Sa'erli" (Foreign collaborator: Sarly), "Shanghaishi jingwuju gonghan" (Official letter of the police bureau of Shanghai municipality), February 6, 1945 (mistaken for 1946), (hereafter: "Jingwuju gonghan"), pp. 9–13; *Shenbao*, December 17, 1945, p. 8.

2 The collaborationist government of Wang Jingwei was set up in Nanking in March 1940. It lasted until the Japanese defeat of August 1945. When Chinese historians refer to it they generally call it "the puppet government."

3 The Chinese parts of Shanghai were occupied by Japanese military forces at the beginning of the Sino-Japanese War, in autumn 1937. The International Settlement was occupied the morning after the attack against Pearl Harbor, on December 8, 1941. The French Concession, which at that time was under Vichyist administration, was not occupied but was nevertheless under strict Japanese control. In July 1943 the French authorities, yielding to Japanese pressure, retroceded the concession to Wang Jingwei's collaborationist regime. The Guomindang government, which had taken refuge in Chongqing, sent a great number of spies, intelligence agents, and *agents provocateurs* to Shanghai. Up to 1943, the non-occupied French Concession was a haven for many of them, although a not very safe one.

4 All these charges were lodged in the file prepared by the Wusong–Shanghai garrison at the time of Sarly's arrest. This file was sent over to the High Court on December 20, 1945. Cf. SMA, 187-2-142, Sarly, 2d vol., 2d part, "Waihuan Sa'erli," "Qian Shanghai Fajing wuchu fuzongjian Sa'erli zhi zuixing diaocha" (Investigation of the criminal activities of Sarly, assistant director of the former French Concession's police force) (hereafter "Sa'erli zhi zuixing diaocha"), pp. 64–82.

5 SMA, 187-2-142, "Jingwuju gonghan."

6 SMA, 187-2-142, "Sa'erli zhi zuixing diaocha."

7 Ibid. The cooperation between the French police and the Green Gang at the eve of the April 12 *coup* was later acknowledged by Acting Consul-general Meyrier, cf. Brian Martin, *The Shanghai Green Gang: Politics and Organized Crime, 1919–1937*, Berkeley: University of California Press, 1966, p. 115.

8 Joseph Hsieh (Xie Gengxin), with Marie Holzman, *Dans le Jardin des aventuriers*, Paris: Le Seuil, 1995, p. 70.

9 Hsieh, *Dans le Jardin des aventuriers*, p. 63.

10 Martin, *The Shanghai Green Gang*, pp. 131–4.

11 "Letter from Roland de Margerie to the Procurator," February 26, 1946. The original as well as a Chinese translation are to be found in SMA, 187-2-142, Sarly, 2d vol., 2d part, "Waihuan Sa'eerli," pp. 59–62 (hereafter "Letter from Roland de Margerie to the Procurator"). R. de Margerie had been the French consul-general in Shanghai from October 1940 to September 1944. As such, he had been hierarchically senior to Sarly.

12 The aim of those who negotiated the agreements of July 1943 was to secure a salary for French employees who had been working for the French municipality and were left jobless after the retrocession of the concession. Because of war operations, these employees could not be repatriated either to France or to Indochina. Generally speaking, the puppet government did not entrust them with any responsibility or real task.

13 During the night of March 9, 1945, Japanese forces disarmed and interned most of the French forces of Indochina. They susbstituted themselves for the French colonial administration that, until now, they had thought it enough to keep under

their control. On March 10, the French garrison of Shanghai, which was under the authority of the French higher command in Indochina, was also disarmed by local Japanese forces and the puppet government broke off relations with the French consul-general.

14 Cf. the praise given to Sarly in an official report, dated May 1944, and appended to a telegram from Consul-general Filliol, Shanghai, January 25, 1946, MAE, Série Asie-Océanie 1944–1955, sous-série Chine, vol. 319 (hereafter MAE, vol. 319); SMA, 187-2-142, "Letter from Roland de Margerie to the Procurator"; MAE, Série Asie-Océanie 1944–55, sous-série Chine, vol. 320 (hereafter: MAE, vol. 320), Consul-general Bouffanais, Shanghai, November 17, 1948 .

15 MAE, vol. 319, File concerning Sarly, prepared by "une personnalité shang-haienne" (a well known Shanghai resident), forwarded to the Quai d'Orsay by Father Germain, Dean of Aurore University, June 18, 1946.

16 Maron was a police inspector who belonged to the Political Service (headed by Sarly). He was in charge of a squad whose particular responsibility was to maintain contact with the Japanese gendarmerie (military police). When these wanted to carry on their operations in the French Concession, they had first to warn Inspector Maron and get his agreement. All arrests made by the Japanese in the French Concession had to be made with Maron and his men in attendance.

17 SMA, 187-2-142, Sarly, 2d vol., 2d part, "Waihuan Sa'erli," "Xunwen bilu" (Transcription of interrogation) (of Sarly by the procurator), December 27, 1945, pp. 33–41 (hereafter "Xunwen," December 27, 1945).

18 SMA, 187-2-142, Sarly, 2d vol., 2d part, "Waihuan Sa'erli," "Xunwen bilu" (Transcription of interrogation) (of Sarly by the procurator), February 14, 1946, pp. 47–52 *bis* (hereafter "Xunwen," February 14, 1946).

19 No. 76 Jessfield Road was the seat of the puppet government's secret police force which was made up of gangsters and thugs.

20 SMA, 187-2-142, Sarly, 2d vol., 2d part, "Waihuan Sa'erli," "Sarly to H.H. the Procurator," March 11, 1946, pp. 86–90.

21 *Xinwenbao* (The News), December 29, 1945, "Shali zai yu shenghuo sushi" (Sarly leads a comfortable life in prison). MAE, vol. 319, Consul-general Filliol, Shanghai, March 22, 1946.

22 MAE, vol. 319, Consul-general Filliol, Shanghai, January 12, 1946; *Xinwenbao*, January 11, 1946, p. 3, "Shali sidang beibu" (Sarly's close friend is arrested). Cf. also *Shenbao*, March 17, 1946, p. 3, "Shali sidang san ren xianhou zai Hu luowang" (Sarly's three close associates arrested in Shanghai).

23 MAE, vol. 320, Consul-general Bayens, Shanghai, April 24, 1947. See appended note concerning Emelianoff.

24 Hsieh, *Dans le Jardin des aventuriers*, p. 19.

25 Ibid., p. 170.

26 The bill of indictment is translated in MAE, vol. 319, Consul-general Filliol, Shanghai, April 18, 1946.

27 *Shenbao*, May 30, 1946, p. 3.

28 MAE, vol. 319, Consul-general Bayens, Shanghai, June 19, 1946; appended is a letter from Premet, Sarly's counsel, which comments on the judgment.

29 MAE, vol. 319, Consul-general Bayens, Shanghai, June 19, 1946.

30 MAE, vol. 319, Consul-general Bayens, Shanghai, July 6, 1946.

31 MAE, vol. 319, Ambassador Jacques Meyrier, Nanking, June 26, 1946.

32 SMA, 187-2-142, "Letter from Roland de Margerie to the Procurator"; Ibid., "Letter from M. Grosbois to Consul-general Filliol," March 8, 1946, p. 124.

33 MAE, vol. 319, File concerning Sarly, prepared by "une personnalité shang-haienne" (a well known Shanghai resident), forwarded to the Quai d'Orsay by Father Germain, Dean of Aurore University, June 18, 1946. One can find in MAE, vol. 319, another report which praises the assistant director of police of the

former French Concession: its title is "The Sarly Trial"; it is dated September 1, 1946, and is unsigned, but attributed to M. de Sayve, who had been Director of Finance of the French municipality.

34 MAE, vol. 319, Draft of a note from the Direction d'Asie-Océanie, dated August 21, 1946, to Mme Bidault.

35 MAE, vol. 320, Translation of the judgment passed by the Supreme Court of Nanking on April 11, 1947.

36 MAE, vol. 320, "Note sur l'affaire Sarly," dated June 1947. This is a non-identified text, but at the end of it may be found a handwritten signature "Sarly."

37 MAE, vol. 320, Acting Consul-general Van Laethem, Shanghai, November 14, 1947.

38 MAE, vol. 320, Acting Consul-general Van Laethem, Shanghai, January 24, 1948; Consul-general Bouffanais, Shanghai, November 17, 1948.

39 MAE, vol. 320, Consul-general Bouffanais, Shanghai, November 17, 1948; Direction d'Asie-Océanie to Consul-general Bouffanais, Paris, November 18, 1948; Consul-general Bouffanais, Shanghai, December 9, 1948. The text of the final acquittal may be found in SMA, 187-2-142, Sarly, 3rd vol., 10th part, pp. 1–3.

40 MAE, vol. 320, Consul-general Bayens, Shanghai, February 18, 1947. MAE, vol. 320, Direction d'Asie-Océanie, to the French embassy in Nanking, Paris, stamped 3 decembre 1947.

41 MAE, vol. 320, Acting Consul-general Van Laethem, Shanghai, October 6, 1947. The consul refers to statements made by Oussanosky's counsel, who himself had received assurances from the Ministry of Justice.

42 SMA, 187-2-142, "Jingwuju gonghan."

43 SMA, 187-2-142, "Sa'erli zhi zuixing diaocha."

44 SMA, 187-2-142, Sarly, 2d vol., 2d part, "Waihuan Sa'erli," Transcription of the interrogation of Kaufman by the procurator, March 26, 1946, pp. 149–52.

45 MAE, vol. 319, Note du sous-secrétariat d'Etat à la Direction d'Asie-Océanie, September 30, 1946.

46 *China Weekly Review*, May 3 and 24, 1947.

47 MAE, vol. 320, Acting Consul-general Van Laethem, Shanghai, September 20, 1947.

48 On the Pétainist currents in the emerging French resistance movement, cf. Laurent Douzou and Denis Peschanski, "Les premiers résistants face à l'hypo-thèque Vichy (1940–1942)," in Laurent Douzou *et al.*, eds, *La Résistance des Français: villes, centres et logiques de décision*, International conference, Cachan, November 16–18, 1995, Paris, CNRS, Institut d'Histoire du Temps Présent.

49 In Chinese, *Quxian jiuguo*. This strategy was adopted by the Nationalists: it led to secret cooperation with Wang Jingwei's services. It may be compared with the spirit of "accommodation" (adaptation) analyzed by Philippe Burin, *La France à l'heure allemande, 1940–1944*, Paris: Le Seuil, 1995.

50 In French, *guerre franco-française*. This term was used for the first time in 1950 by an ex-Vichyist official to describe the confrontations triggered by the postwar purge of collaborators. Generally understood in a broader sense, it designates all the fratricidal struggles which took place during the occupation and more generally refers to the old rift between the left and the right which these struggles reenacted. Cf. Henry Rousso, *The Vichy Syndrome in France: History and Memory Since 1944*, Cambridge, Mass.: Harvard University Press, 1991.

51 MAE, Série Asie-Océanie 1944–55, sous-série Chine, vol. 14, (hereafter MAE, vol. 14), "Rapport de Jean de Montousse," vice-consul at the French embassy, Chongqing, representative of Ambassador Zinovi Pechkoff in Shanghai, (hereafter "Rapport Montousse"), Shanghai, October 19, 1945.

52 *Daily Mail*, September 28, 1945, "Japs in Shanghai are all happy. Share luxury with Nazis."
53 Foreign Office Archives (hereafter FO), 371-46244-7815, Letter from M. Thomas Beesley, Secretary, Executive Committee, Shanghai Municipal Council Employees' Association, dated from Shanghai, Ash camp, September 12, 1945.
54 Howard L. Boorman and Richard Howard, eds, *Biographical Dictionary of China*, New York: Columbia University Press, 1967, I, p. 409.
55 MAE, vol. 14, Consul-general Filliol, Shanghai, December 12, 1945; FO, 371-46214-9469, Report by Ambassador Sir Horace Seymour, October 24, 1945.
56 FO, 371-53573-33, Consul-general Ogden, Shanghai, November 29, 1945; MAE, vol. 14, Consul-general Filliol, Shanghai, December 4 and 12, 1945.
57 MAE, vol. 14, "Rapport Montousse."
58 MAE, vol. 14, Private letter from Consul-general Guy Fain, Shanghai, October 4, 1945.
59 Hsieh, *Dans le Jardin des aventuriers*, p. 190.
60 Ibid.
61 MAE, vol. 318, Consul-general Filliol, Shanghai, January 7, 1946. MAE, vol. 319, Consul-general Filliol, Shanghai, December 31, 1945. FO, 371-53695-1059, Vice-consul E. T. Biggs, Shanghai, February 12, 1946. Paul-François Carcopino-Tusoli, also called Jean Carcopino, was the nephew of Jérôme Carcopino, a well known historian of ancient Rome and a government Minister under the Vichy regime (cf. *Le Figaro*, January 8, 1946).
62 MAE, vol. 319, Consul-general Filliol, Shanghai, December 12, 15 and 22, 1945; Consul-general Bayens, Shanghai, August 23, 1946.
63 MAE, vol. 319, Consul-general Filliol, Shanghai, November 29, December 16 and 22, 1945, January 15, 1946.
64 MAE, vol. 318, Ambassador Jacques Meyrier, Chongqing, January 8, 1946.
65 FO, 371-53574-33, "Note of a conversation with Mr. Eric E. Halphern, of *Finance and Commerce*," Shanghai.
66 Text cited in FO, 371-46244-7823, Ambassador Sir Horace Seymour, Chongqing, September 20, 1945.
67 MAE, vol. 14, Ambassador Zinovi Pechkoff, Chongqing, October 18, 1945.
68 MAE, vol. 318, Consul-general Filliol, Shanghai, December 16, 1945.
69 The French state acquired these municipal buildings and properties in spring and early summer 1943, when the French Concession's reversion to Chinese rule was fast approaching. The move was initiated by French local authorities and supported by the Vichy government. This transfer of property rights was made possible thanks to the funds provided by the Caisse des Oeuvres, a philanthropic organization which drew its revenue from the gambling taxes levied at the Canidrome (grey-hound racing track) and which was under the exclusive authority of the consul-general. Cf. MAE, Série Guerre, sous-série Vichy, vol. 144, numerous telegrams from Consul-general Roland de Margerie, dated February to July 1943.
70 MAE, vol.14, Consul-general Guy Fain, Shanghai, September 25, 1945.
71 Report from the Chinese Police Bureau, December 7, 1945, cited in MAE, Série Asie-Océanie 1944–55, sous-série Chine, vol. 252 (hereafter MAE, vol. 252), Consul-general Filliol, Shanghai, February 12, 1946.
72 MAE, vol. 14, "Rapport Montousse."
73 MAE, vol. 318, Consul-general Filliol, Shanghai, February 13, 1946.
74 The British worried much about delay and obstruction being met with in the return to their legitimate owners of businesses and public utility services which had been taken over from the Japanese by the Chinese authorities. Cf. FO,

371-46245, "Intelligence Report from the Naval Attaché," Chongqing, September 1945.
75 FO, 371-53574-33, "Note of a conversation with Mr Eric E. Halphern, of *Finance and Commerce*," Shanghai.
76 Ibid.
77 Ibid.
78 MAE, vol. 318, Consul-general Filliol, January 4, 1946; a translation of the mayor's letter (dated January 2) is appended. The mayor protested against Carcopino's arrest, which he considered illegal.
79 MAE, vol. 318, Daridan, *chargé d'affaires*, French embassy, Chongqing, January 5, 1946; Ambassador Jacques Meyrier, Chongqing, January 8, 1946.
80 FO, 371-53695-1059, Vice-consul E. T. Biggs, Shanghai, February 12, 1946.
81 *Xinwenbao*, December 26, 1946, "Faling jubu nacui faqiao, you sun woguo faquan" (The French consul-general ordered French Nazis to be arrested: this was a breach of China's sovereign rights.)
82 *Xinwenbao*, January 4, 1946, "Faling bugu wofang kangyi, shanbu zhanfan jie Xigong." (The French consul-general in spite of Chinese opposition took it upon himself to have war criminals arrested and taken to Saigon.)
83 *Xinwenbao*, January 7, 1946, p. 3, "Fa zonglingshi yanhua, cheng wei 'difang shijian'." (The French consul-general in a public address called [the war criminal cases] "local incidents".)
84 MAE, vol. 318, Ambassador Jacques Meyrier, Chongqing, January 8 and 9, 1946.
85 MAE, vol. 318, preserve a specimen of these tracts, appended to a letter from the US Forces Headquarters, China Theater, December 27, 1945: "The French consul-general in Shanghai ... dared to smuggle a French war criminal out of China ... Carcopino-Tusoli, a French resident in Shanghai, collaborator with German Nazis in the last war ..." signed "Students in Shanghai."
86 *Xinwenbao*, January 15, 1945, p. 3, "Kangyi *Bai'erding* shijian xuesheng sanwanren youxing" (Thirty thousand students protested against the *Emile Bertin* incident). MAE, vol. 318, Ambassador Jacques Meyrier, Chongqing, January 25, 1946. According to French diplomatic archives, only 20,000 students took part in the anti-French demonstration and the Shanghai mayor did not support them. In British diplomatic archives, mention is also made of 20,000 demonstrators (FO, 371-53573-33, Naval Staff Office, HM consulate-general, Shanghai, January 18, 1946, "Shanghai general report").
87 FO, 371-53695-1059, Ambassador Sir Horace Seymour, Chongqing, February 17, 1946, marginal comments by FO officials.
88 On the rebellion of Annamese guards of the former municipality, see MAE, vol. 14, several reports by Colonel Artigue, commander of the French detachment in Shanghai, Shanghai, June 4, July 23, n.d., and September 14, 1945. On the protection given to these rebels by Chinese Nationalist authorities, see MAE, vol. 14, Consul-general Filliol, Shanghai, January 14, 1946.
89 MAE, vol. 318, Ambassador Jacques Meyrier, Chongqing, 22 January 1946; Consul-general Filliol, Shanghai, February 13, 1946; FO, 371-53573-33, Naval Staff Office, HM consulate-general, Shanghai, January 18, 1946, "Shanghai general report."
90 MAE, vol. 318, Note de la Direction Asie-Océanie, December 4, 1945.
91 MAE, vol. 318, Consul-general Filliol, Shanghai, January 8, 1946; Note de la Direction Asie-Océanie, January 1946. MAE, vol. 252, Consul-general Filliol, Shanghai, February 12, 1946.
92 MAE, vol. 252, Notes de la Direction d'Asie-Océanie, (signed: Chauvel), more particularly note dated March 26, 1946.
93 MAE, vol. 318, Ambassador Jacques Meyrier, Chongqing, January 8, 1946.

94 MAE, vol. 318, Ministère des Affaires Étrangères to French embassy in Chongqing, January 3, 1946.

95 MAE, vol. 318, Ambassador Jacques Meyrier, Chongqing, January 25, 1946; FO, 371-53695-1059, Ambassador Sir Horace Seymour, Chongqing, February 17, 1946, marginal comments by FO officials.

96 Jacques Guillermaz, *Une Vie pour la Chine: Mémoires (1937–1989)*, Paris: Robert Laffont, 1989, pp. 146–7; François Joyaux, *La Nouvelle question d'Extrême-orient: l'ère de la guerre froide (1945–1959)*, Paris: Payot, 1985, pp. 119–20.

97 FO, 371-53695-1059, Ambassador Sir Horace Seymour, Chongqing, February 17, 1946, marginal comments by FO officials.

98 MAE, vol. 14, Ministry of Colonies (Department of Colonial Social Affairs) to the Ministry of Foreign Affairs (Department of Personnel), Paris, February 3, 1945. SMA, 187-2-142, Sarly, 2d vol., 2d part, "Waihuan Sa'erli," Transcriptions of the interrogation of Kaufman by the procurator, March 11, 1946, pp. 94–5, and March 26, 1946, p. 149.

99 MAE, vol. 14, Consul-general Filliol, Shanghai, November 27, 1945.

100 MAE, vol. 320, Acting Consul-general Van Laethem, Shanghai, September 27, 1947.

101 *Xinwenbao*, November 24, 1945, "Guofu mingling gongbu chuli Hanjian anjian tiaoli" (The National Government published a decree which set the rules for dealing with "Chinese traitors" cases); ibid., November 25, 1945, "Chuli Hanjian tiaoli" (The rules for dealing with "Chinese traitors" cases), expounded and commented upon the rules adopted on November 23.

102 MAE, vol. 320, Acting Consul-general Van Laethem, Shanghai, June 30, 1947.

ACKNOWLEDGMENTS

Research for this article was supported by several travel grants from the Centre d'Etudes Chinoises, Institut National des Langues et Civilisations Orientales (Paris). Oral presentations were made at the Center for Chinese Studies, University of California, Berkeley, and at the Institute of History, Shanghai Academy of Social Sciences. The author would like to thank participants for their stimulating comments. For a critical reading of earlier versions, thanks also go to Henry Rousso and Denis Peschanski, Centre National de la Recherche Scientifique. I am greatly indebted to the staffs of the French Diplomatic Archives and of the Shanghai Municipal Archives for their assistance, and to Dr Wang Ju, who helped me to decipher Chinese handwritten reports.

Bibliography

"Chen Yunxiang zai Shanghai bannian" [Chen Yunxiang in Shanghai for half a year], *Yilin*, no. 69, 1940.

"Kangzhan zhong de Zhongguo jingji" [China's economy during the War of Resistance], in Wei Hongyun, ed., *Zhongguo xiandai shi ziliao xuanji* [A selection of materials on contemporary Chinese history] IV, Harbin: Heilongjiang chubanshe, 1981.

"Interview with Mao Tsu-p'ei," report from Howard Wiens, OSS Headquarters, Chungking. OSS report XL-10952. 31/5/45, Office of Strategic Services Archives, War Department, US National Archives, Military Reference Division.

"Shanghai Mayor Keeps his Promise to the Public," *Shanghai* 1, 3 (1941), pp. 2–4.

"Shanghai tebie shi di yi jingcha ju zhanxing," *Jingcha faling* [Police laws], n.p., n.d. (ca. 1944, probably published by the Wang Jingwei Ministry of Interior). Copy in the Shanghai Municipal Library.

"The High Cost of Living," *Shanghai* 1, 3 (1941), pp. 12–15.

Auswärtiges Amt archives, Bonn, Botschaft China Prot. [AA]

Akira, I., *Power and Culture: The Japanese–American War, 1941–1945*, Cambridge, Mass.: Harvard University Press, 1981.

Allman, N. F., papers, Hoover Institution Archives, Stanford, Calif.

Anderson, B. *Imagined Communities: Reflections on the Origins and Spread of Nationalism*, London: Verso, 1993.

Andô, H., *Mantetsu: Nihon teikokushugi to Chûgoku* [The SMR: Japanese imperialism and China], Tokyo: Ochanomizu shobô, 1965.

Archives du Ministère des Affaires Etrangères.

Banno, J. "Japanese Industrialists and Merchants and the anti-Japanese Boycotts in China, 1919–1928," in P. Duus, R. H. Myers, and M. Peattie, eds, *The Japanese Informal Empire in China, 1895–1937*, Princeton: Princeton University Press, 1989.

Baoshan xianzhi [Baoshan county gazetteer], compiled by Shanghai shi Baoshan qu difangzhi biancuan weiyuanhui, Shanghai: Shanghai renmin chubanshe, 1992.

Barnett, R. W., *Economic Shanghai: Hostage to Politics, 1937–1941*, New York: Institute of Pacific Relations, 1941.

Bell, L. S., "From Comprador to Country Magnate: Bourgeois Practice in the Wuxi County Silk Industry," in J. Esherick and M. B. Rankin, eds, *Chinese Local Elites and Patterns of Dominance*, Berkeley: University of California Press, 1990.

Bergère, M. C., "Zhongguo de minzu qiye yu Zhong-Ri zhanzheng: Rongjia Shenxin fangzhi chang" [China's national industry and the Sino-Japanese War: the Rong family's Shenxin textile company], in Zhang Xianwen *et al.*, eds, *Minguo dang'an yu minguo shixue shu taolun hui lunwen ji* [A collection of essays on the study of

Republican history and the Republican archives], Beijing: Dang'an chubanshe, 1988.

— *The Golden Age of the Chinese Bourgeoisie, 1911–1937*, Cambridge: Cambridge University Press, 1989.

Boorman, H. L. (ed.), *Biographical Dictionary of Republican China*, 5 vols, New York: Columbia University Press, 1979.

Bordwell, D., *Narration in the Fiction Film*, Madison: University of Wisconsin Press, 1985.

Boyle, J. H., *China and Japan at War, 1937–1945: The Politics of Collaboration*, Stanford: Stanford University Press, 1972.

British Foreign Office Records, London: Public Record Office. [BFOR]

British War Office Records, London: Public Record Office. [BWOR]

Brown, C., "Woman as Trope: Gender and Power in Lu Xun's 'Soap'," in Tani Barlow, ed., *Gender Politics in Modern China*, Durham, N. C.: Duke University Press, 1993.

Bulletin d'Information Economique, French consulate, Shanghai.

Bunge, F. M., and Shinn, R. S. (eds), *China: A Country Study*, Washington, D.C., US Government, Department of the Army, 1981.

Bunker, G. E. *The Peace Conspiracy: Wang Ching-wei and the China War, 1937–1941*, Cambridge, Mass.: Harvard University Press, 1972.

Burin, P., *La France à l'heure allemande, 1940–1944*, Paris: Le Seuil, 1995.

Ch'en Li-fu Materials, "Ting Mo-ts'un File," Materials relating to the oral history of Mr Ch'en Li-fu, done with Miss Julie Lien-ying How as part of the Chinese Oral History Project of the East Asian Institute of Columbia University between December 1958 and July 2, 1968, New York: Columbia University.

Ch'ien, C. S., *Fortress Besieged*, trans. J. Kelly and N. K. Mao, Bloomington and London: Indiana University Press, 1979.

Chang, M. H., *The Chinese Blue Shirt Society: Fascism and Developmental Nationalism*, Berkeley: Institute of East Asian Studies, University of California, 1985.

Chatterjee, P., *The Nation and its Fragments: Colonial and Postcolonial Histories*, Princeton: Princeton University Press, 1993.

Chen, C., "The Japanese Adoption of the *Pao-chia* System in Taiwan, 1895–1945," *Journal of Asian Studies* 34 (1975), pp. 391–416.

Chen, C., *Kangzhan shidai shenghuo shi* [History of wartime Shanghai life], Hong Kong, Changxing shuqu, n.d.

Chen, D. (ed.), *Zhongguo yingtan juren* [The giant of Chinese cinema], Hong Kong, n.d.

Chen, G., *Beiguo chujian: Yingxiong wuming diyibu* [Weeding out the evil in the north: anonymous heroes, part 1], Taibei: Zhuanji wenxue chubanshe, 1981.

— *Shanghai kangri dihou xingdong* [Fighting the Japanese behind enemy lines in Shanghai], Taibei: Zhuanji wenxue chubanshe, 1984.

— *Kangzhan houqi fanjian huodong* [Counterespionage activities during the later phase of the War of Resistance], Taibei: Zhuanji wenxue chubanshe, 1986.

Chen, J. and Yao, L. (eds), *Zhongguo jindai gongye shi ziliao* [Historical materials on industry in modern China] I, Beijing: San-lian, 1957.

Cheng, J., Li Shaobai and Xing Zuwen, *Zhongguo dianying fazhan shi* II, Beijing, Zhongguo dianying chubanshe, 1980, originally 1964.

Cheng, N., *The Banker*, trans. B. Dean, San Francisco: China Books and Periodicals, 1992.

China at War 2, 6 (June–July 1939).

China Intelligence Wing Report No. C-35-83, 26 April 1944, in FO371/41680, BFOR.

China Weekly Review.

Chu, S. C., *Reformer in Modern China: Chang Chien, 1853–1926*, New York: Columbia University Press, 1965.

Chûgoku nenkan, 1939 [China yearbook; Shanghai], n.p., 1939.

Clifford, N. R., *Spoilt Children of Empire: Westerners in Shanghai and the Chinese Revolution of the 1920s*, Hanover, N.H.: University Press of New England, 1991.

Coble, P., *The Shanghai Capitalists and the Nationalist Government, 1927–1937*, Cambridge Mass.: Harvard University Press, 1980.

— *Facing Japan: Chinese Politics and Japanese Imperialism, 1931–1937*, Cambridge, Mass.: Harvard University Press, 1991.

Cochran, S., *Big Business in China: Sino-Foreign Rivalry in the Cigarette Industry, 1890–1930*, Cambridge, Mass.: Harvard University Press, 1980.

— "Business, Governments, and War in China, 1931–1949," in A. Iriye and W. Cohen, eds, *American, Chinese, and Japanese Perspectives on Wartime Asia, 1931–1949*, Wilmington, Del.: Scholarly Resources, 1990.

Collar, H., *Captive in Shanghai*, Hong Kong: Oxford University Press, 1990.

Confidential US State Department Central Files, China: Internal Affairs, 1940–1944. [CSDCF]

Daily Mail, London.

Dan D., trans. "Riben dianying de Dalu zhengce ji qi dongxiang zuotan" [Symposium on the mainland policy of Japanese filmmaking and its future development], *Wenxian* 4 (1939), pp. 113–25.

Davidson-Houston, J. V., *Yellow Creek: The Story of Shanghai*, Philadelphia: Defour Editions, 1964.

Deakin, F. W., and G. R. Storry, *The Case of Richard Sorge*, London: Chatto and Windus, 1966.

Deng W., *Congjun baoguo ji* [Record of a military life in the service of the nation], Taibei: Zhengzhong Shuju, 1979

Deng Y., *Sanmin zhuyi lixing she shi* [History of the Vigorous Practice Society of the Three Principles of the People], Taibei: Shijian chubanshe, 1984.

Dianying shenghuo.

Dianying shijie.

Dikang sanri kan [War of resistance], published every three days, no. 8 (September 13, 1937).

Douzou, L., and Peschanski, D., "Les premiers résistants face à l'hypothèque vichy (1940–1942)," in L. Douzou *et al.*, ed., *La Résistance des Français: villes, centres et logiques de décision*, International conference, Cachan, 16–18 November 1995, Paris, CNRS, Institut d'histoire du temps présent.

Dower J. W., *War without Mercy: Race and Power in the Pacific War*, New York: Pantheon Books, 1986.

Duara, P., "The Order of Authenticity: National History and Gender in Modern China," paper presented at "Narratives, Arts, and Ritual: Imagining and Constructing Nationhood in Modern East Asia," University of Illinois, Urbana–Champaign, November 14–17, 1996.

Duus, P., "Zaikabô: Japanese Cotton Mills in China, 1895–1937," in *The Japanese Informal Empire in China*, in P. Duus, R. H. Myers, and M. Peattie, eds, *The Japanese Informal Empire in China, 1895–1937*, Princeton: Princeton University Press, 1989.

DYNQJ. See Guofang Bu Qingbao Ju (ed.), 1979.

Eastman, L.E., *The Abortive Revolution: China under Nationalist Rule, 1927–1937*, Cambridge, Mass.: Harvard University Press, 1974.

— "Facets of an Ambivalent Relationship: Smuggling, Puppets, and Atrocities during the War, 1937–1945," in A. Iriye, ed., *The Chinese and the Japanese: Essays in Political and Cultural Interactions*, Princeton: Princeton University Press, 1980.

— "Nationalist China during the Sino-Japanese War, 1937–1945," in J. K. Fairbank and A. Feuerwerker, eds, *The Cambridge History of China* XIII, *Republican China, 1912–1949*, Part 2, pp. 547–608, Cambridge: Cambridge University Press, 1986.

Ebrey, P., *The Inner Quarters: Marriage and the Lives of Chinese Women in the Sung Period*, Berkeley: University of California Press, 1993.

Ehrlich, E., *Cinema of Paradox: French Filmmaking under the German Occupation*, New York: Columbia University Press, 1985.

Epstein, I., *The Unfinished Revolution in China*, Boston: Little Brown, 1947.

Farmer, R., *Shanghai Harvest: A Diary of Three Years in the China War*, London: Museum Press, 1945.

Fewsmith, J., *Party, State, and Local Elites in Republican China: Merchant Organizations and Politics in Shanghai, 1890–1930*, Honolulu, University of Hawaii Press, 1985.

Finch, P., *Shanghai and Beyond*, New York: Charles Scribner's Sons, 1953.

Fitzgerald, J., "Continuity within Discontinuity: The Case of *Water Margin* Mythology," *Modern China* 12, 3 (1986), pp. 361–400.

Fogel, J. A., "Introduction: Itô Takeo and the Research Work of the South Manchurian Railway Company," in T. Itô, *Life along the South Manchurian Railway*, pp. xiv, xv, xvii–xviii.

— "Senzen Nihon no minkan Chûgokugaku" [Non-academic genres of Sinology in prewar Japan], in *Kôsaku suru Ajia* [Asia entangled], ed. Y. Mizoguchi, T. Hamashita, N. Hiraishi, and H. Miyajima, in the series, *Ajia kara kangaeru* [Reconsiderations from Asia], I, Tokyo: Tokyo University, 1993.

— "The Sino-Japanese Controversy over Shina as a Toponym for China," in J. A. Fogel, *The Cultural Dimension of Sino-Japanese Relations: Essays on the Nineteenth and Twentieth Centuries*, Armonk, N.Y.: Sharpe, 1994.

— "The Voyage of the *Senzaimaru* to Shanghai: Early Sino-Japanese Contacts in the Modern Era," in J. A. Fogel, *The Cultural Dimension of Sino-Japanese Relations*, Armonk, N.Y.: Sharpe, 1994.

— "Japanese Literary Travelers in Prewar China," *Harvard Journal of Asiatic Studies* 49, 2 (1989), pp. 575–602.

— *The Literature of Travel in the Japanese Rediscovery of China, 1862–1945*, Stanford: Stanford University Press, 1996.

Foreign Office Archives, London.

Foreign Relations of the United States, *Diplomatic Papers, 1939*, IV, *The Far East, the Near East, and Africa*, U.S. Department of State, Washington, D.C.: US Government Printing Office, 1955. [FRUS]

Fu, P., "The Ambiguity of Entertainment: Between Collaboration and Resistance in Occupied Chinese Cinema," *Cinema Journal*, 1997 (forthcoming).

— "Intellectual Resistance in Shanghai: Wang Tongzhao and a Concept of Resistance Enlightenment, 1937–1939," paper delivered at the annual meeting of the Association for Asian Studies, San Francisco, March 24, 1988.

— "Selling Fantasies at War: Production and Promotion Practices of the Shanghai Film Industry, 1937–1941," paper presented at "Commercial Culture of Republican Shanghai," Cornell University, July 21–22, 1995.

— "Patriotism or Profit: Hong Kong Cinema during the Second World War," in L. Kar, ed., *Early Images of Hong Kong and China*, Hong Kong: Urban Council, 1995.

— "Struggle to Entertain: The Political Ambivalence of Shanghai Film Industry under the Japanese Occupation, 1941–1945," in L. Kar, ed., *Cinema of Two Cities: Hong Kong–Shanghai*, Hong Kong: Urban Council, 1994.

— *Passivity, Resistance, and Collaboration: Intellectual Choices in Occupied Shanghai, 1937–1945*, Stanford: Stanford University Press, 1993.

Gan G., "Guanyu suowei 'Fuxing she' de zhenshi qingkuang" [Some facts about the "Renaissance Society"], *Zhuanji wenxue* 35, 3 (1979), pp. 32–8; 35, 4 (1979), pp. 68–73; 35, 5 (1979), pp. 81–6.

Ge B., *"A Q zhengzhuan" zai guowai* ["The True Story of A Q" Overseas], Beijing: Renmin chubanshe, 1981.

Gendaishi shiry [Source materials on contemporary history] XXXVIII, Tokyo: Misuzu shobô, 1972.

Gong T., "Rongshi jiazu de shiye juzi—ji Rong Zongjing, Rong Desheng xiongdi" [The Rong family, industrial leaders—remembering Rong Zongjing and Rong Desheng], *Jiangsu wenshi ziliao* 34 (1989), pp. 111–38.

Goodman, B., *Native Place, City and Nation: Regional Networks and Identities in Shanghai, 1853–1937*, Berkeley: University of California Press, 1995.

Gu S., *Dai Li jiangjun yu Kang-Ri zhanzheng*, [General Dai Li and the anti-Japanese War of Resistance], Taibei: Huaxin Chuban Youxian Gongsi.

Guillermaz, J., *Une Vie pour la Chine: mémoires, 1937–1989*, Paris: Laffont, 1989.

Gunn, E., *Unwelcome Muse: Chinese Literature in Peking and Shanghai, 1937–1945*, New York: Columbia University Press, 1980.

Guofang Bu Qingbao Ju (ed.), *Dai Yunong xiansheng quanji* [The complete works of Dai Yunong], 2 vols, Taibei: Guofang Bu Qingbao Ju, 1979. [*DYNQJ*]

— (ed.), *Zhongmei hezuo suo zhi* [History of Sino-American cooperative organization], Taibei: Guofang Bu Qingbao Ju, 1970.

Han Q., *Zhongguo dui Ri zhanshi sunshi zhi guji* [An estimate of China's losses in the war against Japan], Shanghai: Zhonghua shuju, 1946.

Handlin, J., "Lu K'un's New Audience: The Influence of Women's Literacy on Sixteenth Century Thought," in M. Wolf and R. Witke, eds, *Women in Chinese History*, Stanford: Stanford University Press, 1975.

Hara K., *Gendai Ajia kenkyû seiritsu shiron: Mantetsu chôsabu, Tô-A kenkyûjo, IPR no kenkyû* [Historical analysis of the founding of modern Asian studies: Studies of the Research Department of the SMR, the East Asian Research Institute, and the Institute of Pacific Relations], Tokyo: Keisô shobô, 1984.

— *Mantetsu chôsabu to Ajia* [The Research Department of the SMR and Asia], Tokyo: Sekai shoin, 1986.

Harada K., *Mantetsu* [The SMR], Tokyo: Iwanami shoten, 1984.

Haruke Y., "Wo suo zhidao de qishiliu hao" [No. 76 as I knew it], *Shulin* 4 (1983), pp. 45–8.

Hauser, E. O., *Shanghai: City for Sale*, New York: Harcourt Brace, 1940.

Hayward, S., *French National Cinema*, London: Routledge, 1993.

Henriot, C., "Le gouvernement municipal de Shanghai, 1927–1937," thèse pour le doctorat de troisième cycle présenté à l'Université de la Sorbonne Nouvelle (Paris III), 1983.

— *Shanghai, 1927–1937: Municipal Power, Locality, and Modernization*, trans. N. Castelino, Berkeley: University of California Press, 1993.

— *Belles de Shanghai: prostitution et sexualité en Chine aux XIXe–XXe siècles* (English translation forthcoming), Cambridge: Cambridge University Press.

Heppner, E. G., *Shanghai Refuge: A Memoir of the World War II Jewish Ghetto*, Lincoln: University of Nebraska Press, 1993.

Hershatter, G., *Dangerous Pleasures: Prostitution and Modernity in Twentieth Century Shanghai*, Berkeley, University of California Press, 1996.

Honig, E., "Women Cotton Mill Workers in Shanghai, 1919–1949," Ph.D. dissertation, Stanford, 1982.

— *Sisters and Strangers: Women in the Shanghai Cotton Mills, 1919–1949*, Stanford, Cal.: Stanford University Press, 1986.

— *Constructing Chinese Ethnicity: Subei People in Shanghai, 1850–1980*, New Haven: Yale University Press, 1992.

Hsieh, J. (Xie Gengxin), with M. Holzman, *Dans le jardin des aventuriers*, Paris: Le Seuil, 1995.

Hsiung, J., and Levine, S. (eds), *China's Bitter Victory: The War with Japan*, New York, Sharpe, 1992.

Huang H., "Rongjia qiye dizao zhe—Rong Zongjing, Rong Desheng" [The founders of the Rong industries—Rong Zhongjing, Rong Desheng], in Xu Dixin, ed., *Biographies of China's Entrepreneurs* I, 1988.

Huang J., *et al.*, *Dai Li jiangjun ji qi shilue* [General Dai Li and his enterprises], Nanjing: Saodang Congkan She, n.d.

Huang L. and Zhang Y., "KangRi zhanzheng shiqi Zhongguo bingqi gongye neiqian chulun" [A first discussion of the movement to the interior of China's weapons industry during the anti-Japanese War of Resistance period], *Lishi dang'an* [Historical archives] 2 (1991), pp. 118–25.

Huang M. and Zhang Y. (eds), *Wang Jingwei guomin zhengfu chengli* [The founding of Wang Jingwei's Nationalist government], 2 vols, Shanghai: Shanghai remin chubanshe, 1984.

— *Wang Jingwei jituan panguo toudi* [How Wang Jingwei and his followers betrayed the nation and joined the enemy], Kaifeng: Henan renmin chubanshe, 1987.

Huang T., "Zhongguo dianying gongsi tuozhan shilue" [A history of Zhongdian's development], *Xin yingtan* 1, 1 (1942).

— "Yiduan bei yiwang de Zhongguo dianying shi" [A forgotten phase of the Chinese film history], unpublished manuscript.

Huang Y., *Kang-Ri zhanzheng shiqi de heping yundong* [The so-called peace movement during the War of Resistance], Beijing: Jiefangjun chubanshe, 1988.

Hung, C. T., *War and Popular Culture: Resistance in Modern China*, Berkeley, University of California Press, 1994.

India Office Records, London. [IOR]

Ishidô K., *Waga itan no Shôwa shi* [My heretical history in the Shôwa period], Tokyo: Keisô shobô, 1987, and *Zoku waga itan no Shôwa shi* [My heretical history in the Shôwa period, continued], Tokyo: Keisô shobô, 1990.

Itô T., *Life along the South Manchurian Railway: The Memoirs of Itô Takeo*, trans. J. A. Fogel, Armonk, N.Y.: Sharpe, 1988.

Jankowski, P., *Communism and Collaboration: Simon Sabiani and Politics in Marseille, 1919-1944*, Yale University Press, 1989.

Japanese Foreign Ministry Archives, Tokyo.

JGZJ. See Zhongguo Guomindang Zhongyang Weiyuan Hui, Dangshi Weiyuan Hui (ed.), 1984.

Jiang D., "Shanghai lunxian qianqi de 'gudao fanrong'" [The "flourishing solitary island" of the first period of occupied Shanghai], *Jingji xueshu ziliao* [Materials on economic studies] 10 (1983), pp. 25–31.

Jiang Y. (ed.), *Beifa shiqi de zhengzhi shiliao: Yijiuerqi nian de Zhongguo* [Historical sources concerning political events during the Northern Expedition: China in 1927], Taibei: Zhengzhong shuju.

Jin X., *Wang zhengquan shimo ji* [Wang Jingwei regime from start to finish], 2 vols, Hong Kong: Chunqiu zazhi shi n.d..

Jingcha faling [Police laws], n.p., n.d. (ca. 1944, probably published by the Wang Jingwei Ministry of the Interior), copy in the Shanghai Municipal Library.

Johnson, C., *An Instance of Treason: Ozaki Hotsumi and the Sorge Spy Ring*, expanded edition, Stanford: Stanford University Press, 1990.

Jordan, D. A., *Chinese Boycotts versus Japanese Bombs: The Failure of China's "Revolutionary Diplomacy," 1931–32*, Ann Arbor: University of Michigan Press, 1991.

Joyaux, F., *La Nouvelle Question d'extrême Orient: l'ère de la Guerre froide (1945–1959)*, Paris: Payot, 1985.

Katô Y., "Shanhai ryakushi" [A brief history of Shanghai], appended to S. Matsumoto, *Shanhai jidai: jaanarisuto no kaisô* [The Shanghai Years: Memoirs of a Journalist] I, Tokyo: Chûô kôronsha, 1974.

Kawai T., *Aru kakumeika no kaisô* [Memoirs of a revolutionary], Tokyo: Shin jinbutsu ôraisha, 1973.

— *Harukanaru seinen no hibi ni, watakushi no hansei ki* [Days of my distant youth: a record of half my life], Tokyo: Tanizawa shobô, 1979.

— *Zoruge jiken gokuchû ki* [Prison notes from the Sorge case], Tokyo: Shin jinbutsu ôraisha, 1975.

Kedward, H. R., *Resistance in Vichy France*, Oxford: Oxford University Press, 1978.

Kirby, W., "The Chinese War Economy," in James Hsiung and Steven Levine, eds, *China's Bitter Victory: The War with Japan, 1937–1945*, Armonk, N.Y.: Sharpe, 1992.

Kirby, W. and Bergère, M.-C., *China's Mid-century Transition*, Cambridge, Mass.: Harvard University Press, (forthcoming).

Kobayashi, F., "Kawai Teikichi no Chûgoku kan" [Kawai Teikichi's view of China], in *Chûgoku gendai shi no danshô* [Fragments from the contemporary history of China], Tokyo: Tanizawa shobô, 1986.

Kusayanagi D., *Jitsuroku: Mantetsu chôsabu* [The true story of the Research Department of the SMR], Tokyo: Asahi shinbunsha, 1979.

Le Figaro, Paris.

Lee, L. O., "Literary Trends: The Road to Revolution, 1927-1949," in *The Cambridge History of China*, XIII, *Republican China, 1912–1949*, Part 2, Cambridge: Cambridge University Press, 1986.

Li G., "Rongjia jingying fangzhi he zhifen qiye liushi nian" (Sixty years of managing the Rong family textile and flour enterprises), *Gongshang shiliao* [Historical materials on industry and commerce] I, 1980.

Liangxiong (ed.), *Dai Li zhuan* [A biography of Dai Li], 2 vols, Taibei: Dunhuang Shuju, 1979.

Liao L., "Jianli xin wenhua zhongxin" [Establish a new cultural center], *Li bao*, April 2, 1942.

Lieu, D. K., "The Sino-Japanese Currency War," *Pacific Affairs* 12, 4 (1939), pp. 413–26.

— *The Silk Industry of China*, Shanghai: Kelly and Walsh, 1940.

Link, P., *Mandarin Ducks and Butterflies: Popular Fiction in Early Twentieth Century Chinese Cities*, Berkeley and Los Angeles: University of California Press, 1981.

Linz, J. J., "An Authoritarian Regime: Spain," in Eric Allard and Stein Rokkan, eds, *Mass Politics: Studies in Political Sociology*, New York: Free Press, 1987.

Liu G., "Wo suo zhidao de Zhongtong" [The Bureau of Statistics and Investigation of the Nationalist Central Committee that I knew], *Wenshi ziliao xuanji* 36 (1962), pp. 59–117.

Liu P., *Fusheng lueying ji* [Fleeting images from a floating life], Taibei: Zhengzhong shuju, 1968.

Liu, L., "The Female Body and Nationalist Discourse: The Field of Life and Death Revisited," in C. Kaplan (ed.), *Scattered Hegemonies: Postmodernity and Transnational Feminist Practices*, Minneapolis: University of Minnesota Press, 1994.

Lu G., *Zhongguo dianying shihua* [History of Chinese cinema] I, Hong Kong: Chunqiu chubanshe, 1960.

Lu X., *Lu Xun quanji* [Collected works of Lu Xun] XI, Beijing: Renmin daxue chubanshe, 1987.

Lu Y., "Jindai Zhongguo di yige da shiye jia—ji Zhang Jian de nanku chuangye" [Modern China's first big industrialist—remembering Zhang Jian's hard work to begin an undertaking], *Jiangsu wenshi ziliao* [Selections from literary and historical materials, Jiangsu province] 34 (1989), pp. 2–17.

Luo G., *Sanguo yanyi* [A romance of three kingdoms], Hong Kong: Zhonghua shuju, 1970.

Luo G. and Yang Y., *Hongyan* [Red crag], Beijing: Renmin chubanshe, 1961.

Lyell, W. A., Jr, *Lu Hsün's Vision of Reality*, Berkeley: University of California Press, 1976.

Mader, J., *Dr.-Sorge-Report. Ein Dokumentarbericht über Kunderschafter des Friedens mit ausgewählten Artikeln von Richard Sorge*, Berlin: Militärverlag der Deutschen Demokratischen Republik, 1984.

Mao D., *Fushi* [Corrosion], Chengdu: Sichuan renmin chubanshe, 1981. First serialized in *Dazhong shenguo*, May 17–September 27, Hong Kong, 1941.

Mao X. and Wang M., "Wang Wei 'tegong zongbu' qishiliu hao de jianli," *China Weekly Review*, November 16, 1940.

Marsh, S. H., "Chou Fo-hai: The Making of a Collaborator," in A. Iriye, ed., *The Chinese and the Japanese: Essays in Political and Cultural Interactions*, Princeton: Princeton University Press, 1980.

Martin, B., *The Shanghai Green Gang: Politics and Organized Crime, 1919–1937*, Berkeley: University of California Press, 1966.

Maruyama N., "Lu Xun in Japan," in L. O. Lee, ed., *Lu Xun and his Legacy*, Berkeley: University of California Press, 1985.

Masuda Y., *Shina sensō keizai no kenkyū* [Research on China's wartime economy]; Tokyo: Diamondō, 1944.

Masui Y., *Kankan saiban shi* [History of the trial of Chinese collaborators], Tokyo: Misuzu Shobo, 1977.

Matsuzaki K., *Shanhai jibun ki* [Shanghai men of letters], Tokyo: Takayama Shoin, 1941.

Maze Papers, S[chool of] O[riental and] A[frican] S[tudies], University of London.

Meng C., "Kangzhan qianhou de Shanghai xiangjiao shiye" [The Shanghai rubber industry before and during the War of Resistance], *Shangye zazhi* [Commercial magazine] I, (1940), pp. 39–40.

Meng Z., "Zhongtong diandi" [Bits and pieces about *Zhongtong*], *Jiushi niandai*, July 1986, pp. 87–88.

Municipal Gazette of the Council for the Foreign Settlement of Shanghai, Shanghai: Municipal Council, 1941.

Nakamura S., "Nosaka Sanzô to En'an dôkutsu no Nihonjin" [Nosaka Sanzô and the Japanese in the caves of Yan'an], in *Son Bun kara Ozaki Hotsumi e* [From Sun Yat-sen to Ozaki Hotsumi], Tokyo, Nit-Chû shuppan, 1975.

Nakanishi T., *Chûgoku kakumei no arashi no naka de* [In the tempest of the Chinese revolution], Tokyo: Aoki shoten, 1974.

Nathan papers, Bodleian Library, Oxford.

NHK, "Dokyumento Shôwa," part 2, "Shanhai kyôdô sokai" [The international settlement of Shanghai], an hour-long television documentary shown on Japanese educational television (NHK) in 1986.

Nina, "Huanying Chen Yunxiang lai Hu" [Welcome Chen Yunxiang to Shanghai], *Xinhua huabao* 3, 3 (1938).

Nishizato T., *Kakumei no Shanhai de: aru Nihonjin Chûgoku kyôsantôin no kiroku* [In revolutionary Shanghai: the chronicles of a Japanese member of the Chinese Communist Party], Tokyo: Nit-Chû shuppan, 1977.

Oakes, V., *White Man's Folly*, Boston: Houghton Mifflin, 1943.

Ozaki H., *Shanhai 1930 nen* [Shanghai 1930], Tokyo: Iwanami shoten, 1990.

Ozawa M., *Uchiyama Kanzô den: Nit-Chû yûkô ni tsukushita idai na shomin* [Biography of Uchiyama Kanzô: a great commoner in the establishment of Sino-Japanese friendship], Tokyo: Banchô shobô, 1972.

Public Record Office files, London. [PRO]

Pan L., *Old Shanghai: Gangsters in Paradise*, Hong Kong: Heinemann Asia, 1984.

Peattie, M., "Japanese Treaty Port Settlements in China, 1895–1937," in Peter Duus, Ramon H. Myers, and Mark R. Peattie, eds, *The Japanese Informal Empire in China, 1895–1937*, Princeton: Princeton University Press, 1989.

Peng H., "Chuanhe Zhanji de zuji" [The career of Kawai Teikichi], *Zhongguo Zhong-Ri guanxi shi yanjiuhui huikan* [Journal of the Chinese Research Committee on the History of Sino-Japanese Relations] 14 (1988).

Perry, E., *Shanghai on Strike: The Politics of Chinese Labor*, Stanford, Cal.: Stanford University Press, 1993.

Pingjiang Buxiao Sheng, *Jianghu qixia zhuan* [Legendary roving knights of the rivers and lakes], Shanghai: Shijie Shuju, 1923.

Prange, G., *Target Tokyo: The Story of the Sorge Spy Ring*, New York: McGraw-Hill, 1984.

Pu T., "Zaitan *Mulan congjun*" [Reconsider *Hua Mulan joins the Army*], *Dawan bao*, March 25, 1940.

Qian Z., "Minzu ziben jia Rong Zongjing, Rong Desheng" [National capitalists—Rong Zongjing, Rong Desheng], *Jiangsu wenshi ziliao xuanji* 2 (1963), pp. 131–9.

— "Wuxi wuge zhuyao chanye ziben xitong de xingcheng yu fazhan" [The formation and development of Wuxi's five most important industrial capitalist systems] in *Wenshi ziliao xuanji* [Selections from literary and historical materials], 24 (1986), pp. 98–153. Beijing: Zhongguo wenshi chubanshe.

Qiao J., "Dai Li xiansheng de renqing wei" [The human touch of Dai Li], *Zhongwei zazhi* 13, 1 (19), pp. 13–23; 3 (19), pp. 31–5.

— *Dai Li jiangjun he ta de tongzhi* [General Dai Li and his comrades], 2 vols, Taibei: Zhongwai tushu chubanshe, 1981.

— *Haoran ji* [The brave and the imperishable], 4 vols, Taibei: Zhongwai tushu chubanshe, 1981.

Rankin, M., "The Emergence of Women at the End of the Ch'ing: The Case of Ch'iu Chin," in M. Wolf and R. Witke, eds, *Women in Chinese Society*, Stanford: Stanford University Press, 1975.

Records of the Department of State Relating to the Internal Affairs of China, 1930–1939. University of California, Berkeley, Government Documents Library, microfilm 31217. [RDS]

Reynolds, D. R., "China Area Studies in Prewar China: Japan's Tôa Dôbun Shoin in Shanghai, 1900–1945," *Journal of Asian Studies* 45, 5 (1986), pp. 945–70.

— "Recent Sourcebooks on Tô-A Dôbunkai and Tô-A Dôbun Shoin: A Review Article," *Sino-Japanese Studies* 1, 2 (1989), pp. 18–27.

— "Training Young China Hands: Tôa Dôbun Shoin and its Precursors, 1886–1945," in Peter Duus, Ramon Myers, and Mark Peattie, eds, *The Japanese Informal Empire in China, 1895–1937*, Princeton: Princeton University Press, 1989.

Rong S., "Wojia jingying mianfen gongye de huiyi" [Memoirs of management of the flour milling industry by my family], *Gongshang shiliao* 2 (1980), pp. 52–3.

Rousso, H., *The Vichy Syndrome in France: History and Memory Since 1944*, Cambridge, Mass.: Harvard University Press, 1991.

— *The Vichy Syndrome: History and Memory in France since 1949*, trans. Arthur Goldhammer, Cambridge, Mass.: Harvard University Press, 1991.

Scott, P., "Uchiyama Kanzô: A Case Study in Sino-Japanese Interaction," *Sino-Japanese Studies* 2, 1 (1990), pp. 49–52.

Shai, A., *Origins of the War in the East: Britain, China and Japan, 1937–1939*, London: Croom Helm, 1976.

Shang F., "Jindai shiye jia Rongshi xiongdi jingying zhi daoxi" [Modern industrialists: the Rong brothers and their way of management], *Minguo dang'an* 2 (1992), pp. 86–91.

Shanghai Municipal Archives.

Shanghai Municipal Police files. [SMP]

Shanghai shehui kexue yuan, jingji yanjiu suo (ed.), *Rongjia qiye shiliao* [Historical materials on the Rong family enterprises] II, Shanghai: Shanghai renmin chubanshe, 1962.

Shanghai shi dang'an guan (ed.), *Ri wei Shanghai shi zhengfu* [The Japanese puppet government of Shanghai], Shanghai: Dang'an chubanshe, 1988.

Shanghai shi gongshang xingzheng guanli ju *et al.* (eds), *Shanghai minzu xiangjiao gongye* [Shanghai's national rubber industry], Beijing: Zhonghua shuju, 1979.

Shen Z., "Wo suo zhidao de Dai Li" [The Dai Li that I know], in Shen Z. and Wen Q., eds, *Dai Li qiren*, Beijing: Wenshi Ziliao Chuban She, 1980.

Shenbao.

Shi Y., "Li Shiqun," in Huang Meizhen, ed., *Wang wei shi hanjian* [Ten Wang puppet traitors], Shanghai: Shanghai renmin chubanshe, 1986.

Shih, S. M., "Gender, Race, and Semicolonialism: Liu Na'ou's Urban Shanghai Landscape," *Journal of Asian Studies* 35, 4 (1996), pp. 934–56.

Shimizu A., *Shanhai sokai eiga watakushi shi* [Personal history of Shanghai's foreign concession cinema], Tokyo: Shinchosha, 1995.

Shu J., "Guomindang Juntong ju zai Tianjin de huodong gaikuang" [Nationalist Military Bureau of Statistics and Investigation's activities in Tianjin], *Tianjin wenshi ziliao xuanji* 26 (1984), pp. 169–76.

Silliman, A., "Sino-foreign Conflict and the Extra-Settlement Roads of Shanghai," *Annual Report of the Shanghai Municipal Council, 1939.*

Sima Q. *Shiji* [Record of the historian], reprinted Hong Kong: Zhonghua Shuju, n.d.

Smith, H. D. *Japan's First Student Radicals*, Cambridge, Mass.: Harvard University Press, 1972.

SMP (International Settlement) Files, N-1437-1-4, Microfilms from the US National Archives.

Su Y., *Lunjin yinhe* [On Chinese cinema], Hong Kong: Boyi chubanshe, 1982.

Sun C. *et al.*, "Yu Xiaqing shilue" [A biographical sketch of Yu Xiaqing], in *Zhejiang wenshi ziliao xuanji*, [Selections from literary and historical materials, Zhejiang province], 32.

Sun G., "Kangzhan qijian da houfang minzu gongye fazhan yuanyin chutan" [A preliminary investigation of the causes of the development of national industry in the rear areas during the War of Resistance period], *Dang'an yu lishi* [Archives and history] 2 (1986), pp. 60–5.

Swire papers, School of Oriental and African Studies, University of London.

Sydney Morning Herald.

Tôa kenkyûjo, ed., *Shina senryû chi keizai no hatten* [The development of the economy of the occupied areas of China], Tokyo: Tôa kenkyûjo, 1944.

Tan C., "Yige teshu de dianying wenhua xianxiang" [A unique film cultural phenomenon], *Dianying shuanzhoukan* 257 (January 1989).

Tan Z., *Yiye huanghou* [An overnight queen], Hong Kong: Dianying xuanzhoukan, 1996.

Tang Y. and Gong P., "Hankou Fuxin diwu mianfen chang he Shenxin disi fangzhi chang" [Hankou's Fuxin No. 5 flour mill and Shenxin No. 4 textile mill], *Wuhan wenshi ziliao* 33, pp. 5, 14–15.

Tang Z. (ed.), *Shanghai shi* [A history of Shanghai]; Shanghai: Shanghai renmin chubanshe, 1989.

Tao J., *Gudao jianwen: Kang-Ri zhanzheng shiqi de Shanghai* [Things seen and heard on the isolated island: Shanghai during the War of Resistance], Shanghai: Shanghai renmin chubanshe, 1979.

— *Tianliang qian de gudao* [The isolated island before daybreak], Shanghai Zhonghua shuju, 1947.

Toshida M., "Henbo shuru Shanhai Shina eiga kaku-sha" [Chinese production companies in Shanghai], *Eiga hyoron* 16 (1941), p. 67.

Trunk, I., *Judenrat: The Jewish Councils in Eastern Europe under Nazi Control*, New York: Macmillan, 1972.

Tsuji H., *Chunka denei shiwa* [A narrative history of Chinese cinema], Tokyo: Gaifusha, 1987.

Uchiyama K., *Kakôroku* [Diary], Tokyo: Iwanami shoten, 1961.

— "Ro Jin sensei tsuioku" [Remembrances of Lu Xun], in Uchiyama Kanzô, *Ro Jin no omoide* [Memories of Lu Xun], Tokyo: Shakai shisôsha, 1979.

United States National Archives, Washington, D.C. [USNA]

Usui, K., "The Politics of War, 1937–1941," in J. W. Morley, ed., *The China Quagmire: Japan's Expansion on the Asian Continent, 1933–1941*, New York: Columbia University Press, 1983.

Van Slyke, L., "The Chinese Communist Movement during the Sino-Japanese War, 1937–1945," in J. K. Fairbank and A. Feuerwerker, eds, *The Cambridge History of China* XIII, *Republican China, 1912–1949*, Part 2, pp. 609–83, Cambridge: Cambridge University Press, 1989.

Wakeman, F., Jr., "The Evolution of Local Government in Late Imperial China," in F. Wakeman Jr. and C. Grant, eds, *Conflict and Control in Late Imperial China*, Berkeley: University of California Press, 1975.

— "Liberation," manuscript in progress.

— "The Civil Society and Public Sphere Debate: Western Reflections on Chinese Political Culture" *Modern China* 19, 2 (1993), pp. 108–38.

— "Models of Historical Change: The Chinese State and Society, 1938–1989," in K. Lieberthal, J. Kallgren, R. MacFarquhar, and F. Wakeman Jr., eds, *Perspectives on Modern China: Four Anniversaries*, Armonk and London: Sharpe, 1991.

— *Policing Shanghai, 1927–1937*, Berkeley: University of California Press, 1995.

— *The Shanghai Badlands: Wartime Terrorism and Urban Crime, 1937–1941*, New York: Cambridge University Press, 1996.

— and Yeh, W. (eds), *Shanghai Sojourners*, Berkeley: Institute of East Asian Studies, University of California, 1992.

Wan L., "Wuxi Rongshi jiazu baofa shi" [The history of the sudden rise of the Rong family enterprises], *Jingji daobao* [Economic report] 50 (December 14, 1947), p. 1.

Wang G., Feng, J. and Gu Y., "Wuxi jiefang qian zhuming de liujia minzu gongshang ye ziben" [The six well known commercial and industrial capitalist families in Wuxi before liberation], *Jiangsu wenshi ziliao xuanji* 31 (1989).

Wang H., "Wei fazhan Zhongguo siye er xiangji fendou" [The development of the Chinese silk industry and its continued struggle], *Jiangsu wenshi ziliao* 34 (1989).

Wang J. (ed.), *Zhanshi Shanghai jingji* [The wartime Shanghai economy], Shanghai: Shanghai jingji yanjiu suo, 1945.

Wang Q., "Yinian lai zhi Xinhua" [Xinhua in the last year], *Xinhua huabao*, 4, 1 (1939), pp. 1–30.

Wang R., "Jindai hangyun ye jubo Yu Xiaqing" [Modern shipping authority Yu Xiaqing] in Xu Dixin, ed., *Zhongguo qiye jia liezhuan* [Biographies of Chinese entrepreneurs] II, Beijing: Jingji ribao chubanshe, 1988, pp. 42–3.

Wasserstrom, J., *Student Protests in Twentieth Century China: The View from Shanghai*, Stanford, Cal.: Stanford University Press, 1991.

Wei, D., "Pingshu Dai Yunong xiansheng de shigong" [Dai Li's career and accomplishment: comments and accounts], part 1, *Zhuanji wenxue* 38, 2 (1981), pp. 40–5.

— "Pingshu Dai Yunong xiansheng de shigong" [Dai Li's career and accomplishment: comments and accounts], part 2, *Zhuanji wenxue* 38, 2 (1981), pp. 40–5.

Wen Q., "Dai Li qiren" [Dai Li, the man], in Shen Z. and Wen Q., eds, *Dai Li qiren* [Dai Li, the man], Beijing: Wenshi Ziliao chubanshe, 1980.

Wenxian (Shanghai).

Wettern, D., *The Lonely Battle*, London: 1960.

White, L. T., III, "Deviance, Modernization, Rations, and Household Registers in Urban China," in A. A. Wilson, S. L. Greenblatt, and R. W. Wilson, eds, *Deviance and Social Control in Chinese Society*, New York: Praeger, 1977, pp. 151–72.

— "Non-governmentalism in the Historical Development of Modern Shanghai," in L. J. C. Ma and E. W. Hanten, eds, *Urban Development in Modern China*, Boulder, Colo.: Westview Press, 1981.

Wong, S. L., *Emigrant Entrepreneurs: Shanghai Industrialists in Hong Kong*, Hong Kong: Oxford University Press, 1988.

Wu, T. W., "Contending Political Forces during the War of Resistance," in J. C. Hsiung and S. I. Levine, eds, *China's Bitter Victory: The War with Japan, 1937–1945*, Armonk, N.Y.: Sharpe, 1992.

Wu Y., "Guanyu Yue Fei jinzhong paoguo" [On Yue Fei] *Dianying shijie* 2, 12 (1940).

Xia Y., "Wenti yao feng qingchu" [We have to separate the questions], in *Dianying shijie* 8, 1940.

Xinhua huabao.

Xinwenbao.

Xue W., "Ji jiefang qian Wuxi Qingfeng mian fangzhi chang" [On the Qingfeng cotton textile plant in Wuxi before liberation], *Jiangsu wenshi ziliao* 31 (1989), pp. 76–88.

Yamada G., *Mantestu chôsabu, eikô to zasetsu no yonjûnen* [The Research Department of the SMR: forty years of glory and frustration], Tokyo: Nihon keizai shinbunsha, 1977.

Yan X., "Riben dui Nantong Dasheng qiye de lueduo" [Japan's plundering of the Dasheng enterprises of Nantong], in Jiangsu sheng shixue hui, ed., *KangRi zhanzheng shishi tansuo* [Explorations in the history of the anti-Japanese War of Resistance], Shanghai: Shanghai shehui kexue yuan chubanshe, 1988.

Yang C., *Zhongguo dianying sanshi nian* [Thirty years of Chinese cinema], Hong Kong: Shijie chubanshe, 1954.

— *Zhongguo dianying yanyuan cangsang lu* [Vicissitudes of Chinese movie actors], Shanghai: Shijie, n.d.

Yang S. and Hong F., "Zhengtai xiangjiao chang ershi er nian de jingli" [The experience of twenty-two years of the Zhengtai rubber factory], in *Shanghai wenshi ziliao xuanji* [Selections from literary and historical materials (Shanghai)] 32, pp. 148–67.

Yang T., "Wuxi Yangshi yu Zhongguo mianfang ye de guanxi" [The relationship of Wuxi's Yang family and China's cotton textile industry], in Zhongguo renmin zhengzhi xieshang huiyi quanguo weiyuan hui, wenshi ziliao yanjiu weiyuan hui, ed., *Gongshang shiliao* [Historical materials on industry and commerce] II, Beijing: Wenshi ziliao chubanshe, 1981.

Yeh, W. H., "Dai Li and the Liu Geqing Affair: Heroism in the Chinese Secret Service during the War of Resistance," *Journal of Asian Studies* 48, 3 (1989), pp. 545–62.

— *Provincial Passages: Culture, Space, and the Origins of Chinese Communism*, Berkeley and Los Angeles: University of California Press, 1996.

— "On the Republican Origin of the Communist *Danwei*," in W. Kirby and M. C. Bergère, eds, *China's Mid-century Transition*, Cambridge, Mass.: Harvard University Press, forthcoming.

Yilin.

Ying S. (A Ying), "Guanyu Mulan congjun" [On Mulan joins the army], *Wenxian* 6, (1939), p. F32.

Yinhang zhoubao [Bankers' weekly].

Yonezawa H., "Shanhai hôjin hatten shi" [A history of the growth of the Japanese in Shanghai], *Tô-A keizai kenkyû*, part 1, 22, 3 (July 1938), pp. 394–408; part 2, 23, 1 (January–February 1939), pp. 112–26.

Yuan Y., "Rikou jiaqiang lueduo Huazhong zhanlue wuzi paozhi 'Shangtong hui' jingguo" [The Japanese bandits enhance their plundering of central China's strategic material, the development of the "Commerce Control Commission"], *Dang'an yu lishi* 1, 4 (1986), p. 82.

Zarrow, P., *Anarchism and Chinese Political Culture*, New York: Columbia University Press, 1990.

Zhang F., *Jinrong manji* [Random notes on finance], Shanghai: n.p., 1942.

Zhang J., "Dai Li de gushi" [The story of Dai Li], *Zhuanji wenxue* 14, (1969), pp. 8–19.

Zhang J. and Hu X. "Zhongguo huaxue boli gongye xianqu—Wang Xinsheng" [China's vanguard in the chemical glass industry—Wang Xingsheng], *Renwu* [Personalities] 3 (1989), pp. 119–26.

Zhang W., "Dai Li yu 'Juntong ju'" [Dai Li and the Military Statistics Bureau], in Wenshi ziliao yanjiu weiyuanhui, eds, *Zhejiang wenshi ziliao xuanji* 23, Zhejiang: Renmin chubanshe, 1982.

Zhang X. *et al.*, *Zhanshi de Zhongguo jingji* [China's wartime economy], Guilin: Kexue shudian, 1943.

Zhang Y., *Lunxian qianhou de Shanghai.*

Zheng J. (ed.), *Wangni tegong zongbu neimu* [Inside the headquarters of the secret service of Wang Jingwei], Guilin: Guofang Shudian, n.d.

Zheng, Z., "Jindai Shanghai chengshi fengmas de bianqian" [Changing faces of modern Shanghai], paper presented at conference on modern Shanghai, Shanghai Academy of Social Sciences, August, 1994.

Zhongguo di'er lishi dang'an guan (ed.), "Riben dui Huazhong lunxian qu jingji qinlue shiliao yizu" [A group of historical materials on Japan's economic invasion of the occupied district of central China], *Minguo dang'an* [Republican archives]1 (1991), pp. 21–3.

Zhongguo Guomindang Zhongyang Weiyuan Hui, Dangshi Weiyuanhui (ed.) *Xian zongtong Jianggong sixiang yanlun zongji* [Complete collection of the ideas, speeches, and writings of the late President Chiang Kai-shek], Taibei, Zhongguo Guomindang Zhongyang Weiyuan Hui Dangshi Weiyuanhui. [JGZJ]

Zhongguo minguo shi cidian [Historical Dictionary of the Republic of China], ed. Chen Xulu and Li H., Shanghai: Shanghai renmin chubanshe, 1991.

Zhou B., *Xia Yan zhuanlüe* [Short Biography of Xia Yan], Shanghai: Shanghai wenyi chubanshe, 1994.

Zhou Z., "Wuhan de Rongjia qiye" [The Rong family enterprises in Wuhan], *Dang'an yu lishi* 3 (1986), pp. 75–80.

Zhu R., "Zhang Jian yu Nantong Dasheng shachang" [Zhang Jian and the Nantong Dasheng textile mill], *Jiangsu wenshi ziliao* 31 (1989).

Zhu Z. (Jin Xiongbai), *Wang zhengquan de kaichang yu shouchang* [The beginning and end of the drama of the Wang regime] I–IV, Hong Kong: Chunqiu zazhi she, 1959–61; V–VI, Hong Kong: Wuxingji shubao she, 1964, 1971.

Index

Akira, Iriye 66–7
Alessy, René d' 166
American community 18, 27
Anderson, Benedict 86
anti-imperialist collaborators 19, 30, 34–6
Anzai Kuraji 47, 49
Arao Kiyoshi 47
Artigue, A.J.F. 27
Associated American Industries 74–5

Bai Yun 90
Ballard, J.G. 38
Bank of China 3, 4, 7
Bank of Communications 3, 4
Bankers' Association 5
banks/banking 3, 4, 5, 7, 8, 43, 64, 72
Bao Tianqing 126
baojia system 11, 144–5, 147–50
Beggar Girl (film) 88
Bergère, Marie-Claire 22–3, 157–72
Betar movement 26
Bian Yuying 90
black market 13, 146
Blue Shirts (Tewu chu) 114, 115, 116
Bourne, K.M. 29, 141
Brightness Production 90
British community 38; collaboration by 18–19, 27–30, 31–6, 37, 39; resistance groups 37–8
Bu Wancang 88, 89, 94, 95, 97, 98, 102
business *see* industry and commerce
business collaborators 19, 20, 30, 31–4; Chinese 62–80
Butterfield and Swire 31

Cai family (industrialists) 69, 72, 73
Cai Juntu 7
Cai Shenchu 125

Canidrome riot 146
capitalists, Chinese 20, 62–80
Carcopino, Paul-François 166, 168–9
Central Bank 3
Central Chemical Glass Works 67–8
Central China Development Company 66, 71
Central China Silk Reeling Company 71
Central News Agency 4
Central Reserve Bank 8
Cercle Sportif Français 26
Chahua nu (film) 92–3
Chambers of Commerce: Japanese 43; Shanghai 5
Chan, Nancy *see* Chen Yunshang
Chatterjee, Partha 96
Chen Gongbo 14, 23, 141, 142–4
Chen Gongshu 126, 127, 128
Chen Guofu 121
Chen Lifu 121
Chen Lu 92, 117, 119
Chen Mingchu (Chen Dirong) 122, 124, 125
Chen Shu-sun, General 25
Chen Yanyan 89
Chen Yunshang 86, 94, 95, 98, 102–3
Chen Ziyi 125
Cheng family (industrialists) 69, 73
Cheng Fangwu 52
Cheng Jihua 86
Chiang Kai-shek 2, 5, 112, 113, 114, 115, 116, 143, 165
China Merchants' Steam Navigation Company 65
China Movie Company (Zhongdian) 100, 101
China Productions (Guohua dianying gongsi) 90, 98, 99
Chinese Arts Movie Company (Yihua

dianying gongsi) 90, 98, 99
Chinese businessmen, collaboration by
    20, 62–80
Chinese Patriotic League 35
Chinese Problems Study Group 49
Chisholm, Don 36, 37
cinema *see* film industry
Coble, Parks 20, 62–80
Cochin, M. 163
Cochran, Sherman 77–8
collaboration 18–19, 22–3, 24–39;
    anti-imperialist 19, 30, 34–6;
    business 19, 20, 30, 31–4, 62–80;
    by British nationals 18–19, 27–30,
    31–6, 37, 39; by Chinese capitalists
    20, 62–80; by French nationals 18,
    25, 157–8, 160–1, 162–4, 166,
    167, 168–9, 171–2; film industry
    92–3; trials 157–8, 160–1, 162–4,
    171–2
Collar, Hugh 38, 39
commerce and industry *see* industry and
    commerce
commodity exchange 5, 13
Communists: Chinese 9–10, 12, 13, 14,
    53, 133; Japanese 47
Compagnie des Messageries Maritimes
    168
Compagnie Française des Tramways
    168, 169
concessions, foreign *see* French
    Concession; International Settlement
corruption 13, 142–3, 157
Cosme, Henri 165
Cotton Control Commission 76
Creation Society 52
Cuming, James 38
currency control 12

Dai Jingyuan 118
Dai Li, General 6, 92, 111–30 *passim*
Daikô Textile Company 72
Dasheng mills 65
Deng Yanda 48
Deng Zuyou 143
Diaochan (film) 88
Ding Mocun 120, 121, 139, 140
Doihara Kenji 120, 121, 139–40
Dong Guo 102, 103
Dongyang heping zhi dao (film)
    99–100
drug trafficking 142
Du Berrier, Hilaire 37
Du Yuesheng 121, 169–70

East Asian Common Culture Academy
    (Tô-A dôbun shoin) 47, 50
East Asian Sphere of Co-prosperity 6,
    19
economic collaboration *see* business
    collaborators
economy/economic resources 8, 12–13,
    134–5, 146–7
Egal, R. 26–7, 171
electricity supplies 146–7
Emelianoff, George 160
Emile Bertin crisis 168–9, 170
entertainment 4–5, *see also* film
    industry
Escarra, Jean 170
European community 18–19, 24–7
export trade 134

Fabre, L. 27, 159
Fain, Guy 166
Fang Peilin 86
Far East Movie Company 90
Farmers' Bank 3
Fei Mu 98
Filipinos 34
Filliol, General 169, 170
film industry 5, 20–1, 86–105
financial markets 5, 13, 134
Fiori, Captain 158
Fischer, Martin 26
Flour Control Commission 76
flour milling 70, 74, 76, 77, 146
Fogel, Joshua 19–20, 42–57
food supplies 12, 145–6
foreign collaborators *see* collaboration
foreign concessions *see* French
    Concession; International Settlement
Franco-Chinese School 169
Franco-Chinese treaties (1946) 170–1
Franklin, Cornell S. 141
French Concession 2, 3–4, 26, 87, 111,
    133, 140, 147, 157, 158–9;
    declaration of neutrality 3; end of
    164–71; Japanese civilian community
    43; population 43, 133, 147
French nationals 26–7; collaboration by
    18, 25, 157–8, 160–1, 162–4, 166,
    167, 168–9, 171–2
Fu, Poshek 20–1, 24, 62, 86–105
Fu Xiaoan 92
Fu Zongyao 136, 138, 141
Fujimori Seikichi 46
Fujimura Ichinori 68, 69
Funakoshi Hisao 49, 52, 53

gambling casinos 142–3
Gande, W.J. 37
George, A.H. 140–1
Gerspach, Alexandre 166, 167
glass production 67–8
gold prices 13
Gongfei Coffee Shop 46
Gracie, J.K. 36–7
Great World Amusement Palace 89
Green Gang 121, 159
Grosbois, M. 161
Gu Eryi 88
Gu Lanjun 88, 98
Gu Zhuhua 136
Guangming yingye gongsi (Brightness
    Production) 90
gudao period 2–10, 64, 87
Guo Moruo 45, 52
Guo Shaoyi 137
Guohua dianying gongsi (China
    Productions) 90, 98, 99

Han Jun 136
Han Langen 94
Hankow Light and Power Company 31
Haruke Yoshitane 121, 140, 144, 145
Hata Shunroku 145
He Yingqin 167
Hirabayashi Taiko 46
hokô system 144
Holland, John Joseph 36
Honda Kumataro 143
Hong Fumei 68, 69
household registration 11, 21, 22, 145,
    147–9
Hu Anbang 136
Hu Die 87
Hua Mulan Joins the Army (film) 87,
    94–8, 101–3, 105
Huang Chujiu 89
Huang Jinrong 89
Huang Tianshi 92, 100
Huang Tianzuo 92, 100

Imperial Military Reserve Association
    44
Independent Australia League 36
Indians 34
industry and commerce 134, 146;
    Chinese 62–80; French 167–8;
    Japanese 43, *see also* banks/banking
inflation 12, 13, 134, 135, 146, 147
International Settlement 3–4, 87, 111,
    133, 134; *baojia* system in 147–9;

Chinese capitalists in 64; declaration
    of neutrality 3; Japanese civilian
    population 43; Japanese seizure of 2;
    population 43, 134, 147
Ishidô Kiyotomo 54
Ishigawa Aya 92
Itô Takeo 54, 56
Iwabashi Takeji 50

Jankowski, Paul 24
Japanese civilians 19–20, 42–4; leftwing
    activists 20, 42–57
Japanese Residents' Association (JRA)
    43, 44, 51
Jewish community 18, 25, 26
Jian Dajun 165
Jiang Tingyao 147
Jiangsu Provincial Bank 7
Jin Dianyang 137
Jin Shan 88
Jing Ke of Yan 113
Johnson, Chalmers 47
journalism/journalists, Japanese 43
Juntong 6, 7, 92, 111–30, 139

Kagesa Sadaaki 140
Kailan Mining Administration 31–4
Kanegafuchi Company 65, 74
Kaneko Yôbun 46
Kaneya Military Police 135
Kaufman, Horace 162–3, 171
Kawai Teikichi 48, 49, 50–1, 52–3,
    56
Kawakami Hajime 49
Kawakita Nagamasa 99–100, 101
Kedward, H.R. 24
Kegesa Sadaaki 121
Kentwell, Lawrence 19, 34–6, 37, 39
Keswick, W.J. 141
Kita Ikki 48
Kobayashi Takiji 46
Komatsu Shigeo 48, 49
Konoe Atsumaro 47

Lambalot 160, 172
League of Leftwing Writers 46
League of Ten 114
leftwing activists, Japanese 19–20,
    42–57
Li Dashen 91
Li Guowei 77–8
Li Hongzhang 70
Li Lihua 86, 90, 99
Li Lisan 48

Li Shiqun 120, 121, 122, 124, 126, 127, 139, 140, 142, 145
Liang Hongzhi 6
Lianhua dianying gongsi 87
Lihua Cloth Company 73
Lin Bosheng 7
Lin Kanghou 12, 14
Lin Zhijiang 122
Liu Geqing 117–20, 126, 127, 128
Liu Naou 92, 100
Liu Qiong 98
Liu Shaoqi 48
Liu Zhan'en 125
Liu Zongliang 90
Liu Zonghao 90
Lixin Cloth Printing and Dyeing Company 73
Lixing she (Vigorous Practice Society) 113
loyalty, political 86
Lu Ming 98
Lu Xun 45, 46, 52
Lu Ying 136, 137, 141, 143, 143–4

McFarlane, J.A. 29–30
Maklaevsky, B. 30
Manchuria 5
Manchurian Incident 51
Margerie, Roland de 26, 159, 161, 165, 167
Matsuzaki Keiji 92
Ma Yanxiang 101
Maze, Sir Frederick 39
Mei Xi 94, 98
Meyrier, Jacques 159, 170
Military Bureau of Statistics and Investigation *see* Juntong
military units: European 27; Japanese 11, 44, 136
Mingxing dianying gongsi 87
Mitsubishi 43, 66
Mitsui 43, 66
Mizuno Shigero 49
'model peace zones' 144–5
Moy, Herbert 34, 37
Mu Mutian 52
Mulan congjun see Hua Mulan Joins the Army
mutual responsibility system (*baojia*) 144–5, 147–50

Nakajima, General 136
Nakanishi Tsutomu 47, 49, 54–5, 56
Nakano Shigeharu 46

Nanhuai anti-Communist Self-defense Corps 137
Nanjing, fall of 3
Nanjing Bankers' Association 64
Nathan, Edward J. 31–4, 37
National Commercial Bank 72
Nationalists 4, 6–8, 9–10, 12–13, 14, 133
Negishi Tadashi 48
New China Movie Company (Xinhua yingye gongsi) 88–90, 91, 98, 102
New Fourth Army 9, 11
New Man Society 54
newspapers 4; Japanese 43
Neyrone, L. 140
Nezu Hajime 47
Nis-Shi tôsô dômei 49–50
Nishimura, Colonel 136
Nishizato Tatsuo 46–7, 49, 50, 53
No. 76 organization 7, 12, 92, 98, 120–5, 139–41
North China Development Company 66
Nosaka Sanzô 49
Nottingham, E.A. 31, 37

Oakes, Vanya 145–6
Ogawa Goro 76
opportunist collaborators 31, 36–7
Osaka Shipping Company 43
Oussakovsky 160
Ouyang Yuqian 45, 94
Ozaki Hotsumi 46, 50–1, 52, 54, 56
Ozaki Shôtarô 47

Pan Hannian 62
Pan Zhijie (Pan Da) 141, 143, 144
paramilitary groups, Japanese 44, 136
People's Liberation Army 14
People's Self-protection Corps 148–9
Phillips, Godfrey 138, 140
police force 11, 98, 135–8, 149; British members of 28–30, 135, 148; Japanese military and consular 44, 135, 136, 137; Shanghai Municipal Police (SMP) 135, 136, 137, 140–1, 147, 148; Western Shanghai Area Special Police Force (WSP) 141–2, 144, *see also* secret service organizations
prices 12, 13, 134, 135, 146, 147
publishing houses 4
puppet regime 5–8, 138–9

Qian Fenggao 71–2, 79
Qiao Jiacai 128

Qigai qianjin (film) 88

racial inequality, and collaboration 19,
    39
Ransome, Arthur 38
rationing 12, 145–7
Raymond, Alan 36
religious groups, Japanese 43
resistance 21, 22, 24, 25, 37–8, 111–30
resources: control over allocation of
    11–12, 145–7, *see also* economy
Reuters 43
rice 12, 145–6
Rivelain-Kauffman, Georges 27
Rong family 69, 74–8, 80
rubber production 68–9
Russian community 18, 25–6

San Bei Steam Navigation Company 65
Sarly, Roland 22–3, 157–61, 162–3, 164,
    165, 168, 171
Satô Haruo 45
Sawada Shigeru 144
schools, Japanese 43, 47
secret service organizations 7, 12, 21, 92,
    98, 111–30
Semenov, Ataman 25
Shanghai Bankers' Association 64
Shanghai Federation of Industrial and
    Trade Associations 169
Shanghai Incident 52
Shanghai Municipal Council 28, 30, 138,
    148
Shanghai Municipal Police (SMP) 135,
    136, 137, 140–1, 147, 148
Shanghai Power Company 134
Shanghai Textile Company 74
Shanghai Times 31
Shen Tianyin 90, 92
Shi Fuhou 76
Shieh, Joseph 158, 160
Shimizu Akira 100
Shimonoseki, Treaty of 42, 43
Shinjinkai 54
shipping industry 65, 134
Shirai Yukiyoshi 49
Sino-Italian Steamship Navigation
    Company 65
Sino-Japanese Struggle Alliance 49–50
Smedley, Agnes 50
smuggling 13, 146
social clubs 5
Société d'Oxygène et d'Acétylène
    d'Extrême-Orient 167

Soejima Tatsuoki 48
Sofer brothers 166, 169
Soong, T.V. 161
Sorge spy ring 10, 46, 50–3, 56
South Manchurian Railroad Company
    10, 54–5, 66
Star Studio (Mingxing dianying gongsi)
    87
stock market 5, 13, 134
Su Xiwen 5
Sun Yat-sen 6, 112–13, 114

Tachibana Shiraki 48
Tan Wenzhi 125
Tanaka Tadao 48, 49
Tang Enpo 165
Tang family (industrialists) 69, 72–3
Tang Shaoyi 6, 119–20
Tanizaki Jun'ichirô 45
Tao Jingsun 52
Tejima Hirotoshi 48
Tewu chu (Blue Shirts) 114, 115, 116
textile industry 5, 65–6, 69–78, 134,
    146
Tian Han 45
Tô-A dôbun shoin 47, 50
Toho Productions 92
Toii Minfu, General 25
Tong Luqing 76
Tosoli, Paul-François 27
trade, export 134
trade organizations 5, 169
trade routes 8, 13
Trunk, Isaiah 24

Uchiyamo Kanzô 20, 44–6, 56
United China Productions (Lianhua
    dianying gongsi) 87
United Front 9, 10
urban control 10–12, 21–2, 133–50

Vanhoong, Nguyen 160
Vigorous Practice Society 113

Wakeman, Frederic 8, 21–2, 133–50
Wang Duqing 52
Wang Jingwei 6–7, 13–14, 119, 121–2,
    123, 138, 143
Wang Tianmu 117, 119, 122–6
Wang Xinsheng 67–8
Wang Xuewen 49, 50, 53
Wang Yuanlong 98
Wang Yuncheng 78
Wasserstein, Bernard 18–19, 24–39

Wavell, General 28
Wen Lanting 12, 14
Wen Shengguang 48, 49
Western Shanghai Area Special Police
    Force (WSP) 141–2, 144
Wheat Flour Control Commission 70
Wong Siu-lun 80
Wu Shaoshu 166
Wu Shibao 122, 139, 142, 143, 144
Wu Yonggang 98

Xia Yan 46–7, 102
Xi'an Incident 114–15
Xiang Zhongfa 48
Xie Gengxin (Joseph Shieh) 158, 160
Xingzhong company 66
Xinhua yingye gongsi (New China
    Movie Company) 88–90, 91, 98, 102
Xu Chang 147
Xu Enzeng 121
Xue family 69, 70–1, 73

Yamagami Masayoshi 52
Yan Chuntang 90, 93, 104
Yan Hua 99
Yan Jun 86
Yang family (industrialists) 70, 73
Yang Liuqing 49, 50
Yang Shaozhen 68, 69
Yang Xiaozong 88
Yeh, Wen-hsin 1–14, 18–23, 111–30
Yellow Way Association 92
Yeqin enterprise group 70
Yihua dianying gongsi (Chinese Arts
    Movie Company) 90, 98, 99

Yin Zhongli 136, 137
Ying Sun (A Ying) 96
YMCA 5
Yokohama Specie Bank 43
Yorke, R.W. 140
Young, Colonel P.C. 33
Yu Dafu 52
Yu Xiaqing 65
Yuan Liangchu 118
Yuan Ludeng 12, 14
Yuan Meiyun 89, 98
Yuan Muzfi 87
Yuandong yingpan gongsi (Far East
    Movie Company) 90
Yue Feng 86
Yuho Textile Company 74
Yung, Larry 78

Zeng Che 125
Zhang Shankun 20, 21, 88–90, 92, 93–4,
    97, 98, 99, 100–1, 102, 104–5
Zhang Shichuan 104
Zhang Xueliang 114
Zhao Dan 87
Zhao Gangyi 125
Zhengtai Rubber Works 68–9
Zhongdian (China Movie Company)
    100, 101
Zhou Fengqi 6
Zhou Fohai 14, 139, 142, 165
Zhou Guangshi 125
Zhou Menhua 98
Zhou Xuan 90, 99
Zhu Shanyuan 126
Zhu Shilin 89